The 100 most influential painters &
sculptors of the Renaissance
709.024 ONE

THE 100 MOST INFLUENTIAL
PAINTERS & SCULPTORS
OF THE RENAISSANCE

THE BRITANNICA GUIDE TO THE WORLD'S MOST INFLUENTIAL PEOPLE

THE 100 MOST INFLUENTIAL PAINTERS & SCULPTORS OF THE RENAISSANCE

EDITED BY KATHLEEN KUIPER, MANAGER, ARTS AND CULTURE

Britannica
Educational Publishing

IN ASSOCIATION WITH

ROSEN
EDUCATIONAL SERVICES

Published in 2010 by Britannica Educational Publishing
(a trademark of Encyclopædia Britannica, Inc.)
in association with Rosen Educational Services, LLC
29 East 21st Street, New York, NY 10010.

Distributed exclusively by Rosen Educational Services.
For a listing of additional Britannica Educational Publishing titles, call toll free (800) 237-9932.

First Edition

Britannica Educational Publishing
Michael I. Levy: Executive Editor
Marilyn L. Barton: Senior Coordinator, Production Control
Steven Bosco: Director, Editorial Technologies
Lisa S. Braucher: Senior Producer and Data Editor
Yvette Charboneau: Senior Copy Editor
Kathy Nakamura: Manager, Media Acquisition
Kathleen Kuiper: Manager, Arts and Culture

Rosen Educational Services
Jeanne Nagle: Senior Editor
Nelson Sá: Art Director
Matthew Cauli: Designer
Introduction by Janey Levy

Library of Congress Cataloging-in-Publication Data

The 100 most influential painters & sculptors of the Renaissance / edited by Kathleen Kuiper. — 1st ed.
    p. cm. — (The Britannica guide to the world's most influential people)
"In association with Britannica Educational Publishing, Rosen Educational Services."
Includes index.
ISBN 978-1-61530-004-4 (library binding)
1. Painting, Renaissance — Juvenile literature. 2. Sculpture, Renaissance — Juvenile literature. 3. Painters — Europe — Biography — Juvenile literature. 4. Sculptors Painters — Europe — Biography — Juvenile literature. I. Kuiper, Kathleen. II. Title: One hundred most influential painters & sculptors of the Renaissance.
ND170.A14 2010
709.02'4 — dc22

                                                                    2009023697

Manufactured in the United States of America

On the cover: Self-portrait of Leonardo da Vinci, one of the most influential artists of the Renaissance or any other period. *Stuart Gregory/Photographer's Choice RF/Getty Images*

Photo Credits: pp. 8, 355, 357, 359 © www.istockphoto.com.

CONTENTS

INTRODUCTION

One of the best known and most celebrated of all periods in history, the Renaissance was a time of momentous change in European art and civilization, representing a transition from the medieval world to the modern one. In fact, when historians speak of early modern Europe, they are referring to the period encompassed by the Renaissance.

For most people, the idea of the Renaissance is tightly bound with Italy, and fully two-thirds of the painters and sculptors surveyed in this book are Italian. Yet the Renaissance was hardly confined to Italy. One has only to think of some of the most famous and familiar names of the period: Albrecht Dürer and Hans Holbein the Younger (Germany), or Hiëronymus Bosch and Pieter Bruegel the Elder (the Netherlands). These and other great artists from France, Spain, and England are among those treated here.

Still, the Renaissance remains closely identified with Italy, and part of the reason for this rests on the term's inception and original meaning. As is often the case with periods of art history, the Renaissance received its name from scholars of a later time. The term "Renaissance," which literally means "rebirth," was first employed in the late 18th century, when it was used to describe the reappearance of Classical (ancient Greek and Roman) architectural forms in 16th-century Italian buildings. (Interestingly, it was French, not Italian, art historians who coined the term.) Over time, the term came to be applied not only to architecture but also to painting, sculpture, metalwork, ivory carving, and other art forms.

Generally speaking, scholars consider the Renaissance to cover the period in Europe from about 1400 to around 1600, although those dates are not hard and fast. Precise dates vary among regions and among art forms. Within the period of the Renaissance, art historians recognize three primary divisions. The early Renaissance extends from about 1420 to 1495. The High Renaissance covers a much shorter span of time—from 1495 to 1520. Late Renaissance painting and the style known as Mannerism comprise the remainder of the period.

Of course, it would be a mistake to believe the early Renaissance represented a sudden and complete break with previous art styles, mysteriously springing into being fully formed, like Athena from the brow of Zeus. Although the Renaissance was an era of far-reaching transformations, it nonetheless rests firmly on foundations that date back to earlier centuries.

Perhaps the element that stands out most widely and clearly in Renaissance art, and sets it apart from medieval art, is its emphasis on humanity and the human realm. This is not to say that the religious subjects that dominated earlier art disappeared from Renaissance art; that was hardly the case. However, the figures in Renaissance religious art—no matter how idealized they might be— were not the two-dimensional, sometimes ethereal and abstract figures of medieval art, but solid human figures who occupied three-dimensional space and were placed firmly on Earth.

Godly themes and earthly representation meld in the art of Fra Angelico, a 15th-century Dominican friar and painter who incorporated both religious attitude and Classical influences into his work. Sharply drawn and delineated human figures adorn his many altarpieces and frescoes. Angelico's influence reportedly extended throughout his native Florence, to amateurs and respected masters alike. The accomplished painter Fra Filippo Lippi, who was in great demand in the mid-1400s, is said to have borrowed heavily from Fra Angelico, mimicking the latter's style but infusing it with his own techniques and narrative spirit.

In addition, the creators of religious Renaissance art expressed drama and emotion in human terms. Beyond this development of more human qualities in religious art, the Renaissance also saw the growth of art categories that had little place in the medieval world—including portraits that were independent artworks and not secondary elements in religious images, subjects from Classical mythology, landscapes, and genre painting (scenes of daily life). One of the Renaissance's most important and beloved painters, Sandro Botticelli, was adept at both the period's firmly entrenched religious and the emerging secular aspects. In fact, many art scholars believe Botticelli's historical canvases are equal or superior to the devotional pieces he was commissioned to create for a number of Florentine churches. He also was frequently called upon to paint portraits of his patrons, who were members of the infamous Medici family. Botticelli was even know to serve both masters at once; three patriarchs of the Medici clan are depicted as the Magi (the kings who paid homage to Jesus at his birth) in one of the master's most famous works, *Adoration of the Magi*, which adorned the chapel at Santa Maria Novella.

Confidence in human intellectual and creative ability and in the human capacity to understand and control the natural world, along with an increasing sense of individualism, marked the Renaissance throughout Europe. These developments were manifestations of the Renaissance intellectual movement known as humanism. Nineteenth-century German scholars coined the term to describe the Renaissance emphasis on Classical studies. However, although "humanism" may be a 19th-century invention, it's based on the word used in 15th-century Italy to describe a teacher of the humanities—*umanista* (plural: *umanisti*). That word in turn derives from *studia humanitatis*, the term applied to the course of Classical studies that included Classical Latin, Greek, grammar, poetry, rhetoric, history, and moral philosophy.

Humanism emphasized the fullest possible development of human virtue, including qualities such as understanding, compassion, mercy, fortitude, judgment, eloquence, and love of honour. It stressed a life of involvement in the world as well as one of contemplation. In humanist thought, people were the centre of the universe, possessed of personal freedom and an intelligence capable of understanding the world and accomplishing whatever they set their minds to. At the heart of humanism was belief in human dignity and individualism.

Humanism's beliefs gave rise to the notion of the *uomo universale* (universal man), known today as the Renaissance man. This was someone who was a master in all areas of knowledge, in physical skills, in social accomplishments, and in the arts. The idea originated in the writings of Leon Battista Alberti (1404–72), whose books on art theory did much to shape Renaissance art and elevate the artist's status from craftsman to intellectual. Alberti was, in fact, a prime example of the *uomo universale*—he was not only a scholar but also an architect, painter, classicist, poet, scientist, and mathematician.

Alberti's 1435 book *On Painting* laid out the rules for depicting a three-dimensional scene on a two-dimensional surface. This is known as perspective, a technique that makes paintings more vibrantly alive and that had been a particular forte of Paolo Uccello. His experiments with various forms of perspective—showing an almost analytical, mathematic obsession with the style—are credited with ushering in the common use of this most crucial Renaissance artistic component. It is believed that Uccello's perspective studies made an impression on the likes of fellow artists such as Piero della Francesca and, perhaps the best-known Italian *uomo universale*, Leonardo da Vinci.

As an inventor, musician, writer, scientist, and engineer as well as a painter, Leonardo was indeed a Renaissance man. Labeled by author Giorgio Vasari as the "founder of the High Renaissance," Leonardo was a master of perspective and composition. Masquerading as a simple portrait, his *Mona Lisa* is actually a complex study of favourite Renaissance themes — the human figure (the smiling, enigmatic woman in the foreground) and nature (the rolling hills and wandering river of the landscaped background).

Another multifaceted artist, Michelangelo worked as a sculptor, painter, architect, poet, and fortification designer. First and foremost a sculptor, as well as a disavowed acolyte of Leonardo, Michelangelo transformed static marble into detailed human bodies in motion. The technique and mastery of anatomy he used in sculpting translated beautifully onto the ceiling of the Sistine Chapel—where he visually retold the biblical story of Genesis instead of simply portraying the twelve apostles, as he'd been contracted to do.

Meanwhile, in Northern Europe, early Renaissance artists were less preoccupied with Classical antiquity than their Italian contemporaries. Their works do reveal, however, the humanist's profound and abiding interest in humanity and the human realm. In the late 14th and early 15th centuries, innovative sculptor Claus Sluter fashioned figures of unprecedented monumentality whose faces and gestures expressed deeply felt human emotions. One of Sluter's patrons was Philip the Bold, duke of Burgundy and ruler of the Low Countries. In Northern Europe, Philip and his successors played the same important role as art patrons that the Medici did in Italy.

Around the same time Sluter was working, painter Robert Campin created works whose subject matter was traditionally religious but whose style was decidedly not. He placed his heavy, solid figures in three-dimensional space and set the scenes in ordinary settings familiar to the emerging middle class, filled with carefully observed details of daily life.

Jan van Eyck, often hailed as the founder of Flemish painting, perfected the newly developed technique of oil painting at a time when Italian painters were still using medieval tempera (ground pigments mixed with egg yolk). Using this technique, he depicted a world of extraordinary detail, rich colour, and brilliant luminosity. He was also the first Flemish painter to sign his works — an expression of the artist's new status in the Renaissance, which he carried even further by adding an aristocratic motto to some paintings.

A contemporary of van Eyck's, Rogier van der Weyden produced paintings that explored with great subtlety not so much the physical as the emotional world. At the end of the 15th century, Hans Memling, a German painter working in the Low Countries, produced portraits of extraordinary sensitivity and observation. His religious paintings, though popular at the time and widely imitated, are usually viewed today as unexceptional.

Working in Germany in the late 15th and early 16th centuries, Albrecht Dürer was one of the giants of the Renaissance, perhaps closer to the ideal of the *uomo universale* than any other Northern artist. Exceptionally talented, he produced paintings, prints, and drawings of a wide range of subjects, including carefully observed and detailed studies of the natural world.

After his death in the second half of the 16th century, the painter Pieter Bruegel the Elder was mourned by one of his friends as "the most perfect painter of his age." His works covered a wide range of subject matter, but he is perhaps best known today for his paintings that exemplify the humanist's interest in humans and their world. He painted numerous scenes of daily life—but not the life of the nobles or even that of the merchant middle class. Rather, he portrayed the daily life of peasants and villagers; the effect was almost like an anthropologist studying a culture. Bruegel also created paintings that gave visual form to popular sayings found in *The Netherlands Proverbs*.

What follows will provide more detailed narratives of the artists mentioned here, as well as dozens more. The accounts of their lives and works will offer greater insight into the complex and fascinating period known as the Renaissance.

CLAUS SLUTER

(b. *c.* 1340/50, Haarlem?, Holland [now in the Netherlands] — d. between Sept. 24, 1405, and Jan. 30, 1406, Dijon, Burgundy [now in France])

An influential master of early Netherlandish sculpture, Claus Sluter moved beyond the dominant French taste of the time and into highly individual monumental, naturalistic forms. His works infuse realism with spirituality and monumental grandeur. His influence was extensive among both painters and sculptors of 15th-century northern Europe.

Sluter, whose first name appears variously as Claus, Claes, or Klaas, is known through his works rather than accounts of his person. He is thought to be the Claes de Slutere van Herlam (Haarlem) who was listed in the records of the stonemasons' guild in Brussels about 1379. From ducal archives he is known to have entered in 1385 the service of Philip II the Bold, duke of Burgundy, who was ruler of the Netherlands and regent of France in the last decades of the century. Philip founded the Carthusian monastery of Champmol at Dijon in 1383 and made its chapel a dynastic mausoleum adorned with sculpture by Sluter.

All of the surviving sculpture known to be by Sluter was made for Philip. Two compositions are still to be found at the site of Champmol. The figures on the central pillar that divided the portal of the chapel show the duke and duchess presented by their patron saints John the Baptist and Catherine to the Virgin and Child. The *Well of Moses* in the cloister consists of the remains of a wellhead that had been surmounted by a group showing the Calvary of Christ. The other extant work is the duke's own tomb, which once stood in the chapel at Champmol but which has been reassembled in the Museum of Fine Arts in Dijon.

The archives in Dijon provide some information on Sluter's sculptural commissions. In 1389 he succeeded Jean de Marville as chief sculptor to the duke, and in that year he began carving the portal sculptures, which had been planned as early as 1386. He replaced the portal's damaged central canopy, and by 1391 had completed the statues of the Virgin and Child and the two saints. By 1393 the statue of the duchess was completed, and it is presumed that the duke's statue also was finished by then. In 1395 he began the Calvary group for the cloister.

In 1396 Sluter brought to Dijon his nephew Claus de Werve and sculptors from Brussels to assist in his numerous ducal commissions. The architectural portion of the duke's tomb had been completed by 1389, but only two mourning figures of the sculptural composition were ready when the duke died in 1404. Philip's son, Duke John the Fearless, contracted in 1404 for the completion of his father's tomb within four years, but Sluter's nephew did not finish it until 1410, and he used it as the model for Duke John's own tomb. Many of the mourning figures around the base are copies of what must be Sluter's work, though the problem of establishing his exact contribution is difficult because the two tombs were disassembled in the French Revolution and extensively restored from 1818 to 1823.

Sluter, an innovator in art, moved beyond the prevailing French taste for graceful figures, delicate and elegant movement, and fluid falls of drapery. In his handling of mass, he also moved beyond the concern with expressive volumes visible in the sculptures of André Beauneveu, an eminent contemporary who worked for Philip's brother Jean, Duke de Berry. The grandeur of Sluter's forms can only be paralleled in Flemish painting (by the van Eycks and Robert Campin) or in Italian sculpture (by Jacopo della Quercia and Donatello) several decades later.

The portal of the Champmol chapel is now somewhat damaged. The Virgin's sceptre is missing, as are the angels, once the object of the child's gaze, holding symbols of the Passion. This work, though begun by Marville, must have been redesigned by Sluter, who set the figures strongly before an architecture with which they seem intentionally not closely aligned, the doorway becoming a background for the adoring couple of Duke Philip and his wife. This transforms traditional portal design into a pictorial form in which architecture has become a foil, the framework for a figured triptych. Projecting canopies and jutting corbels carved with figures, deep undercut-tings, and swirling draperies aid Sluter's dynamic naturalism. This is a weighty, massive art of dominantly large, balanced forms.

The six-sided *Well of Moses*, now lacking its crowning Calvary group, which made the whole a symbol of the "fountain of life," presents six life-sized prophets holding books, scrolls, or both. The figures, beginning with Moses, proceed counterclockwise to David, Jeremiah, Zechariah, Daniel, and Isaiah. Moses was placed directly below the face of Christ, and the location of Zechariah, father of John the Baptist, was at Jesus' back, as befits a precursor. Zechariah looks down sadly as Daniel vigorously points to his prophecy. On the other side of Daniel, and serving to balance Daniel's passionate temperament, is the calm reflective Isaiah. This juxtaposition reveals Sluter's use of alternating naturalistic balances. The head and torso frag-ment of Christ from the Calvary reveal a power and intensity of restrained expression that conveys over-whelming grandeur. Suffering and resignation are mingled, a result of the way the brow is knitted, though the lower part of the face, narrow and emaciated, is calm and with-out muscular stress. The *Well of Moses* was originally painted in several colours by Jean Malouel, painter to the duke, and gilded by Hermann of Cologne. The figures of the composition dominate the architectural framework but also reinforce the feeling of support that the structure provides through their largeness of movement.

Sluter's latest preserved work, the tomb of Philip the Bold, was first commissioned from Jean de Marville, who is responsible only for the arcaded gallery below the sepulchral slab of black marble from Dinant. Forty figures, each about 16 inches (41 cm) high and either designed or executed by Sluter, made up the mourning procession. Not all the figures are still in position at the tomb; three are lost, three are in the Cleveland Museum of Art, and one is in a French private collection. They served as models for Sluter's nephew Claus de Werve, Juan de la Huerta, and other artists for sculptured tombs in France and beyond its borders. Sluter did not invent the mourning procession nor did he design the setting. But he conceived of the figures as mourners, of whom no two are alike; some are openly expressing their sorrow, others are containing their grief, but all are robed in heavy wool, draping garments that occasionally veil a bowed head and face to convey a hidden mourning. Spiritualist and naturalist in one, Sluter epitomized in sculpture the growing awareness of an individualized nature with discoverable laws and an enduring grandeur.

JACOPO DELLA QUERCIA

(b. c. 1374, Siena [Italy]—d. Oct. 20, 1438, Bologna, Papal States)

Jacopo della Quercia was one of the most original Italian sculptors of the early 15th century. His innovative work influenced a number of Italian artists, including Francesco di Giorgio, Niccolò dell'Arca, and Michelangelo.

Jacopo came from a family of craftsmen; his father, Piero d'Angelo, was also a sculptor, and his brother Priamo was a painter. In 1401 Jacopo participated in the competition for the bronze doors of the baptistery in Florence, which was won by Lorenzo Ghiberti. About 1406 Jacopo carved the tomb of Ilaria del Carretto in the Cathedral of Lucca. The effigy and sarcophagus alone survive. In 1408, at Ferrara, he made the statue of the Virgin and Child, which still exists in the Museo dell'Opera del Duomo. A year later he received the commission for the Fonte Gaia in the Piazza del Campo at Siena, now replaced by a copy; the original is in the loggia of the town hall. The scheme of this celebrated and highly original fountain seems to have been repeatedly modified, the most effective work being done between 1414 and 1419. At the same time, Jacopo was working on the statue of an apostle for the exterior of the cathedral at Lucca, the Trenta altar for the Church of San Frediano in Lucca, and tomb slabs for Lorenzo Trenta and his wife.

In 1417 he undertook the creation of two gilt bronze reliefs for the baptismal font in San Giovanni in Siena. Being a dilatory artist, he completed only the *Zacharias in the Temple*, the second being assigned to Donatello. Jacopo's main work is the sculpture around the portal of San Petronio at Bologna. The 10 scenes from Genesis, including *The Creation of Eve*, five scenes from the early life of Christ, the reliefs of prophets, and the statues of the Virgin and Child with Saints Petronius and Ambrose give a sense of depth often seen in the paintings of Masaccio.

In 1435 Jacopo was appointed superintending architect of Siena Cathedral, for which he was employed on the decoration (unfinished) of the Cappella Casini. His innovative sculptural style found no immediate followers in Siena, Bologna, or Lucca, but it later became a profound influence on Michelangelo.

ROBERT CAMPIN

(b. *c.* 1378, Tournai, France—d. April 26, 1444, Tournai)

O ne of the earliest and greatest masters of Flemish painting was Robert Campin. He has been identified with the Master of Flémalle on stylistic and other grounds. Characterized by a naturalistic conception of form and a poetic representation of the objects of daily life, Campin's work marks the break with the prevailing International Gothic style and prefigures the achievements of Jan van Eyck and the painters of the Northern Renaissance.

Documents show that Campin was established as a master painter in Tournai in 1406. Two pupils are mentioned as entering his studio in 1427—Rogelet de la Pasture (generally identified with the great Rogier van der Weyden) and Jacques Daret. The only documented work by Jacques Daret, an altarpiece executed for the Abbey of St. Vaast near Arras, shows close stylistic analogies with works by van der Weyden on one hand and works earlier in style by the Master of Flémalle on the other. Both seem to proceed from common models, for they obviously are not copies of one another. As the Tournai records give the name of Campin as master of both Daret and van der Weyden, it has been generally assumed that the Master of Flémalle may be reasonably identified with Campin. Some scholars, however, have stylistically considered the works ascribed to the Master of Flémalle as early works by van der Weyden himself.

Campin's art is indebted to that of manuscript illumination, but his work displays greater powers of observation and ability to render plastic forms than is found in contemporary manuscript illumination. One of his masterpieces is the Mérode Altarpiece (*c.* 1428), a triptych of the Annunciation with the donors and St. Joseph on the wings. The Virgin is portrayed in a setting of bourgeois realism in which interior furnishings are rendered with the frank and loving attention to detail that was to become a characteristic tradition of Flemish art. Another important work, at the Städelsches Kunstinstitut in Frankfurt am Main, consists of two wings of an altarpiece dating *c.* 1440 that are said to have come from the Abbey of Flémalle. They depict the Virgin and Child and St. Veronica (with Trinity on the reverse). Among other works generally ascribed to Campin are the *Virgin and Child Before a Firescreen* and a double portrait at the National Gallery, London, a *Nativity* at Dijon (dated *c.* 1430), and the Werl Altarpiece (1438) in the Prado, Madrid.

LORENZO GHIBERTI

(b. *c.* 1378, Pelago [Italy]—d. Dec. 1, 1455, Florence)

The early Italian Renaissance sculptor Lorenzo Ghiberti is best known for his doors for the baptistery of Florence Cathedral (Gates of Paradise; 1425–52), which are considered one of the greatest masterpieces of Italian art in the Quattrocento. His other works include three bronze statues for Or San Michele (1416–25) and the reliefs for Siena Cathedral (1417–27). Ghiberti also wrote *I Commentarii*, three treatises on art history and theory from antiquity to his time.

Ghiberti's mother had married Cione Ghiberti in 1370, and they lived in Pelago, near Florence. At some point she went to Florence and lived there as the common-law wife of a goldsmith named Bartolo di Michele. They were married in 1406 after Cione died, and it was in their home that Lorenzo Ghiberti spent his youth. It is not certain which man was Ghiberti's father, for he claimed each as his father at separate times. But throughout his early years, Lorenzo considered himself Bartolo's son, and it was Bartolo who trained the boy as a goldsmith. Ghiberti also received training as a painter; as he reported in the autobiographical part of his writings, he left Florence in 1400 with a painter to work in the town of Pesaro for its ruler, Sigismondo Malatesta.

Ghiberti returned quickly to his home city when he heard, in 1401, that a competition was being held for the commission to make a pair of bronze doors for the baptistery of the cathedral of Florence. He and six other artists were given the task of representing the biblical scene of Abraham's sacrifice of Isaac in a bronze relief of quatrefoil shape, following the tradition of the first set of doors

Isaac, Jacob, and Esau, gilded bronze relief panel from the east doors (Gates of Paradise) of the Baptistery of San Giovanni in Florence, by Lorenzo Ghiberti, 1425–52. SCALA/Art Resource, New York

produced by Andrea Pisano (1330–36). The entry panels of Ghiberti and of Filippo Brunelleschi are the sole survivors of the contest. Ghiberti's panels displayed a graceful and lively composition executed with a mastery of the goldsmith's art. In 1402 Ghiberti was chosen to make the doors by a large panel of judges; their decision brought immediate and lasting recognition and prominence to the young artist. The contract was signed in 1403 with Bartolo di Michele's workshop—overnight the most prestigious in Florence—and in 1407 Ghiberti legally took over the commission.

The work on the doors lasted until 1424, but Ghiberti did not devote himself to this alone. He created designs for the stained-glass windows in the cathedral; he regularly served as architectural consultant to the cathedral building supervisors, although it is unlikely that he actually collaborated with Brunelleschi on the construction of the dome as he later claimed. The Arte dei Mercanti di Calimala, the guild of the merchant bankers, gave him another commission, about 1412, to make a larger than life-size bronze statue of their patron saint, John the Baptist, for a niche on the outside of the guilds' communal building, Or San Michele. The job was a bold undertaking. As well as Ghiberti's first departure from goldsmith-scale work it was, in fact, the first large bronze in Florence. Ghiberti successfully finished the *St. John* in 1416, adding gilding in the following year. The technical achievement and the modernity of its style brought Ghiberti commissions for two similarly large bronze figures for guild niches at Or San Michele: the *St. Matthew* in 1419 for the bankers' guild and the *St. Stephen* for the wool guild in 1425.

These last two commissions brought Ghiberti into open competition with the newly prominent younger sculptors Donatello and Nanni di Banco, who had made

stone statues for Or San Michele after Ghiberti's first figure there. Ghiberti's *St. John* still followed many of the
conventions of the Gothic tradition. It combined small-
scale details with a larger-than-life scale that made the
figure appear overwhelmed by the drapery. Donatello's *St.
Mark* and *St. George* and Nanni di Banco's *St. Philip* and
Four Crowned Saints were as large as Ghiberti's figure but
were designed with monumental proportions to match
their scale. The boldness and strength of the weighty new
Classical figures constituted a challenge for Ghiberti, but
he met it with success in his next sculptures, and maintained his preeminent position as a leading artist in
Florence.

The teens and '20s were years of flourishing expansion
for Ghiberti and his firm. He had completed a great deal of
the modelling and casting of the panels for the baptistery
doors by 1413, and he was in control of a smoothly functioning workshop with many assistants. In 1417 Ghiberti
was asked to make two bronze reliefs for the baptismal font
of the cathedral in Siena. He was so busy that he finished
them, under pressure from the Sienese authorities, 10 years
later. In 1419, when Pope Martin V was in Florence, Ghiberti
was called on as a goldsmith to fashion a morse and mitre
for the pontiff. Unfortunately, these pieces, like other
examples of Ghiberti's art in rare stones and precious metals, have disappeared. During these years, too, Lorenzo
found a wife—Marsilia, the 16-year-old daughter of
Bartolomeo di Luca, a wool carder. She soon bore him two
sons: Tommaso was born in 1417 and Vittorio the next year.
His sons later joined Ghiberti in his business, and Vittorio
continued its operation after his father's death.

Ghiberti's artistic success also had its financial rewards.
A surviving tax return of 1427 lists property in Florence,
land out of town, and a substantial amount of money
invested in government bonds to his credit. Over the

Bronze doors from the north side of the baptistery of San Giovanni in Florence, by Lorenzo Ghiberti, c. 1403–24. Alinari/Art Resource, New York

years, his real estate and monetary holdings continued to grow. In addition to being well paid, Ghiberti was a businessman who managed his affairs shrewdly. He was a well-to-do member of Florentine society and a rich man among the artists of his time.

Ghiberti was actively involved with and interested in other artists and their work. Some (Donatello, Paolo Uccello, Michelozzo, Benozzo Gozzoli) had worked for a time in his workshop as young assistants. Ghiberti's association with the painter Fra Angelico is documented: Ghiberti designed the frame for his Linaiuoli Altarpiece. In his commentaries, Ghiberti exaggerates only a bit when he proudly claims that "few important things were done in our city which were not devised or designed by my hand." Among his undocumented works may be noted some half-dozen floor tombs and sarcophagi, but the vast extent to which Ghiberti's providing of designs and models influenced Florentine art is hard to measure. He appears to have shared his knowledge and talent generously and freely. Long before the completion of his second pair of doors (the Gates of Paradise) in 1452, the fund of figures and models assembled in connection with this work, which the public saw only later, was open to painters of frescoes in the Chiostro Verde (Green Cloister) of Santissima Annunziata and the sculptor Luca della Robbia, who was working on a marble singing gallery for the cathedral. Naturally, the impact of the Gates increased after they were installed.

When he was 45 years old, Ghiberti finished the first doors. They are the effort of more than 20 years of work and the major sculptural complex of the International Gothic style in Italy. They show some changes in the latest parts, however, to a more Classical style that emphasizes the bodies of figures more than the elegant draperies that enfold them. Ghiberti created expressive, strong faces based on examples he knew of ancient Roman art—portrait busts and carved sarcophagi. Because of the success of the first doors, a contract was soon signed with the Calimala for a second pair, but the political and financial fortunes of the city and the guild did not permit work to get under way for about five years.

Following the completion of the first doors, Ghiberti embarked on a decade of intense exploration of new ways of forming pictorial space and making gracefully active and lifelike figures. His works of the late 1420s show him able to make space increasingly intelligible in a series of clearly receding planes; using shallow relief, Ghiberti depicted volumes of bodies and deep architectural spaces. Examples of these are the reliefs in Siena; the Dati Tomb (the bronze plaque for the floor tomb of the Dominican general Leonardo Dati); and the two shrines in Florence, Cassa di S. Zenobius (a bronze casket with relief panels of stories from the saint's life) and Shrine of Saints Protus, Hyacinth, and Nemesius (a bronze container for the relics of three martyrs).

It is likely that at this time Ghiberti encountered Leon Battista Alberti, a young humanist scholar, who, inspired by the new art in Florence, was composing theoretical treatises on the visual arts. Their mutual belief that beauty was synonymous with the conception they shared of antique art makes it difficult to know whether or not Alberti's ideas in *De pictura* (*On Painting*) precede the three panels of the second door (Isaac, Joseph, and Solomon), which are the visual equivalent of those ideas. The beauty of antique art meant for both Alberti and Ghiberti an idealization of nature; capturing its essence meant revealing life by depicting movement, life's most salient visible characteristic. For the representation of a realistic spatial setting for these naturalistic figures, Alberti's treatise sets forth a perspective system for projecting such spaces onto the picture plane of a painting or bas-relief. Ghiberti's three panels seem an embodiment of the humanist's formulations for Renaissance pictorial art, and it is clear that any assessment of his art must account for the incorporation of the new theory as well as for the beauty and charm of these works. Ghiberti was himself so proud that he claimed to have made, in all, 10 panels, ". . . architectural settings in the relation with which the eye measures them, and real to such a degree that . . . one sees the figures which are near appear larger, and those that are far off smaller, as reality shows it."

Ghiberti's writings, *I Commentarii* (probably completed around 1447), shed more light on his humanist interests. The commentaries are composed of three books. The first, a history of art in ancient times, is Ghiberti's digest of writings of Latin authors on the subject. In it he reveals his belief that the inseparability of practice and theory is responsible for the excellence of ancient art. In the second book, which records the art of the immediate past, Ghiberti expresses his admiration for certain Sienese painters and for a late 14th-century northern goldsmith named Gusmin, who is known only through Ghiberti's pages. This book includes an autobiography, in which Ghiberti establishes his place in the history of art. The last book was apparently more theoretical, but in the surviving manuscript it is fragmentary. The commentaries demonstrate Ghiberti's confidence in his position as an important leader in the Florentine Renaissance—one interested in recapturing the art of the ancients and studying it as a humanist scholar would, and one who developed a new style, *all'antica,* in which he freely created art works with a grace and beauty that have been found winning since their invention.

DONATELLO

(b. *c.* 1386, Florence [Italy]—d. Dec. 13, 1466, Florence)

Donatello was a master sculptor who worked in both marble and bronze. He is one of the greatest of all Italian Renaissance artists.

A good deal is known about Donatello's life and career, but little is known about his character and personality, and what is known is not wholly reliable. He never married, and he seems to have been a man of simple tastes. Patrons often found him hard to deal with in a day when artists' working conditions were regulated by guild rules. Donatello seemingly demanded a measure of artistic freedom. Although he knew a number of humanists well, the artist was not a cultured intellectual. His humanist friends attest that he was a connoisseur of ancient art. The inscriptions and signatures on his works are among the earliest examples of the revival of Classical Roman lettering. He had a more detailed and wide-ranging knowledge of ancient sculpture than any other artist of his day. His work was inspired by ancient visual examples, which he often daringly transformed. Though he was traditionally viewed as essentially a realist, later research indicates he was much more.

EARLY CAREER

Donatello (diminutive of Donnato) was the son of Niccolò di Betto Bardi, a Florentine wool carder. It is not known how he began his career, but it seems likely that he learned stone carving from one of the sculptors working for the cathedral of Florence about 1400. Some time between 1404 and 1407, he became a member of the workshop of Lorenzo Ghiberti, a sculptor in bronze who in 1402 had won the competition for the doors of the Florentine baptistery. Donatello's earliest work of which there is certain knowledge, a marble statue of David, shows an artistic debt to Ghiberti, who was then the leading Florentine exponent of International Gothic, a style of graceful, softly curved lines strongly influenced by northern European art.

The full power of Donatello first appeared in two marble statues, *St. Mark* and *St. George* (both completed *c.* 1415), for niches on the exterior of Or San Michele, the church of Florentine guilds. Here, for the first time since Classical antiquity and in striking contrast to medieval art, the human body is rendered as a self-activating, functional organism, and the human personality is shown with a confidence in its own worth. The same qualities came increasingly to the fore in a series of five prophet statues that Donatello did beginning in 1416 for the niches of the campanile, the bell tower of the cathedral. These works, with their highly individual features inspired by ancient Roman portrait busts, are so different from the traditional images of Old Testament prophets that by the end of the 15th century they could be mistaken for portrait statues.

Donatello continued to explore the pictorial possibilities of sculpture begun by Ghiberti on the baptistery doors in his marble reliefs of the 1420s and early 1430s. The most highly developed of these are *The Ascension, with Christ Giving the Keys to St. Peter*, which is so delicately carved that its full beauty can be seen only in a strongly raking light; and the *Feast of Herod* (1433–35), with its perspective background. Meanwhile, Donatello had also become a major sculptor in bronze. His earliest such work was the more than life-size statue of St. Louis of Toulouse (*c.* 1423) for a niche at Or San Michele. Donatello had been commissioned to do not only the statue but the niche and its framework. The niche may have been a collaboration with Michelozzo, a sculptor and architect with whom he entered into a limited partnership. Michelozzo was responsible for the architectural framework and the decorative sculpture.

The architecture of these partnership projects resembles that of Brunelleschi and differs sharply from that of comparable works done by Donatello alone in the 1430s. All of his work done alone shows an unorthodox ornamental vocabulary drawn from both Classical and medieval sources and an un-Brunelleschian tendency to blur the distinction between the architectural and the sculptural elements. Both the Annunciation tabernacle in Santa Croce and the *Cantoria* (the singer's pulpit) in the Duomo show a vastly increased repertory of forms derived from ancient art, the harvest of Donatello's long stay in Rome (1430–33). His departure from the standards of Brunelleschi produced an estrangement between the two old friends that was never repaired.

During his partnership with Michelozzo, Donatello carried out independent commissions of pure sculpture, including several works of bronze for the baptismal font of San Giovanni in Siena. The earliest and most important of these was the *Feast of Herod* (1423–27), an intensely dramatic relief with an architectural background that first displayed Donatello's command of scientific linear perspective, which Brunelleschi had invented only a few years earlier. To the Siena font Donatello also contributed two statuettes of Virtues, austerely beautiful figures whose style points toward the Virgin and angel of the Santa Croce Annunciation, and three nude putti, or child angels. These putti, evidently influenced by Etruscan bronze figurines, prepared the way for the bronze *David*, the first large-scale, free-standing nude statue of the Renaissance. Well-proportioned and superbly poised, it was conceived independently of any architectural setting. Its harmonious calm makes it the most Classical of Donatello's works.

Whether the *David* was commissioned by the Medici or not, Donatello worked for them (1433–43), producing sculptural decoration for the old sacristy in San Lorenzo, the Medici church. Works there included 10 large reliefs in coloured stucco and two sets of small bronze doors, which showed paired saints and apostles disputing with each other in vivid and even violent fashion.

PADUAN PERIOD

In 1443 Donatello was lured to Padua by a commission for a bronze equestrian statue of a famous Venetian condottiere, Erasmo da Narmi, popularly called Gattamelata ("The Honeyed Cat"), who had died shortly before. Such a project was unprecedented—indeed, scandalous—for since the days of the Roman Empire bronze equestrian monuments had been the sole prerogative of rulers. The execution of the monument was plagued by delays. Donatello did most of the work between 1447 and 1450, yet the statue was not placed on its pedestal until 1453. It portrays Gattamelata in pseudo-Classical armour calmly astride his mount, the baton of command in his raised right hand. The head is an idealized portrait with intellectual power and Roman nobility. This statue was the ancestor of all the equestrian monuments erected since. Its fame, enhanced by the controversy, spread far and wide. Even before it was on public view, the king of Naples wanted Donatello to do the same kind of equestrian statue for him.

In the early 1450s, Donatello undertook some important works for the Paduan Church of San Antonio: a splendidly expressive bronze crucifix and a new high altar, the most ambitious of its kind, unequaled in 15th-century Europe. Its richly decorated architectural framework of marble and limestone contains seven life-size bronze statues, 21 bronze reliefs of various sizes, and a large limestone relief, *Entombment of Christ*. The housing was destroyed a century later, and the present arrangement, dating from 1895, is wrong both aesthetically and historically. Donatello's mastery in handling large numbers of figures (one relief has more than 100) anticipates the compositional principles of the High Renaissance.

Donatello was apparently inactive during the last three years at Padua, clearly passing through a crisis that prevented him from working. He was later quoted as saying that he almost died "among those frogs in Padua." In 1456 the Florentine physician Giovanni Chellini noted in his account book that he had successfully treated the master for a protracted illness. Donatello completed only two works between 1450 and 1455: the wooden statue *St. John the Baptist* in Santa Maria Gloriosa dei Frari, Venice, shortly before his return to Florence; and an even more extraordinary figure of Mary Magdalen in the Florentine baptistery. Both works show new insight into psychological reality; Donatello's formerly powerful bodies have become withered and spidery, overwhelmed, as it were, by emotional tensions within.

LATE FLORENTINE PERIOD

During Donatello's stay in Padua, a new generation of sculptors who excelled in the sensuous treatment of marble surfaces had arisen in Florence. Thus Donatello's wooden figures must have been a shock. With the change in Florentine taste, all of Donatello's important commissions came from outside Florence. They included the dramatic bronze group *Judith and Holofernes* and a bronze statue of St. John the Baptist for Siena Cathedral.

The last years of Donatello's life were spent designing twin bronze pulpits for San Lorenzo, and thus, again in the service of his old patrons the Medici, he died. Covered with reliefs showing the passion of Christ, the pulpits are works of tremendous spiritual depth and complexity.

JAN VAN EYCK

(b. before 1395, Maaseik, Bishopric of Liège, Holy Roman Empire [now in Belgium]—d. before July 9, 1441, Bruges)

Flemish painter Jan van Eyck is notable for having perfected the newly developed technique of oil painting. His naturalistic panel paintings, mostly portraits and religious subjects, made extensive use of disguised religious symbols. His masterpiece is the altarpiece in the cathedral at Ghent, the *Adoration of the Lamb* (1432; also called Ghent Altarpiece).

Jan van Eyck must have been born before 1395, for in October 1422 he is recorded as the *varlet de chambre et peintre* ("honorary equerry and painter") of John of Bavaria, count of Holland. He continued to work in the palace of The Hague until the count's death in 1425 and then settled briefly in Bruges before he was summoned, that summer, to Lille to serve Philip the Good, duke of Burgundy, the most powerful ruler and foremost patron of the arts in Flanders. Jan remained in the duke's employ until his death. On behalf of his sponsor he undertook a number of secret missions during the next decade, of which the most notable were two journeys to the Iberian Peninsula, the first in 1427 to try to contract a marriage for Philip with Isabella of Spain, and a more successful trip in 1428–29 to seek the hand of Isabella of Portugal. As a confidant of Philip, Jan may have participated directly in these marriage negotiations, but he also was charged to present the duke with a portrait of the intended.

In 1431 Jan purchased a house in Bruges and, about the same time, married a woman named Margaret, about whom little more is known than that she was born in 1406 and was to bear him at least two children. Residing in Bruges, Jan continued to paint, and in 1436 he again made a secret voyage for Philip. After his death in 1441, he was buried in the Church of Saint-Donatian, in Bruges.

Securely attributed paintings survive only from the last decade of Jan's career; therefore, his artistic origins and early development must be deduced from his mature work. Traditionally, Jan has been acclaimed the founder of Flemish painting, and scholars have sought his artistic roots in the last great phase of medieval manuscript illumination. It is clear that the naturalism and elegant composition of Jan's later painting owe much to such early 15th-century illuminators as the anonymous Boucicaut Master and Pol, Herman, and Jehanequin de Limburg (the "Limburg Brothers"), who worked for the Burgundian dukes. A document of 1439 reports that Jan van Eyck paid an illuminator for preparing a book for the duke; but central to the discussion of his ties to manuscript illustration has been the attribution to Jan of several miniatures, identified as H and G, in a problematic prayer book known as the Turin-Milan Hours. So long as these "Eyckian" miniatures were dated in the 1420s or even earlier, Jan's authorship seemed indubitable; but recent investigations strongly indicate that these miniatures were painted at least 20 years later and, hence, that they are by an imitator. With the elimination of the Turin-Milan Hours from Jan van Eyck's early oeuvre, his connections with International Gothic style illumination appear to have been less direct than had been thought.

Certainly as important for Jan's artistic formation were the panel paintings of Robert Campin (c. 1378–1444), a Tournai painter whose important role in the history of Flemish art has only recently been reestablished. Jan must have met Campin at least once, when he was feted by the Tournai painter's guild in 1427, and from Campin's art he seems to have learned the bold realism, the method of disguised symbolism, and perhaps the luminous oil technique that became so characteristic of his own style. In contrast to Campin, who was a Tournai burgher, Jan was a learned master at work in a busy court, and he signed his paintings, the first Flemish artist to do so. The majority of Jan's panels present the proud inscription "IOHANNES DE EYCK," and several bear his aristocratic motto, "*Als ik kan*" ("As best I can"). It is small wonder that Campin's reputation faded and his influence on Jan was forgotten, and it is of little surprise that many of Campin's achievements were credited to the younger master.

Despite Jan van Eyck's having signed 9 paintings and dated 10, the establishment of his oeuvre and the reconstruction of its chronology present problems. The major difficulty is that Jan's masterpiece, the *Adoration of the Lamb* altarpiece, has a probably reliable inscription that introduces another painter, Hubert van Eyck, as its principal master. (Hubert van Eyck is believed to have been Jan's brother.) This has caused art historians to turn to less ambitious but more secure works to plot Jan's development, including, most notably: the *Portrait of a Young Man* (*Leal Souvenir*) of 1432, the wedding portrait *Giovanni Arnolfini and Giovanna Cenami* of 1434, the *Madonna with Canon van der Paele* of 1434–36, the triptych *Madonna and Child with Saints* of 1437, and the panels of *St. Barbara* and the *Madonna at the Fountain*, dated, respectively, 1437 and 1439. Although they fall within a brief span of seven years, these paintings present a consistent development in which Jan moved from the heavy, sculptural realism associated with Robert Campin to a more delicate, rather precious, pictorial style.

On stylistic grounds there seems little difficulty in placing the Ghent Altarpiece at the head of this development as indicated by the date 1432 in the inscription, but the question of Hubert's participation in this great work has yet to be completely resolved. The inscription itself is definite about this point: "The painter Hubert van Eyck, greater than whom no one was found, began [this work]; and Jan, his brother, second in art [carried] through the task . . ." On the basis of this claim, art historians have attempted to distinguish Hubert's contribution to the Ghent Altarpiece and have even assigned to him certain of the more archaic "Eyckian" paintings, including *The Annunciation* and *The Three Marys at the Tomb*.

The confusion concerning Jan's relationship to Hubert, the doubt about his activities as an illuminator, and the reemergence of Robert Campin as a preeminent master do not diminish the achievement and significance of Jan van Eyck. He may not have invented oil painting as early writers asserted, but he perfected the technique to mirror the textures, light, and spatial effects of nature. The realism of his paintings—admired as early as 1449 by the Italian humanist Cyriacus D'Ancona, who observed that the works seemed to have been produced "not by the artifice of human hands but by all-bearing nature herself"—has never been surpassed. For Jan, as for Campin, naturalism was not merely a technical tour de force, however. For him, nature embodied God, and so he filled his paintings with religious symbols disguised as everyday objects. Even the light that so naturally illuminates Jan van Eyck's landscapes and interiors is a metaphor of the Divine.

Because of the refinement of his technique and the abstruseness of his symbolic programs, the successors of Jan van Eyck borrowed only selectively from his art. Campin's foremost student, Rogier van der Weyden, tempered his master's homey realism with Eyckian grace and delicacy. In fact, at the end of his career, Campin himself succumbed somewhat to Jan's courtly style. Even Petrus Christus, who may have been apprenticed in Jan's atelier and who finished the *Virgin and Child, with Saints and Donor* after Jan's death, quickly abandoned the intricacies of Jan's style under the influence of van der Weyden. During the last third of the century, the Netherlandish painters Hugo van der Goes and Justus van Gent revived the Eyckian heritage, but, when such early 16th-century Flemish masters as Quentin Massys and Jan Gossart turned to Jan's work, they produced pious copies that had little impact on their original creations. In Germany and France the influence of Jan van Eyck was overshadowed by the more accessible styles of Campin and van der Weyden, and only in the Iberian Peninsula—which Jan had visited twice—did his art dominate. In Italy his greatness was recognized by Cyriacus and by the humanist Bartolomeo Facio, who lists Jan, together with van der Weyden and the Italian artists Il Pisanello and Gentile da Fabriano, as one of the leading painters of the period. But Renaissance artists, as painters elsewhere, found him easier to admire than to imitate.

Interest in his painting and acknowledgment of his prodigious technical accomplishment have remained high. Jan's works have been copied frequently and have been avidly collected. He is referred to in the Treaty of Versailles, which specifies the return of the Ghent Altarpiece to Belgium before peace with Germany could be concluded after the end of World War I.

IL PISANELLO

(b. *c.* 1395, Pisa [Italy]—d. 1455)

Antonio Pisano, known as Il Pisanello, was an Italian medalist and painter and a major exponent of a style known as International Gothic because it was unusually common to several countries. It was characterized by a delicate naturalism. Pisanello's early work suggests that he

Madonna with SS. Anthony and George, *painting by Pisanello, after 1422; in the National Gallery, London.* Courtesy of the trustees of the National Gallery, London; photograph, J.R. Freeman & Co. Ltd Photograph, J.R. Freeman & Co. Ltd.

was the pupil of Stefano da Zevio, a Veronese artist. (He was wrongly identified as "Vittore Pisano" by Giorgio Vasari, and only in 1907 was his personal name verified as Antonio.)

Pisanello collaborated with Gentile da Fabriano on frescoes in the Doges' Palace in Venice (c. 1415–22) and in St. John Lateran in Rome (after 1427). After Gentile's death, Pisanello probably completed the Roman frescoes, known only through drawings, which show Gentile's great influence over the young Pisanello. Until 1969, when layers of plaster were removed from the walls of the Sala del Pisanello in Mantua's Palazzo Ducale to reveal a series of Pisanello's frescoes depicting scenes of war and chivalry, his only surviving frescoes were thought to have been an Annunciation at the tomb of Niccolò di Brenzoni in San Fermo (c. 1423–24) and the legend of St. George in the Pellegrini Chapel in San Anastasia (c. 1433–38), both in Verona. These works are characterized by the curvilinear design, calligraphic draperies, and decorative detail typical of the International Gothic style that Pisanello used throughout his career. Even a mature work such as his *St. Eustace* is encrusted with rich detail that tends to work against spatial clarity. The *Madonna with SS. Anthony and George* displays a simpler conception. It is dominated by the monumental figures of the two saints and the bust of the Virgin in a mandorla, or almond-shaped aureole.

Pisanello's fame and his importance in court circles rested more upon his medals than upon his painting. They are thought to have resulted from his study of ancient Greek and Roman numismatic portraits. He had virtually no recent predecessors, and, with him, the art reached its highest point. His work includes the medal of the Greek emperor John VIII Palaeologus (1438), the wedding medal of Lionello d'Este (1444), Sigismondo Pandolfo Malatesta

(1445), and the medal of Alfonso of Aragon (1448), generally cited as his most successful work in the genre. Most of Pisanello's painted portraits, such as the *Margherita Gonzaga* (c. 1438), and *Lionello d'Este* (c. 1440), show the sitter in profile—a convention of Pisanello's portrait medals—against a background of delicate, colourful flowers and butterflies.

Pisanello's drawings have been preserved in the Codex Vallardi. This is the only instance in which the drawings of a 15th-century workshop have been preserved virtually intact. They are of unique value, therefore, for the study of the style and techniques of draftsmanship of the period. Pisanello uses a large variety of techniques and materials to produce masterful drawings (some coloured) of animals, plants, costume design, and perspective studies. His drawings of various views of horses are particularly well known. He was one of the first 15th-century artists to draw from life instead of adhering to the medieval tradition of copying the drawings of others. These drawings reveal Pisanello's breadth of interest and his sensitive eye. They combine delicately rendered early Renaissance naturalism with the beauty of late Gothic line and are one of his most important contributions to the history of art.

FRANCESCO SQUARCIONE

(b. c. 1395, Padua [Italy]—d. after 1468, Padua)

Early Renaissance painter Francesco Squarcione founded the Paduan school of art. He is known for being the teacher of Andrea Mantegna and other noteworthy painters.

Squarcione was the son of a notary of Padua. From an early age he began to collect and draw copies of ancient sculptures. According to the 16th-century historian

Bernardino Scardeone, who is the main source of information on Squarcione, he traveled widely in search of
these objects and may have even visited Greece. After
returning to Padua, he began teaching, taking his first student in 1431. He was associated in 1434 with the influential
Tuscan painter Fra Filippo Lippi during the latter's stay
in Padua. In 1440 Squarcione purchased a house in which
he displayed his collection of antique sculptures and
architectural fragments. Squarcione's two extant panel
paintings, a Madonna and Child in Berlin and the polyptych *St. Jerome and Saints* (1449–52) in the Civic Museum
of Padua, show the influence of the Florentine early
Renaissance style, especially that of the sculptor Donatello,
who worked in Padua from 1443 to 1453. The only record
of Squarcione's mature style is contained in a cycle of frescoes of scenes from the life of St. Francis on the exterior
of San Francesco at Padua (*c.* 1452–66). Such compositions
as can be reconstructed confirm the traditional view of
Squarcione as one of the channels through which the early
Renaissance style of Florence diffused in Padua.

More significant than his painting, however, was his
establishment of a private school, a place for learning that
differed from the traditional workshop and apprenticeship. According to Scardeone, Squarcione had 137 pupils.
One of the noteworthy features of his school was his incli-
nation to adopt the more skilled students and enlist them
in painting for him. Among the artists he taught or influenced were Mantegna and Marco Zoppo (both of whom
he adopted and both of whom rejected his authority),
Giorgio Schiavone, and Cosmè Tura. Squarcione's school
was renowned as one of the most advanced in the area,
although later scholars credit his students rather than
Squarcione with innovation. The claim that he was one of
the first to understand linear perspective has also been
challenged and seems unlikely.

PAOLO UCCELLO

(b. 1397, Pratovecchio, near Florence [Italy] — d. Dec. 10, 1475, Florence)

The work of Florentine painter Paolo Uccello represents a unique attempt to reconcile two distinct artistic styles — the essentially decorative late Gothic and the new heroic style of the early Renaissance. Probably his most famous paintings are three panels representing *The Battle of San Romano* (c. 1456). His careful and sophisticated perspective studies are clearly evident in *The Flood* (1447–48).

APPRENTICESHIP AND EARLY WORK

By the time Paolo Uccello, born Paolo di Dono, was 10 years old he was already an apprentice in the workshop of the sculptor Lorenzo Ghiberti, who was then at work on what became one of the masterpieces of Renaissance art — the bronze doors for the baptistery of the Florence Cathedral. In 1414 Uccello joined the confraternity of painters (Compagnia di San Luca), and in the following year he became a member of the Arte dei Medici e degli Speziali, the official guild in Florence to which painters belonged. Though Uccello must by then have been established as an independent painter, nothing of his work from this time remains, and there is no definite indication of his early training as a painter, except that he was a member of the workshop of Ghiberti, where many of the outstanding artists of the time were trained.

Uccello's earliest, and now badly damaged, frescoes are in the Chiostro Verde (the Green Cloister, so called because of the green cast of the frescoes that covered its walls) of Santa Maria Novella. They represent episodes from the Creation. These frescoes, marked with a pervasive concern for elegant linear forms and insistent, stylized patterning of landscape features, are consistent with the late Gothic tradition that was still predominant at the beginning of the 15th century in Florentine studios.

From 1425 to 1431, Uccello worked in Venice as a master mosaicist. All his work in Venice has been lost, however. Uccello may have been induced to return to Florence by the commission for a series of frescoes in the cloister of San Miniato al Monte depicting scenes from monastic legends. While the figural formulations of these ruinous frescoes still closely approximate those of the Santa Maria Novella cycle, there is also a fascination with the novel perspective schemes that had appeared in Florence during Uccello's Venetian sojourn and with a simplified and more monumental treatment of forms deriving from the recent sculpture of Donatello and Nanni di Banco.

LATER YEARS

In 1436 in the Florence Cathedral, Uccello completed a monochrome fresco of an equestrian monument to Sir John Hawkwood, an English mercenary who had commanded Florentine troops at the end of the 14th century. In the Hawkwood fresco, a single-point perspective scheme, a fully sculptural treatment of the horse and rider, and a sense of controlled potential energy within the figure all indicate Uccello's desire to assimilate the new style of the Renaissance that had blossomed in Florence since his birth. Following the Hawkwood monument, in 1443 Uccello completed four heads of prophets around a colossal clock on the interior of the west facade of the cathedral; between 1443 and 1445 he contributed the designs for two stained-glass windows in the cupola.

After a brief trip to Padua in 1447, Uccello returned to the Chiostro Verde of Santa Maria Novella. In a fresco illustrating the Flood and the recession of the water, Uccello presented two separate scenes united by a rapidly receding perspective scheme that reflected the influence of Donatello's contemporary reliefs in Padua. Human forms in *The Flood*, especially the nudes, were reminiscent of figures in Masaccio's frescoes in the Brancacci Chapel (*c.* 1427), perhaps the most influential of all paintings of the early Renaissance. More than any other painting by Uccello, *The Flood* illustrates the artist's love for perspective.

Perhaps Uccello's most famous paintings are three panels representing the Battle of San Romano, now in the Louvre, Paris; the National Gallery, London; and the Uffizi, Florence. These panels represent the victory in 1432 of Florentine forces under Niccolò da Tolentino over the troops of their archrival, Siena. There are Renaissance elements, such as a sculptural treatment of forms and fragments of a broken perspective scheme in this work, but the bright handling of colour and the elaborate decorative patterns of the figures and landscape are indebted to the Gothic style. The older style continued to be used through the 15th century in Florence to enrich the environments of the new princes of the day, such as the Medici, who acquired all three of the panels representing the Battle of San Romano.

Uccello is justly famous for his careful and sophisticated perspective studies in the underdrawing (sinopia) for his last fresco, *The Nativity*, formerly in San Martino della Scala in Florence, and in three drawings universally attributed to him that are now in the Uffizi. These drawings indicate a meticulous, analytic mind, keenly interested in the application of scientific laws to the reconstruction of objects in a three-dimensional space. In these studies he was probably assisted by a noted mathematician, Paolo Toscanelli. Uccello's perspective studies were to influence the Renaissance art treatises of artists such as Piero della Francesca, Leonardo da Vinci, and Albrecht Dürer. Uccello apparently led an increasingly reclusive existence during his last years.

ASSESSMENT

Uccello was long thought to be significant primarily for his role in establishing new means of rendering perspective that became a major component of the Renaissance style. The 16th-century biographer Giorgio Vasari said that Uccello was "intoxicated" by perspective. Later historians found the unique charm and decorative genius evinced by his compositions to be an even more important contribution.

ROGIER VAN DER WEYDEN

(b. 1399/1400, Tournai, France—d. June 18, 1464, Brussels)

Rogier van der Weyden (French: Rogier de la Pasture) was a Flemish painter who, with the possible exception of Jan van Eyck, was the most influential northern European artist of his time. Though most of his work was religious, he produced secular paintings (now lost) and some sensitive portraits.

Rogier van der Weyden was the son of a master cutler, and his childhood must have been spent in the comfortable surroundings of the rising class of merchants and craftsmen. He may even have acquired a university education, for in 1426 he was honoured by the city as "Maistre (Master) Rogier de la Pasture" and began his painting career only the next year at the rather advanced age of 27. It was then, on March 5, 1427, that van der Weyden enrolled as an apprentice in the workshop of Robert Campin, the foremost painter in Tournai and dean of the painters' guild.

Van der Weyden remained in Campin's atelier for five years, becoming an independent master of the guild on Aug. 1, 1432. From Campin, he learned the ponderous, detailed realism that characterizes his earliest paintings, and so alike, in fact, are the styles of these two masters that connoisseurs still do not agree on the attribution of certain works. But the theory that the entire sequence of paintings credited to Campin (who, like van der Weyden, did not sign his panels) are actually from the brush of the young van der Weyden cannot be maintained. Careful study of secure works by van der Weyden and by his colleague in Campin's workshop, Jacques Daret, permit scholars to reestablish a basic series of works by the older master and to distinguish the style of these from that of van der Weyden.

Campin was not the only source of inspiration in van der Weyden's art. Jan van Eyck, the great painter from Bruges, also profoundly affected the developing artist, introducing elegance and subtle visual refinements into the bolder, Campinesque components of such early paintings by van der Weyden as *St. Luke Painting the Virgin*. Although as an apprentice van der Weyden must certainly have met Jan van Eyck when the latter visited Tournai in 1427, it was more likely in Bruges, where van der Weyden may have resided between 1432 and 1435, that he became thoroughly acquainted with van Eyck's style.

By 1435, van der Weyden, now a mature master, settled in Brussels, the native city of his wife, Elizabeth Goffaert, whom he had married in 1426. The next year he was appointed city painter; and it was from this time that he began to use the Flemish translation of his name (van der Weyden). He remained in Brussels the rest of his life, although he never completely severed his ties with Tournai. He was commissioned to paint a mural (now destroyed) for the town hall of Brussels showing famous historical examples of the administration of justice. During this same period, around 1435–40, he completed the celebrated panel of the *Descent from the Cross* for the chapel of the Archers' Guild of Louvain. In this deposition there is evident a tendency to reduce the setting of a scene to a shallow, shrinelike enclosure and to orchestrate a rich diversity of emotions.

These devotional qualities are even more striking in van der Weyden's works of the 1440s such as the twin Granada-Miraflores altarpieces and the Last Judgment Polyptych in Beaune, France (Hôtel-Dieu). In these the settings are stark, the figures are delicate Gothic types, and the action, though stilled, is exquisitely expressive. The removal of van der Weyden's art from concern with outward appearances and his return to medieval conventions is surprising; for it was during this decade that his international reputation was secured and commissions increased from noblemen such as Philip the Good, duke of Burgundy, and his powerful chancellor, Nicolas Rolin. Van der Weyden may well have also been influenced by the writings of Thomas à Kempis, the most popular theologian of the era, whose "practical mysticism," like van der Weyden's painting, stressed empathetic response to episodes from the lives of Mary, Christ, and the saints.

Perhaps as an extension of a journey to install the Last Judgment Altarpiece in Rolin's chapel at Beaune or possibly to obtain a plenary indulgence for his daughter Margaret, one of van der Weyden's four children, who had died that year, the renowned painter visited Rome during the Jubilee of 1450. He was warmly received in Italy. Praise from the humanist Bartolomeo Fazio and the eminent theologian Nicholas of Cusa is recorded; van der Weyden also received commissions from the powerful Este family of Ferrara and the Medici of Florence. He painted a portrait of Francesco d'Este (originally thought to be Leonello d'Este), and his painting of the Madonna and Child that still remains in Florence (Uffizi) bears the arms and patron saints of the Medici.

While on his pilgrimage, van der Weyden apparently tutored Italian masters in painting with oils, a technique in which Flemish painters of the time were particularly adept. He also seems to have learned a great deal from what he viewed. Although he was primarily attracted to the conservative painters Gentile da Fabriano and Fra Angelico, whose medievalizing styles paralleled his own, van der Weyden was also acquainted with more progressive trends. In the St. John Altarpiece and the *Seven Sacraments* triptych, executed between 1451 and 1455, shortly after van der Weyden's return north, his characteristic austerity was tempered by his recollection of the more robust Italian styles. In both, the panels are unified from a single point of view. Despite this enrichment, however, van der Weyden's conceptions remained essentially iconic. He pushed the figures into the foreground and isolated them from their surroundings as subjects for devotion.

The last 15 years of his life brought van der Weyden the rewards due an internationally famous painter and exemplary citizen. He received numerous commissions, which he carried out with the assistance of a large workshop that included his own son Peter and his successor as city painter, Vranck van der Stockt, a mediocre imitator. Even before his death, however, van der Weyden's impact extended far beyond his immediate associates. The influence of his expressive but technically less intricate style eclipsed that of both Campin and van Eyck. Every Flemish painter of the succeeding generation—Petrus Christus, Dirck Bouts, Hugo van der Goes, and Hans Memling (who may have studied in van der Weyden's atelier)—depended on his formulations; during the 16th century, his ideas were transformed and revitalized by Quentin Massys and Bernard van Orley. Van der Weyden's art was also a vehicle for transporting the Flemish style throughout Europe, and during the second half of the 15th century his influence dominated painting in France, Germany, and Spain.

Nevertheless, van der Weyden's fame quickly waned, and no painting by him had been signed or dated. By the end of the 16th century the biographer Carel van Mander had referred mistakenly to two Rogiers in *Het Schilderboek* (1603; "Book of Painters"), and by the middle of the 19th century his fame and art had all but been forgotten. Only through a meticulous evaluation of the documents have scholars since then been able to reconstruct van der Weyden's work and to restore the reputation of one of 15th-century Flanders' leading masters.

LUCA DELLA ROBBIA

(b. 1399/1400, Florence [Italy]—d. Feb. 10, 1482)

The sculptor Luca della Robbia was a pioneer of Florentine Renaissance style and the founder of a family studio primarily associated with the production of works in enameled terra-cotta. Before developing the process with which his family name came to be associated, Luca apparently practiced his art solely in marble.

In 1431 he began what is probably his most important work, the *Cantoria*, or "singing gallery," that was originally over the door of the northern sacristy of the Cathedral of Florence. Taken down in 1688 and reassembled in the Opera del Duomo Museum, it consists of 10 figurated reliefs: two groups of singing boys; trumpeters; choral dancers; and children playing on various musical instruments. The panels owe their great popularity to the innocence and naturalism with which the children are portrayed. The most important of Luca's other works in marble are a tabernacle carved for the Chapel of San Luca in the Santa Maria Nuova Hospital in Florence (1441), and the tomb of Benozzo Federighi, bishop of Fiesole (1454–57).

The earliest documented work in polychrome enameled terra-cotta, executed wholly in that medium, is a lunette of the Resurrection over the door of the northern sacristy of the cathedral (1442–45). According to Luca's contemporary, the writer Giorgio Vasari, the glaze with which Luca covered his terra-cotta sculptures consisted of a mixture of tin, litharge antimony, and other minerals. The Resurrection lunette in the cathedral was followed by a corresponding relief of the Ascension over the southern sacristy door, in which a wider range of colour is employed.

Of the many decorative schemes for which enameled terra-cotta was employed by Luca della Robbia, some of the most important are the roundels of Apostles in Filippo Brunelleschi's Pazzi Chapel in Florence (soon after 1443); the roof of Michelozzo's Chapel of the Crucifix in San Miniato al Monte, Florence (c. 1448); and a lunette over the entrance of San Domenico at Urbino (c. 1449). Luca's last major work in this medium is an altarpiece in the Palazzo Vescovile at Pescia (after 1472). There are also many notable works by Luca outside Italy.

FRA ANGELICO

(b. c. 1400, Vicchio, Republic of Florence [Italy] – d. Feb. 18, 1455, Rome)

One of the greatest painters of the 15th century, Fra Angelico created works within the framework of the early Renaissance style that embody a serene religious attitude and reflect a strong Classical influence. A great number of works executed during his career are altarpieces and frescoes created for the church and the priory of San Marco in Florence while he was in residence there.

San Domenico Period

Baptized Guido di Pietro, Angelico appeared in a document of 1417 as a lay painter. Later, between the years 1420 and 1422, he became a Dominican friar and resided in the priory of San Domenico at Fiesole, there taking the name of Fra Giovanni da Fiesole. At Fiesole he was probably influenced by the teachings of Giovanni Dominici, the militant leader of the reformed Dominicans; the writings of Dominici defended traditional spirituality against the onslaught of humanism. Angelico was also influenced by his fellow friar St. Antoninus Pierozzi, who became the archbishop of Florence when Fra Angelico refused the post and who may have consolidated Angelico's faith. It is believed that Antoninus also may have inspired some of Angelico's compositions.

According to the painter and biographer Giorgio Vasari, Angelico was trained by the greatest painter and miniaturist of the Gothic tradition, Lorenzo Monaco, whose influence may be seen in the clear, painstaking delicacy of execution and the vibrant luminosity that seem to spiritualize the figures in Angelico's paintings. These qualities are notably apparent in two small altarpieces, *Madonna of the Star* and *The Annunciation*.

Angelico's *Deposition* for Santa Trinità in Florence was once attributed to Monaco, who had begun it before he died in 1425. Monaco had divided it into a triptych and executed the pinnacles. Angelico, however, made it a unified altarpiece with a vast landscape dominated by a varicoloured hill town. It is perhaps an imaginative evocation of Cortona, where Fra Angelico spent some time and where some of his important works are to be found. Against that background are sharply outlined human figures in interconnected groups; their features are so delicately traced that attempts have been made to identify them as portraits. These arrangements of figures attest to Angelico's deep knowledge of the formalism that characterized the art of the early Renaissance.

Two strands were interwoven in Angelico's life at Fiesole: the pious life of a friar and continuous activity as a painter. Vasari described him as "saintly and excellent," and, not long after his death, he was called *angelico* ("angelic") because of his moral virtues. This subsequently became the name by which he is best known, often preceded by the word *beato* ("blessed").

Angelico knew and followed closely the new artistic trends of his time, above all the representation of space by means of perspective. In works such as the large *Last Judgment* and *The Coronation of the Virgin*, for example, the human figures receding toward the rear themselves create a feeling of space similar to that in the paintings of Angelico's great Florentine contemporary Masaccio. The earliest work by Angelico that can be dated with certainty is a triptych of huge dimensions that he painted for the linen merchants' guild (or Arte dei Linaiuoli; hence its name, the Linaiuoli Altarpiece); it is dated July 11, 1433. Enclosed in a marble shrine designed by the Florentine sculptor Lorenzo Ghiberti, this altarpiece represents the Virgin and Son facing forward, monumentally, and, surrounding them in a minor key, charming angels, developing the motif of the *Madonna of the Star*. The group has affinities with the Florentine Maestà (i.e., Madonna and Child Enthroned in Majesty) of the 14th century, but the influence of Masaccio may be seen in the formalism of the construction and in the innovative use of light and colour. Angelico finished the work with a predella, or narrow strip of paintings along the bottom of the altarpiece; this group of paintings includes *The Adoration of the Magi* and *The Martyrdom of St. Mark*, which are lucid and compact in their narrative and have a strictly defined perspective, a technique that is even more effective in the small painting depicting the naming of John the Baptist.

In the early 1430s, Angelico was commissioned to paint the *Deposition* for the sacristy of the Church of Santa Trinità as a companion piece to Gentile da Fabriano's *Adoration of the Magi*. As mentioned earlier, Angelico took over this painting after the death of Lorenzo Monaco in 1425. In Angelico's painting, the dead Christ is gently lowered from the cross and is mourned in silent grief by the Virgin Mary and a group of women on the left of the composition. On the right, a group of men clothed in contemporary Florentine dress stand in mute contemplation. One of these figures might be the portrait of Palla Strozzi, the patron of the chapel and of the altarpiece. Strozzi, who was at the time one of the richest men in Europe and a rival to Cosimo de' Medici, was exiled in 1434. The altarpiece might have been finished after his exile, possibly about 1440. The *Deposition* is one of the first paintings in the Italian Renaissance to depict figures in a receding landscape rather than in a space set as a foreground stage. In the background, Angelico depicted the city of Jerusalem.

Also in the 1430s, Angelico painted one of the most inspired works of the Florentine Renaissance, *The Annunciation*, an altarpiece significantly superior to his two other paintings on the same subject. It shows the Garden of Eden with Adam and Eve being driven out by the Angel yet also under the sway of the radiant messenger and pure maiden who are portrayed in the space of a Renaissance-style portico. The predella is skillfully divided into stories of the Virgin Mary, naturalistically portrayed—especially the Visitation, which has a realistic panorama. Angelico always followed reality closely, even when he used a miniaturist technique. Occasionally, he resorted to medieval techniques, such as a gold background, in deference to the taste of those who commissioned the work, but his figures still emerge quite distinctly from the panels, in the Renaissance manner, revealing the painter's increasingly sure and harmonious pictorial idiom. Angelico's Annalena Altarpiece, also of the 1430s, is, so far as is known, the first *sacra conversazione* (i.e., "sacred conversation," a representation of the Holy Family) of the Renaissance.

YEARS AT THE PRIORY OF SAN MARCO

Angelico remained in the Fiesole priory until 1439, when he entered the priory of San Marco in Florence. There he worked mostly on frescoes. San Marco had been transferred from the Sylvestrine monks to the Dominicans in 1436, and the rebuilding of the church and its spacious priory began about 1438, from designs by the Florentine architect and sculptor Michelozzo. The construction was generously subsidized by the Medici family. Angelico was commissioned about 1438 by Cosimo de' Medici the Elder to execute the altarpiece, for which he again painted a *sacra conversazione*. When the church was consecrated at Epiphany in 1443, the altarpiece must have dominated the place of worship. Angelico portrayed the Virgin and Child raised high on a throne, with saints on either side receding into space; among them are the two patron saints of the Medici, Cosmas and Damian. This work, one of the most compelling Fra Angelico created, ends in a dense grove of cypresses, palms, and pines against a deep but toneless sky. His figures seem cleansed of any human passion and appear to have supreme serenity of spirit. A predella, showing eight little legends of the two Medicean saints separated by a Pietà (Virgin Mary holding the body of Christ), completed the work. These paintings are now scattered among various museums.

The Annunciation, *fresco by Fra Angelico, 1438–45; in the Museum of San Marco, Florence.* SCALA/Art Resource, New York

On the walls of the priory of San Marco in Florence are the paintings that mark the high point of Angelico's career. In the chapter hall, he executed a large *Crucifixion* that seems akin to the "Moralities" of the 14th century, which urged detachment from worldly vanities and salvation through Christ alone. In addition to the three crucified figures against the sky, Angelico painted groups of ritual figures, rhythmically arranged, with a chorus of martyrs, founders of religious orders, hermits, and defenders of the Dominican order (whose genealogical tree is depicted beneath this striking scene), as well as the two Medicean saints. Thus, in the comprehensiveness of this work, Fra Angelico developed a concept that was barely suggested in his earlier altarpieces.

He portrayed the exaltation of the Redeemer in many other paintings in the priory's first cloister and in its cells. In one corridor he executed an Annunciation that broadened the pattern of his earlier one in Cortona. In the cells, he proclaimed devotion to Christ crucified in at least 20 examples, all related to monastic life. The pictorial work in these narrow spaces is intricate, probably the work of numerous hands directed by the master, including Benozzo Gozzoli, the greatest of Fra Angelico's disciples, and Zanobi Strozzi, another pupil better known as a miniaturist, as well as his earliest collaborator, Battista Sanguigni. The hand of Fra Angelico himself is identifiable in the first 10 cells on the eastern side. Three subjects merit particular attention: a Resurrection, a coronation of the Virgin, and, especially, a gentle Annunciation, presented on a bare white gallery, with St. Peter Martyr in prayer, timidly facing the group, his coloured habit contrasting with the delicate two tones of pink in the garments of the Virgin and the Angel. The cells, originally hidden from public view because of monastic vows of reclusion, reveal the secret joy of the painter-friar in creating figures of purity to move his fellow friars to meditation and prayer. The images in these paintings are the lyrical expressions of a painter who was also their prior.

ROMAN PERIOD

At the end of 1446, Fra Angelico was called to Rome by Pope Eugene IV, and he remained there until about 1450. In the summer of 1447, however, he had undertaken to decorate the chapel of San Brizio in the cathedral of Orvieto. Angelico's assistants, above all Gozzoli, worked closely with him on two canvases, crowded with figures, in this chapel. These canvases, of Christ the Judge amid the hierarchy of angels and the chorus of the prophets, respectively, were only partially executed by Angelico; they were continued more than 50 years later by Luca Signorelli.

In Rome the frescoes that Angelico executed in a chapel of St. Peter's (*c.* 1446–47), in the chapel of the Sacrament in the Vatican (not before 1447), and in the studio of Pope Nicholas V (1449) have all been destroyed. But the Vatican still possesses his decorative painting for the Chapel of Niccolò V. There he painted scenes from the lives of Saints Stephen and Lawrence, along with figures of the Evangelists and saints, repeating some of the patterns of the predella on his altarpiece of San Marco. The consecration scene of St. Stephen and that of St. Lawrence are both set in solemn cathedral interiors, and the almsgiving of St. Lawrence is set against the background of a temple. In this scene particularly, Angelico imbued the poor and afflicted who surround the deacon-saint with a serenity that purifies them and illuminates them with an inner light, rendering them equals of the blessed figures on the altarpieces. At the same time, the organization of these works and the rendering of architecture in them mark the culmination of his development as a Renaissance artist.

About 1450 Fra Angelico returned to Florence, where, still a friar, he became prior of the priory of San Domenico in Fiesole (1450–*c.* June 1452). His most notable work of this time was the cycle of 35 paintings of scenes from the life of Christ and other subjects for the doors of a silver chest in the sanctuary of the Church of Santissima Annunziata in Florence. These works, which have been extensively repainted, are probably distant echoes of the destroyed paintings in the Chapel of Niccolò V. Although the authenticity of these works is disputed, the *Massacre of the Innocents*, *Flight into Egypt*, and *Presentation in the Temple* seem to be Angelico's because of the bright spontaneity of the slender figures, as well as the spatiality of the surroundings and the landscape. Such traits derived from the artist's vast experience in mural painting. In most of these little pictures, however, there is a kind of disconnectedness and weariness, indicating the hand of pupils whose art was a far cry from Fra Angelico's ineffable poetry. There is still a certain monumental tone in the late altarpiece he executed in the monastery of Bosco ai Frati in the Mugello. With the completion of this altarpiece and several other minor works, Fra Angelico's fertile artistic labours drew to a close.

In 1453 or 1454 Fra Angelico again went to Rome, where he died in the Dominican priory in which he had stayed during his first visit to that city. He was buried in the nearby church of Santa Maria sopra Minerva, where his tomb remains an object of veneration.

ASSESSMENT

In addition to the influence he had on his followers, Fra Angelico exerted a significant influence in Florence, especially between 1440 and 1450, even on such an accomplished master as Fra Filippo Lippi. As a friar, Fra Angelico was lauded in writings of the 15th century and later, some of which bestowed a legendary halo on him. As a painter, he was acclaimed as early as 1438 by the contemporary painter Domenico Veneziano. Vasari, in his section on Angelico in *Lives of the Most Eminent Painters, Sculptors, and Architects*, was largely inaccurate in his biographical data but correctly situated Fra Angelico in the framework of the Renaissance.

JACOPO BELLINI

(b. *c.* 1400, Venice [Italy] — d. *c.* 1470, Venice)

The painter responsible for introducing the principles of Florentine early Renaissance art into Venice was Jacopo Bellini. He was trained under the Umbrian artist Gentile da Fabriano, and in 1423 he had accompanied his master to Florence. There the progress made in fidelity to nature and in mastery of Classic grace by such masters as Donatello and Ghiberti, Masaccio and Paolo Uccello offered Jacopo further inspiration.

By 1429 Jacopo was settled at Venice and had established himself as the city's most important painter. The use of gold pigment in highlights of such works as his *Madonna* (*c.* 1438) shows that Jacopo long retained elements derived from Byzantine art, while the Child's rich robes and the patterned background of angels reveal his continued interest in the higher decorative style in which he was trained, conventionally called International Gothic. The modeling of the figures, the confident rendering of folds of cloth, and the accurate perspective, however, indicate an excellent understanding of the progressive art of 15th-century Florence. In the life-sized *Crucifixion* the spare and sombre scene strictly conforms to the Florentine Renaissance style of Masaccio and repudiates the rich colouring and courtly grace of Bellini's earlier known works.

More important than his paintings are his two books of drawings (*c.* 1450). The Louvre in Paris and the British Museum in London each own one of these sketchbooks. The drawings depict a great variety of scenes, and artists used them as models for compositions well into the 16th century. In such drawings as the *Nativity*, the *Flagellation*, and *St. John the Baptist Preaching*, Jacopo experimented with linear perspective and was among the first to make figures diminish in space using rules of perspective formerly applied only to depictions of architecture. The *Crucifixion* is among Jacopo's boldest compositional experiments. Possibly for the first time in art, the three crosses are viewed at an angle instead of frontally, and the soldiers' backs are turned to the viewer, lending a spontaneity and immediacy rare in Italian art of the time. Jacopo's great influence upon Venetian art was heightened through the work of his sons, Gentile and Giovanni, and his son-in-law, Andrea Mantegna, all of whom were prominent painters in the vicinity of Venice.

MASACCIO

(b. Dec. 21, 1401, Castel San Giovanni [now San Giovanni Valdarno, near Florence, Italy]—d. autumn 1428, Rome)

Masaccio was a Florentine painter of the early Renaissance noted particularly for his frescoes in the Brancacci Chapel of the Church of Santa Maria del Carmine in Florence (*c.* 1427), which remained influential throughout the Renaissance. Masaccio's art eventually helped create many of the major conceptual and stylistic foundations of Western painting. His use of light and shadow, the solidity and realism of his figures, and the use of the perspective in his paintings were entirely different from the work of the medieval and late Gothic artists who preceded him. The feeling of space and depth found in his frescoes and the naturalness and humanity of the religious figures he painted greatly influenced the Renaissance painters who followed him. In the span of only six years, he radically transformed Florentine painting. Seldom has such a brief life been so important to the history of art.

EARLY LIFE AND WORKS

Masaccio, as Tommaso di Giovanni di Simone Guidi became known, did not become an artist by inheriting his father's trade, as was typical in the Renaissance. His father was a notary, but Masaccio's paternal grandfather was a maker of chests (*cassoni*), which were often painted. It was perhaps through his grandfather's connection with artists that he became one.

From his birthdate in 1401 until Jan. 7, 1422, absolutely nothing is known about Masaccio. On the latter date he entered the Florentine Arte dei Medici e Speziali, the guild to which painters belonged. It is safe to assume that by his matriculation, he was already a full-fledged painter ready to supervise his own workshop. Where he had been between his birth and his 21st year, the painter or painters with whom he apprenticed, all that and more, remains, like so much about him, a tantalizing mystery.

Masaccio's earliest extant work is a small triptych dated April 23, 1422, or about three months after he matriculated in the Florentine guild. This triptych, consisting of the Madonna enthroned, two adoring angels, and saints, was painted for the Church of San Giovenale in the town of Cascia, near San Giovanni Valdarno, and is now in the Uffizi Gallery in Florence. It displays an acute knowledge of Florentine painting, but its eclectic style is strongly influenced by Giotto and Andrea Orcagna. The triptych, nonetheless, is a powerfully impressive demonstration of the skill of the young, but already highly accomplished, artist. Masaccio's forms are startlingly direct and massive. The triptych's tight, spare composition and the unidealized and vigorous portrayal of the plain Madonna and Child at its centre does not in the least resemble contemporary Florentine painting. The figures do, however, reveal a complete understanding of the revolutionary art of

Donatello, the founder of the Florentine Renaissance sculptural style, whose early works Masaccio studied with care. Donatello's realistic sculptures taught Masaccio how to render and articulate the human body and provide it with gestural and emotional expression.

Masaccio's next important work was a sizable, multi-paneled altarpiece for the Church of Santa Maria del Carmine at Pisa in 1426. Unfortunately, the Pisa Altarpiece was dismantled in the 18th century and many of its parts lost, but 13 sections of it have been rediscovered and identified in museums and private collections. The altarpiece's images, which include the *Madonna and Child* originally at its centre, amplify the direct, realistic character of the 1422 triptych. Ensconced in a massive throne inspired by Classical architecture, the Madonna is viewed from below and seems to tower over the spectator. The contrast between the bright lighting on her right side and the deep shadow on her left impart an unprecedented sense of volume and depth to the figure.

Originally placed beneath the Madonna, the rectangular panel depicting the *Adoration of the Magi* is notable for its realistic figures, which include portraits, most likely those of the donor and his family. Like the *Madonna and Child*, the *Adoration* is notable for its deep, vibrant hues so different from the prevailing pastels found in contemporary Florentine painting. Unlike his fellow artists, Masaccio used colour not as pleasing decorative pattern but to help impart the illusion of solidity to the painted figure.

THE BRANCACCI CHAPEL

Shortly after completing the Pisa Altarpiece, Masaccio began working on what was to be his masterpiece and what was to inspire future generations of artists: the frescoes of the Brancacci Chapel (*c.* 1427) in the Florentine Church of

Santa Maria del Carmine. He was commissioned to finish painting the chapel's scenes of the stories of St. Peter after Masolino (1383–1447) had abandoned the job, leaving only the vaults and several frescoes in the upper registers finished. Previously, Masaccio and Masolino were engaged in some sort of loose working relationship. They had already collaborated on a *Madonna and Child with St. Anne* in which the style of Masaccio, who was the younger of the two, had a profound influence on that of Masolino. It has been suggested, but never proven, that both artists were jointly commissioned to paint the Brancacci Chapel. The question of which painter executed which frescoes in the chapel was much discussed in the 19th and 20th centuries. It is now generally thought that Masaccio was responsible for the following sections: the *Expulsion of Adam and Eve* (or *Expulsion from Paradise*), *Baptism of the Neophytes*, *The Tribute Money*, *St. Peter Enthroned*, *St. Peter Healing the Sick with His Shadow*, *St. Peter Distributing Alms*, and part of the *Resurrection of the Son of Theophilus*.

The radical differences between the two painters are seen clearly in the pendant frescoes of the *Temptation of Adam and Eve* by Masolino and Masaccio's *Expulsion of Adam and Eve*, which preface the St. Peter stories. Masolino's figures are dainty, wiry, and elegant, while Masaccio's are highly dramatic, volumetric, and expansive. The shapes of Masaccio's Adam and Eve are constructed not with line but with strongly differentiated areas of light and dark that give them a pronounced three-dimensional sense of relief. Masolino's figures appear fantastic, while Masaccio's seem to exist within the world of the spectator illuminated by natural light. The expressive movements and gestures that Masaccio gives to Adam and Eve powerfully convey their anguish at being expelled from the Garden of Eden and add a psychological dimension to the impressive physical realism of these figures.

The boldness of conception and execution—the paint is applied in sweeping, form-creating bold slashes—of the *Expulsion of Adam and Eve* marks all of Masaccio's frescoes in the Brancacci Chapel. The most famous of these is *The Tribute Money*, which rivals Michelangelo's *David* as an icon of Renaissance art. *The Tribute Money*, which depicts the debate between Christ and his followers about the rightness of paying tribute to earthly authorities, is populated by figures remarkable for their weight and gravity. Recalling both Donatello's sculptures and antique Roman reliefs that Masaccio saw in Florence, the figures of Christ and his apostles attain a monumentality and seriousness hitherto unknown. Massive and solemn, they are the very embodiments of human dignity and virtue so valued by Renaissance philosophers and humanists.

For the first time in Florentine painting, religious drama unfolds not in some imaginary place in the past but in the countryside of Tuscany or the city streets of Florence, with St. Peter and his followers treading the palace-lined streets of an early 15th-century city. By setting his figures in scenes of such specificity, Masaccio sanctified and elevated the observer's world. His depiction of the heroic individual in a fixed and certain place in time and space perfectly reflects humanistic thought in contemporary Florence.

In *The Tribute Money*, with its solid, anatomically convincing figures set in a clear, controlled space lit by a consistent fall of light, Masaccio decisively broke with the medieval conception of a picture as a world governed by different and arbitrary physical laws. Instead, he embraced the concept of a painting as a window behind which a continuation of the real world is to be found, with the same laws of space, light, form, and perspective that obtain in reality. This concept was to remain the basic idiom of Western painting for the next 450 years.

THE TRINITY

The Trinity, a fresco in the Church of Santa Maria Novella, also presents important pictorial innovations that embody contemporary concerns and influences. Painted about 1427, it was probably Masaccio's last work in Florence. It represents the Trinity (Father, Son, and Holy Spirit) set in a barrel-vaulted hall before which kneel two donors. The deep coffered vault is depicted using a nearly perfect one-point system of linear perspective, in which all the orthogonals recede to a central vanishing point. This way of depicting space may have been devised in Florence about 1410 by the architect Filippo Brunelleschi. Masaccio's *Trinity* is the first extant example of the systematic use of one-point perspective in a painting. One-point perspective fixes the spectator's viewpoint and determines his relation with the painted space. The architectural setting of *The Trinity* is derived from contemporary buildings by Brunelleschi which, in turn, were much influenced by Classical Roman structures. Masaccio and Brunelleschi shared a common artistic vision that was rational, human-scaled and human-centred, and inspired by the ancient world.

INFLUENCE

Documentation suggests that Masaccio left Florence for Rome, where he died about 1428. His career was lamentably short, lasting only about six years. He left neither a workshop nor any pupils to carry on his style, but his paintings, though few in number and done for patrons and locations of only middling rank, made an immediate impact on Florence, influencing future generations of important artists. Masaccio's weighty, dignified treatment of the human figure and his clear and orderly depiction of space, atmosphere, and light renewed the idiom of the early 14th-century Florentine painter Giotto, whose monumental art had been followed but not equaled by the succeeding generations of painters. Masaccio carried Giotto's more realistic style to its logical conclusion by utilizing contemporary advances in anatomy, chiaroscuro (a technique employed in the visual arts to represent light and shadow as they define three-dimensional objects), and perspective.

The major Florentine painters of the mid-15th century—Filippo Lippi, Fra Angelico, Andrea del Castagno, and Piero della Francesca—were all inspired by the rationality, realism, and humanity of Masaccio's art. But his greatest impact came only 75 years after his death, when his monumental figures and sculptural use of light were newly and more fully appreciated by Leonardo da Vinci, Michelangelo, and Raphael, the chief painters of the High Renaissance. Some of Michelangelo's earliest drawings, for example, are studies of figures in *The Tribute Money*, and through his works and those of other painters, Masaccio's art influenced the entire subsequent course of Western painting.

FRA FILIPPO LIPPI AND FILIPPINO LIPPI

Respectively, (b. *c.* 1406, Florence [Italy]—d. Oct. 8/10, 1469, Spoleto, Papal States) and (b. *c.* 1457, Prato, Republic of Florence [Italy]—d. April 18, 1504, Florence)

The Florentine painter Filippo Lippi belongs to the second generation of Renaissance artists. While exhibiting the strong influence of Masaccio (e.g., in *Madonna and Child*, 1437) and Fra Angelico (e.g., in *Coronation of the Virgin, c.* 1445), his work achieved a distinctive clarity of expression. Legend and tradition surround his unconventional life. The son of Fra Filippo Lippi and his wife, Lucrezia Buti, Filippino Lippi was a painter of the Florentine school, like his father. His works influenced the Tuscan Mannerists of the 16th century.

FRA FILIPPO LIPPI'S LIFE AND WORKS

Filippo Lippi was born into a very large and poor family in Florence. After the death of both his father and mother, the young Filippo was raised by an aunt for some years; later, she placed him with his brother in the Convent of Carmelite monks at Santa Maria del Carmine. The Brancacci chapel of the monastery was at that time being decorated with frescoes by Masaccio. These frescoes, which were to be among the most glorious and influential paintings of the Renaissance, were Lippi's first important contact with art.

In 1432, after having painted some frescoes there, Lippi left the monastery. According to the Renaissance biographer Giorgio Vasari, who wrote a lively and fanciful profile of the painter, Lippi was abducted with some companions by the Moors on the Adriatic, held as a slave for 18 months, and then freed after he painted a portrait of his owner. It is known that in 1434 the artist was at Padua. None of the works executed while he was at Padua are known, but the effect of his presence may be recognized in the paintings of others there, such as Andrea Mantegna.

In 1437 Lippi returned to Florence, protected by the powerful Medici family, and was commissioned to execute several works for convents and churches. The qualities he acquired during his years of travel are affirmed with clarity in two works of 1437, painted immediately after his return from Padua: *The Virgin and Child Between SS. Frediano and Augustin* and the *Madonna and Child*. In both of these altarpieces, the influence of Masaccio is still evident, but it is absorbed into a different style, having the pictorial effect of bas-relief, rendered more evident by lines, so that it resembles the reliefs of the sculptors Donatello and Jacopo della Quercia. In these works, the colour is warm, toned down with shadings, approaching the limpid chromatics of his great contemporary Fra Angelico. Still further testimony to Lippi's development is the *Annunciation*, once believed to be a late work but now dated between 1441 and 1443. It is composed in a new way, using the newly discovered effects of perspective and skillful contrasts between colour and form; the suggested movement of the light garments of the two frightened girls at the door is rendered with such sensitivity as to anticipate Sandro Botticelli.

A famous altarpiece of the same time, Lippi's well-known *Coronation of the Virgin* is a complex work crowded with figures. The celebrated altarpiece is exquisitely sumptuous in appearance and marks a historic point for Florentine painting for its success in uniting as one scene the various panels of a polyptych.

The altarpieces are characterized by a solemnity of composition that is absent from the paintings in which he developed a typical motif of 15th-century Florentine art: the Madonna with the Child at her breast. The masterpiece of these is the tondo (circular painting) *Madonna with Child and Scenes from the Life of Mary*; it is a clear and realistic mirror of life, transfigured in a most intimate way, and it had a great effect on Renaissance art. A second *Coronation of the Virgin*, executed about 1445, displays a marked change in the style of Lippi—from the plastic values suggested by his study of Masaccio to the serene chromatics of Angelico.

In 1442 Lippi had been made rector of the church of San Quirico at Legnaia. His life, however, became constantly more eventful. Tradition has given him the reputation (borne out in great part by documents) of a man dominated by love affairs and impatient of methodical or tranquil conduct. His adventures culminated in 1456 in his romantic flight from Prato—where he was painting in the convent of the nuns of Santa Margherita—with a young nun of the convent, Lucrezia Buti. From 1456 to 1458 Lippi lived with Lucrezia, her sister, and a few other nuns. Lippi's conduct, together with his apparent inability to fulfill contracts in time, got him in trouble. He was arrested, tried, and tortured. It was only thanks to the intervention of Cosimo de' Medici that Lippi was released and allowed to renounce his vows. The pope later gave permission for the former priest-painter and the nun to marry, and from this union was born a son, Filippo, called Filippino, who was to be one of the most noted Florentine painters of the second half of the 15th century.

The bright and active city of Prato, a short distance from Florence, was Lippi's second home. He returned to Prato often, staying there for long periods, painting frescoes and altarpieces. Accompanied by Fra Diamante, who had been his companion and collaborator since he was a young man, Lippi began to redecorate the walls of the choir of the cathedral there in 1452. He returned in 1463 and again in 1464, remaining in the city this time until 1467. At the centre of his activity in Prato stand the frescoes in the chancel of the cathedral, with the four Evangelists and scenes from the lives of St. John the Baptist and St. Stephen. Perhaps the most solemn scene of the life and death of St. Stephen is the burial; at the sides of the funeral bed of the saint stand a crowd of prelates and illustrious persons in mourning, among them Cardinal Carlo de' Medici, Fra Diamante, and the artist himself.

The Virgin Adoring the Child, *oil on wood panel by Fra Filippo Lippi, c.
1460; in the Staatliche Museen Preussischer Kulturbesitz, Berlin.* Staatliche
Museen Preussischer Kulturbesitz, Berlin

In 1467 Lippi, his son Filippino, and Fra Diamante left
for Spoleto, where Lippi had received a commission for
another vast undertaking, the decorations and frescoes of
the choir of the cathedral. These included the *Nativity*,
the *Annunciation*, the *Death of Mary*, and, in the centre of
the vault of the apse, the *Coronation*. These frescoes were

Lippi's final work. They were interrupted by his death, for which there are two documented dates—in the monks' necrology of Santa Maria del Carmine in Florence and in the archives of Spoleto. Later the Medici had a splendid sepulchre, designed by Lippi's son, erected for him (1490) in the cathedral of Spoleto.

ASSESSMENT

Posthumous judgments of Filippo Lippi were often coloured by the traditions of his adventurous life. Moreover, his works have been criticized from time to time for their borrowings from other painters. Nevertheless, it has also been recognized that his art was not diminished but rather enriched and rendered more balanced by what he took from Masaccio and Fra Angelico. He was constantly seeking the techniques to realize his artistic vision and the new ideas that made him one of the most appreciated artists of his time.

The 20th-century critic Bernard Berenson, who maintained that Lippi's true place as an artist was among the "painters of genius," also described him as "a high-class illustrator," intending by this to underline the importance of expressive content and the presentation of reality in his works. Later critics have recognized in Lippi a "narrative" spirit that reflected the life of his time and translated into everyday terms the ideals of the early Renaissance.

FILIPPINO LIPPI'S LIFE AND WORKS

After his father's death, Filippino entered the workshop of Sandro Botticelli. By 1473 he had finished his apprenticeship. The style of Filippino's earliest works stems from that of Botticelli, but Filippino's use of line is less sensitive and subtle than Botticelli's. In a group of paintings executed about 1480–85 he developed a harder and more individual style. Among the most notable works of this period is the *Journey of Tobias* in the Galleria Sabauda, Turin, Italy. He was employed, along with Botticelli, Perugino, and Domenico Ghirlandaio, on the frescoed decoration of Lorenzo de' Medici's villa at Spedaletto and at the end of 1482 was commissioned to complete work left unfinished by Perugino in the Palazzo della Signoria in Florence. No trace of either work survives. Soon after (probably 1483–84) he was entrusted with the completion of the frescoes in the Brancacci Chapel in the Carmine, which had been left unfinished on Masaccio's death in 1428.

His most popular picture, the beautiful altarpiece of *The Vision of St. Bernard* (Badia, Florence), has been variously assigned to the years 1480 and 1486. In Rome Filippino decorated the Carafa Chapel in St. Maria sopra Minerva. Nothing in Filippino's earlier works hints of the inspiration he found while at work on the Carafa Chapel.

After his return from Rome, Filippino executed a fresco of the *Death of Laocoön* for the villa of Lorenzo de' Medici at Poggio a Caiano, in which some of the decorative devices used in the Carafa Chapel are again employed, and resumed work in the Strozzi Chapel (completed 1502), the frescoes of which anticipate Tuscan Mannerism of the 16th century.

DOMENICO VENEZIANO

(b. c. 1410, Venice [Italy]—d. May 15, 1461, Florence)

One of the protagonists of the 15th-century Florentine school of painting, the Italian Renaissance painter

Domenico Veneziano was born Domenico di Bartolomeo. Little is known about his early life and training. He was in Perugia (central Italy) in 1438, and from there he wrote a letter to Piero de' Medici soliciting work. He settled in Florence in 1439 and, except for brief periods, worked there until his death. It is likely that he had been in Florence prior to this date, possibly as an assistant to Gentile da Fabriano. Even his early works, in fact, reflect the influence of Florentine art, in particular that of Fra Angelico, Fra Filippo Lippi, and Lorenzo Ghiberti.

Two signed works by Domenico survive. The first, a much-damaged fresco of the Virgin and Child enthroned and two damaged heads of saints, formed part of the Carnesecchi Tabernacle and may have been the first work Domenico executed in Florence. Its accurate perspective and the sculptural quality of the figures suggest he was influenced by Masaccio. The second work is an altarpiece for the Church of Santa Lucia dei Magnoli, usually called the St. Lucy Altarpiece, which was probably painted about 1447. The central panel, the Virgin and Child with four saints, is one of the outstanding paintings produced in Florence in the middle of the 15th century. It is remarkable for the soft contours of its figures, its fresh and delicate palette, its mastery of light, and its precise and subtle space construction. The five panels of the predella (the base of the altarpiece) are now dispersed. The *Annunciation* is the most successful of Domenico's experiments in rendering outdoor light: the pale morning light fills and defines the space of the courtyard, and the cool light on the broad plane of white wall heightens the sense of moment and loneliness in the two figures.

A tondo of the *Adoration of the Magi* is of uncertain date. It combines bright colour with careful realism and has an expansive and accurately drawn landscape background.

Domenico's two profile portraits (the only two that can reasonably be considered his work) of Matteo and Michele Olivieri are in the tradition of Pisanello.

DIRCK BOUTS

(b. *c.* 1415, Haarlem, Holland [now in the Netherlands]—d. May 6, 1475, Louvain, Brabant [now in Belgium])

Though by most lights he lacks the grace of expression and intellectual depth of his great Flemish contemporaries Rogier van der Weyden and Jan van Eyck, the painter Dirck Bouts was without doubt an accomplished master.

Little is known of Bouts's early years in Haarlem, although it is possible that he studied in Brussels with van der Weyden, whose influence is obvious in his early works. In 1448 he visited Louvain in the southern Netherlands, where he married the daughter of a local merchant. After 1457 his name appeared almost every year in the archives of Louvain. Bouts's earlier works, dated on stylistic evidence before 1457, are strongly Rogierian in their expression of strong emotion through symbolic gestures. Passionate subjects such as *The Entombment*, *Pietà*, and scenes of the Crucifixion, descent from the Cross, and the Resurrection depicted in an impressive triptych in the Royal Chapel in Granada, Spain, were appropriate vehicles for this expression. They lack van der Weyden's anatomical correctness, however, and Bouts's compositions appear stiff and angular; these differences are perhaps due as much to the sober religious intensity of the northern Netherlands in comparison with the more relaxed spirit of Flanders as to a deficiency in skill or feeling. The overall design of Bouts's early works shows the influence of the elegant and intellectual van Eyck.

In the paintings ascribed to Bouts's mature period after he settled in Louvain, van der Weyden's influence gives way to a greater severity and dignity in the treatment of figures; there is a shift toward grander, more allegorical subjects as well. The facial expressions of the figures in these paintings show an extraordinary restraint that appears as a deliberately controlled intensity with great spiritual effect. Bouts's two best-known works, which exemplify all of these characteristics of his mature style, belong to the last 20 years of his life. One, ordered by the Confraternity of the Holy Sacrament for the Church of St. Peter in Louvain in 1464, is a triptych, the wings of which are divided into two smaller panels, one above the other. The central panel represents the Last Supper, and on the wings are shown four scenes from the Old Testament foreshadowing the institution of the Eucharist: the *Feast of the Passover*, *Elijah in the Desert*, the *Gathering of Manna*, and *Abraham and Melchisedek*.

The second painting, commissioned by the city of Louvain in 1468, the year in which Bouts became official painter to the city, was to be an ambitious project on the theme of the Last Judgment, but the work remained uncompleted at Bouts's death. Panels representing heaven and hell survive, as well as two thematically related panels illustrating an episode from the legend of the Holy Roman emperor Otto III.

ANTONIO VIVARINI

(b. c. 1415, Murano?, Republic of Venice [Italy] — d. c. 1480)

Antonio Vivarini was one of the most important and prolific Venetian artists of the first half of the 15th century and one of the first Venetian painters to utilize Renaissance style. He founded the studio of the influential Vivarini family of painters.

Vivarini's first signed work was an altarpiece executed for the Basilica Eufrasiana di Parenzo (now in Poreč, Croatia) in 1440. The piece contained both the Venetian Gothic and Renaissance elements that would characterize much of his work. From 1444 he collaborated with his brother-in-law Giovanni d'Alemagna. Surviving altarpieces executed by the two are in the churches of San Zaccaria (1443–44) and San Pantalon (1444) and in the Accademia (1446), all in Venice; there is also a polyptych in the Brera in Milan (1448).

One of Vivarini's most important joint commissions with d'Alemagna was the three altars for the Church of San Zaccaria, in which their depictions of saints appear to be three-dimensional—unusual for the time. They also painted the *Coronation of the Virgin* for the Church of San Pantalon. Between 1447 and 1450, the two artists lived in Padua, where, together with Andrea Mantegna and Niccolò Pizzolo, they executed a cycle of frescoes in the Ovetari Chapel of Eremitani Church (destroyed in World War II).

After d'Alemagna's death in 1450, Vivarini abandoned both his work on Eremitani Church, which was never completed, and the city of Padua in order to work with his younger brother, Bartolomeo, in Venice. The styles of Vivarini and d'Alemagna are not easily distinguished, but Antonio was certainly the dominant partner. The soft, rounded figures in his heavily ornamented polyptychs are influenced by Gentile da Fabriano and, more superficially, by Masolino. The earliest work signed by Antonio and Bartolomeo is a polyptych commissioned by Pope Nicholas V in 1450. It is couched in the same idiom as the paintings of Antonio's first period, but, in later works, the intervention of his more progressive younger brother resulted in the introduction of Renaissance elements into Antonio's style.

In addition to his collaborations with Giovanni and Bartolomeo, Antonio completed many independent projects. These included altarpieces for the Benedictine abbey of Praglia (*c.* 1448) as well as the large-scale *St. Peter*, *St. Paul*, and *St. Ursula and Her Virgins* (*c.* 1450s) for a church in Brescia. Antonio continued to produce altarpieces into the late 1460s, including his last signed piece, the polyptych for San Maria Vetere in Andria (1467).

PIERO DELLA FRANCESCA

(b. *c.* 1416/17, Sansepolcro, Republic of Florence [Italy]—d. Oct. 12, 1492, Sansepolcro)

Noted for his serene, disciplined exploration of perspective, the painter Piero della Francesca had little influence on his contemporaries, but these explorations came to be recognized in the 20th century as a major contribution to the Italian Renaissance. The fresco cycle *The Legend of the True Cross* (1452–66) and the diptych portrait of Federico da Montefeltro, duke of Urbino, and his consort (1465) are among his best known works.

FORMATIVE PERIOD

Piero di Benedetto dei Franceschi's father was apparently a tanner and shoemaker, prosperous enough for his son to become well educated and literate in Latin. Nothing is known about Piero's early training as a painter, though it is assumed that he was instructed by local masters who had been influenced by Sienese art.

In 1439 Piero worked as an associate of Domenico Veneziano, who was then painting frescoes for the hospital of St. Maria Nuova in Florence, where the early Renaissance style was beginning to flourish. In Florence he probably studied the statuary of Donatello and Luca della Robbia, the buildings of Filippo Brunelleschi, and the paintings of Masaccio and Fra Angelico, and he might have read a theoretical treatise on painting by the human-ist and architect Leon Battista Alberti. Undoubtedly, he would have been directed to these luminaries by Domenico, whose own works demonstrate a Renaissance emphasis on colour and light as elements of pictorial construction. This contact with the early Renaissance art of Florence pro-vided the foundation of Piero's own style.

Back in Sansepolcro by 1442, Piero was elected to the town council. Three years later the Confraternita della Misericordia commissioned a polyptych from him. The Misericordia Altarpiece shows Piero's indebtedness to the Florentines Donatello and Masaccio, his fondness for geo-metric form, and the slowness and deliberation with which he habitually worked—for the Misericordia Altarpiece was not completed until 1462.

Periodic retreat to the provincial isolation of Sansepolcro seems to have been necessary for Piero's work. For the rest of his life he alternated between the calm of Sansepolcro and contact with the humanistic life of the Renaissance in artistic and intellectual centres such as Ferrara and Rimini.

In about 1448 Piero probably worked in the service of Marchese Leonello d'Este in Ferrara, where he may have been influenced by northern Italian art. In 1451, at another northern Italian city, Rimini, he executed a splendidly heraldic fresco (i.e., resembling a heraldic emblem in design) of *Sigismondo Malatesta Before St. Sigismund* in the Tempio Malatestiano, a memorial church built according to the architectural designs of Alberti. Also to this early formative period before 1451 belongs *The Baptism of Christ*. This painting, probably the central panel for an altarpiece for the Pieve of Sansepolcro, shows the elements that remained a constant in Piero's style to his death. The vig-orous volume of the figures, the spatial definition, and, above all, the very original use of colour and light—his paintings appear almost "bleached"—define a style that has all the elements of the Renaissance but that remained one of the most original of all times.

MATURE PERIOD

Piero della Francesca's mature style is revealed in frescoes painted in the choir of the church of San Francesco at Arezzo. The decorations had been begun in 1447 by the elderly Bicci di Lorenzo, who died in 1452; Piero presumably was retained to complete the work shortly thereafter. The narrative cycle, depicting *The Legend of the True Cross*, was completed by 1466. Its simplicity and clarity of structure, controlled use of perspective, and aura of serenity are all typical of Piero's art at its best. Contemporary with the Arezzo cycle are a fresco of the *Magdalen* in Arezzo Cathedral, the *Resurrection* in the Palazzo Comunale at Sansepolcro, and a *Madonna del Parto* in the chapel of the cemetery at Monterchi. In 1454 a burgher of Sansepolcro, Agnolo di Giovanni di Simone d'Angelo, commissioned an altarpiece for San Agostino that Piero, characteristically, did not complete until 1469. The surviving panels of the altarpiece reveal Piero's interest in the creation of monumental human figures through the sculptural use of line and light.

In 1459 Piero was in Rome to paint frescoes (now destroyed) for Pope Pius II in the Vatican. *St. Luke*, executed at the same time, was probably done by assistants in the studio he had established in Rome. More fruitful was Piero's long association with Count (later Duke) Federico da Montefeltro, whose highly cultured court was considered "the light of Italy." In the late 1450s Piero painted the *Flagellation of Christ*, the intended location of which is still debated by scholars. Its lucid perspectival construction contrasts with treatment of the subject wherein Christ is relegated to the background while three unidentified figures dominate the foreground.

A famous diptych portrait of Duke Federico and his consort, Battista Sforza, was probably begun to commemorate their marriage in 1465. The paintings show Piero's respect for visual fact in the unidealized features of the Duke and in the enchanting landscape backgrounds, which also indicate that he had discovered Netherlandish painting. The reverse depicts the couple in a triumphal procession accompanied by the Virtues. The Duke reappears as a kneeling donor in an altarpiece from St. Bernardino, Urbino (now in the Brera, Milan). He, the Madonna and Child, and accompanying saints are placed before the apse (semicircular choir) of a magnificent Albertian church. The painting may have been a memorial to Countess Battista, who died after giving birth to the couple's ninth child and first son, and it has been dated between 1472 and 1474. The altarpiece is one of the most accomplished Renaissance presentations of forms in space and exerted a decided influence on the development of monumental devotional paintings in northern Italian and Venetian art.

LAST YEARS

The last two decades of Piero's life were spent in Sansepolcro, where paintings, now lost, were commissioned by local churches in 1474 and 1478. In 1480 Piero became prior of the Confraternita di San Bartolomeo. Among the few extant paintings from this period are the harmonious *Nativity*, in London, the *Madonna* from the church at St. Maria delle Grazie near Senigallia, now in Urbino, and an awkwardly constructed altarpiece in Perugia, *Madonna with Child and Saints. The Annunciation* from that altarpiece, however, indicates that Piero's interest in perspectival problems remained keen.

In his old age Piero seems to have abandoned painting in favour of more abstruse pursuits. Between 1474 and 1482 he wrote a treatise on painting, *De prospectiva pingendi* ("On Perspective in Painting"), dedicated to his patron, the Duke of Urbino. In its range of topics and method of organization, the book follows Alberti and the ancient Greek geometer Euclid. The principal manuscript, now in the Biblioteca Palatina, Parma, was handwritten by the artist himself and illuminated by him with diagrams on geometric, proportional, and perspectival problems. A second treatise, the *De quinque corporibus regularibus* ("On the Five Regular Bodies"), written some time after 1482, follows Plato and Pythagoras in dealing with the notion of perfect proportions. The manuscript, again illustrated by Piero, is in the Vatican Library. *Del abaco* ("On the Abacus") is a pamphlet on applied mathematics.

Piero's fascination with geometry and mathematics is a corollary of his own art; his manner of theoretical expression owes much to his mentor Alberti and is analogous to that of his younger contemporary Leonardo da Vinci; the rigour and logic of the arguments, however, are unique to Piero.

A reliable 16th-century tradition claimed that Piero was blind in his last years. If true, this must have occurred after 1490 because several autographs from that year survive. Moreover, his will of 1486 refers to the painter as aged but sound of mind and body.

Piero did not establish a lasting tradition in central Italy. Luca Signorelli and Perugino, who are presumed to be his most important pupils, followed the examples of other masters. Although Piero's reticent art had little influence on the experiments of his great Florentine contemporaries, he enjoyed great fame for his scientific contributions. In

1497 he was described as "the monarch of our times of painting and architecture," and the biographer Giorgio Vasari gave him high praise two generations later. In the 20th century, Piero's career was reconstructed and his position reevaluated, giving proper credit to both the science and the poetry of his art.

ANDREA DEL CASTAGNO

(b. *c.* 1419, Castagno d'Andrea, near Florence [Italy] — d. Aug. 19, 1457, Florence)

Andrea del Castagno, pseudonym of Andrea di Bartolo di Simone, was one of the most influential 15th-century Italian Renaissance painters, best known for the

The Last Supper, *fresco by Andrea del Castagno, 1447; in the Cenacolo di Sant'Apollonia, Florence.* SCALA/Art Resource, New York

emotional power and naturalistic treatment of figures in his work. Little is known of Castagno's early life, and it is also difficult to ascertain the stages of his artistic development owing to the loss of many of his paintings and to the scarcity of documents regarding his extant works.

As a youth, he was precocious. He executed a mural of Cosimo de' Medici's adversaries (rebels hanging by their heels) at the Palazzo del Podestà in Florence, earning himself the byname Andreino degli Impiccati ("Little Andrea of the Hanged Men"). It is known that he went to Venice in 1442, and frescoes in the chapel of Saint Tarasio in San Zaccaria are signed and dated by both him and Francesco da Faenza.

His first notable works were a *Last Supper* and three scenes from the *Passion of Christ*—a *Crucifixion*, a *Deposition*, and a *Resurrection*—all executed in 1447 for the refectory of the former Convent of Sant'Apollonia in Florence, now known as the Cenacolo di Sant'Apollonia. These monumental frescoes, revealing the influence of Masaccio's pictorial illusionism and Castagno's own use of scientific perspective, received wide acclaim.

In 1451 Castagno continued the frescoes at San Egidio begun earlier by Domenico Veneziano. The light tones that Castagno adopted for his outstanding *St. Julian* (1454–55) show Domenico's influence.

In a work for a loggia of the Villa Carducci Pandalfini at Legnaia, Castagno broke with earlier styles and painted a larger-than-life–size series of *Famous Men and Women*, within a painted frame. In this work, Castagno displayed more than mere craftsmanship; he portrayed movement of body and facial expression, creating dramatic tension. He also framed the figures in painted architectural niches, to heighten the impression that they are actual sculptural forms. He achieved similar force in his *David with the Head of Goliath* (*c.* 1450–55), painted on a shield. His last dated work (Florence Cathedral) is an equestrian portrait of Niccolò da Tolentino.

Castagno's emotionally expressive realism was strongly influenced by Donatello, Domenico, and perhaps Piero della Francesca. Castagno's work, in turn, influenced succeeding generations of Florentine painters, including Antonio del Pollaiuolo and Sandro Botticelli.

JEAN FOUQUET
(b. *c.* 1420, Tours, France — d. *c.* 1481, Tours)

Jean Fouquet was a preeminent French painter of the 15th century whose work consistently displays clear, dispassionate observation rendered with intricate delicacy and alternates accurate perspective with a flat, non-illusionistic sense of space.

Little is known of Fouquet's early life, but his youthful work suggests that he was trained in Paris under an artist (or group of artists) known as the Bedford Master (or Master of the Bedford Hours) for his work illuminating a Book of Hours for the duke of Bedford. Fouquet's portrait of Charles VII (*c.* 1447), though a panel painting, displays the use of brittle, incisive line characteristic of miniature painting. This work must have helped to establish his international reputation for, before 1447, he executed in Rome the portrait of Pope Eugenius IV. While in Italy he absorbed the progress that such painters as Masaccio, Fra Angelico, and Piero della Francesca had made in the handling of central perspective and foreshortening and in the rendering of volume.

Upon his return to Tours, Fouquet created a new style, combining the experiments of Italian painting with the exquisite precision of characterization and detail of

Flemish art. For the royal secretary and lord treasurer, Étienne Chevalier, he executed between 1450 and 1460 his most famous works: a large *Book of Hours* with about 60 full-page miniatures, 40 of which are among the great treasures of the château of Chantilly; and the diptych from Notre Dame at Melun (*c.* 1450) with Chevalier's portrait on one panel and a Madonna with the features of Agnès Sorel, the king's mistress, on the other. Also to this period of the reign of Charles VII belong the two richly illuminated manuscripts of a French translation of Boccaccio's *De casibus virorum illustrium* ("On the Fates of Famous Men") and *De claris mulieribus* ("On Famous Women"), *Cas des nobles hommes et femmes malheureux* (1458), and a copy of the *Grandes Chroniques de France*; and finally, the large altarpiece of the *Pietà* discovered in the church at Nouans, his only monumental painting.

In 1469 King Louis XI founded the Order of St. Michael, and Fouquet illuminated the statutes of the order. In 1474 he worked with the sculptor Michel Colombe on the design of the king's tomb and in the following year received the official title of royal painter. About the same time he completed the illustration of two volumes of a French translation of Josephus's *Antiquities of the Jews*, in which he broadened the range of miniature painting to include vast panoramas of architecture and landscape, making brilliant use of aerial perspective and colour tonality to achieve compositional unity.

ALESSIO BALDOVINETTI

(b. Oct. 14, 1425, Florence [Italy] — d. Aug. 29, 1499, Florence)

The work of Alessio, or Alesso, Baldovinetti exemplified the careful modeling of form and the accurate depiction of light that is characteristic of the most progressive style of Florentine painting during the last half of the 15th century. He also contributed importantly to the fledgling art of landscape painting.

Baldovinetti's father was a merchant. Though as the oldest male child he might have been expected to follow his father's trade, Baldovinetti chose instead to become an artist. He began his studies in 1448 at the Compagnia di San Luca (painters' guild) before working independently. His earliest work includes paintings for the doors of the Chapel of the Annunciation in Santissima Annunziata (*c.* 1449) and an altarpiece (1450) for the Pieve di Borgo San Lorenzo in Mugello.

It is presumed that he worked as an assistant to Domenico Veneziano, whose influence is reflected in the clear, pervasive light of his earliest surviving works: *The Baptism of Christ*, *Marriage at Cana*, and *The Transfiguration*. Baldovinetti was also greatly influenced by Fra Angelico and Andrea del Castagno, with whom he collaborated on the last fresco cycle in the high chapel of Sant'Egidio, in addition to other works. He achieved his fully mature style in his masterpiece, *The Nativity* (1460–62), a fresco in the Church of Santissima Annunziata, Florence. Although Baldovinetti's technical experiments led to the fresco's rapid decay, it shows the pale colours, atmospheric light, and integration of detail with large-scale design that characterized most of his later works, such as *Madonna and Child* (*c.* 1465). Both *The Nativity* and *Madonna* include views of the Arno River valley and are among Europe's earliest paintings of actual landscapes.

Baldovinetti also did two strips of mosaic decoration over Lorenzo Ghiberti's doors on the baptistery in Florence (1453–55) and a St. John the Baptist over the south doorway of Pisa Cathedral (1462). He also prepared designs for intarsias, or wood inlays, and for stained glass; a good example of the latter is his design for a window of the Gianfigliazzi Chapel in Florence (1466).

GENTILE BELLINI

(b. *c.* 1429, Venice [Italy] — d. before Feb. 23, 1507, Venice)

A member of the founding family of the Venetian school of Renaissance painting, Gentile Bellini is best known for his portraiture and his scenes of Venice.

Gentile was trained by his father, Jacopo Bellini, a painter who introduced Renaissance concerns and motifs into Venice. At the beginning of Gentile's career, he worked with his father and his brother, Giovanni. Jacopo's influence may be seen in Gentile's early *Madonna*. As an independent artist, Gentile contracted with the officers of the San Marco School in 1466 to decorate the doors on the case of their organ. These paintings represent four saints, colossal in size and designed with the harsh austerity and daring perspective that characterized the style of his brother-in-law, Andrea Mantegna, then the most prominent painter of the Paduan school. The same influence may be seen in Gentile's *Banner of Blessed Lorenzo Giustiniani* (1465), with its sharp incisive outlines and stiff drapery. In 1474 Gentile was commissioned to execute a series of paintings for a room in the Doges' Palace in Venice.

In 1479 the doge ("duke") of Venice sent him to Constantinople as a painter to the court of the Sultan Mehmed II. The most important of the extant works that Gentile painted there is the *Portrait of Mohammad II* (*c.* 1480), a masterful characterization of the shrewd, cultivated ruler. In his pen-and-gouache drawing *Seated Scribe* (1479–80), Gentile employs a flat patterned style similar to that of the Turkish miniatures that influenced such later works as his *Portrait of Doge Giovanni Mocenigo* (1478–85).

Among Gentile's best-known works are the scenes of Venice painted for the School of San Giovanni Evangelista, one of the many religious confraternities of the city. Those works deal with episodes related to a relic of the Holy Cross that the school owned. Those events are all but lost in the panorama of *Procession in St. Mark's Square* (1496) and the *Miracle of the True Cross at the Bridge of S. Lorenzo* (1500), huge canvases painted with painstaking attention to the smallest detail and crowded with small, rather rigid figures, including many portraits. A similar but lesser-known work is his *St. Mark Preaching in Alexandria* (1493–1507), which was finished after Gentile's death by his brother, Giovanni, one of the best Venetian painters of the Renaissance. Gentile's paintings are of great interest today primarily as records of Venetian life and architecture during the 15th century.

Miracle of the True Cross at the Bridge of S. Lorenzo, *oil painting by Gentile Bellini, 1500; in the Gallerie dell'Accademia, Venice.* SCALA/Art Resource, New York

ANTONELLO DA MESSINA

(b. *c.* 1430, Messina, Sicily—d. *c.* Feb. 19, 1479, Messina)

Antonello da Messina is noted as the painter who prob-ably introduced oil painting and Flemish pictorial techniques into mid-15th-century Venetian art. His prac-tice of building form with colour rather than line and shade greatly influenced the subsequent development of Venetian painting.

Little is known of Antonello's early life, but it is clear that he was trained in Naples, then a cosmopolitan art centre, where he studied the work of Provençal and Flemish artists, possibly even that of Jan van Eyck. His earliest known works, a *Crucifixion* (*c.* 1455) and *St. Jerome in His Study* (*c.* 1460), already show Antonello's characteris-tic combination of Flemish technique and realism with typically Italian modeling of forms and clarity of spatial arrangement.

In 1457 Antonello returned to Messina, where he worked until 1474. The chief works of this period, the polyptych of 1473 and the *Annunciation* of 1474, are rela-tively conservative altarpieces commissioned by the church, but the *Salvator Mundi* (1465), intended for private devotions, is bold and simple, showing a thorough under-standing of the human form and the depiction of personality. It was but a short step from the *Salvator Mundi* to such incisive characterizations of human psychology as seen in *Portrait of a Man* (*c.* 1472), a work that presaged the uncanny vitality and meticulous realism of such panels as *Portrait of a Condottiere* (1475), which established his repu-tation in northern Italy. During this period Antonello might have traveled to Rome and come into contact with the works of Fra Angelico and Piero della Francesca.

From 1475 to 1476 Antonello was in Venice and possi-bly Milan. Within a short time of his arrival in Venice, his work attracted so much favourable attention that he was supported by the Venetian state, and local painters enthusiastically adopted his oil technique and compositional style. In *St. Sebastian* (*c.* 1476), his most mature work, Antonello achieved a synthesis of clearly defined space, monumental, sculpture-like form, and luminous colour, which was one of the most decisive influences on the evolution of Venetian painting down to Giorgione's day. In 1476 he was again in Messina, where he completed his final masterpiece, *The Virgin Annunciate* (*c.* 1476).

GIOVANNI BELLINI
(b. *c.* 1430, Venice [Italy]—d. 1516, Venice)

The increasing interest of the Venetian artistic milieu in the stylistic innovations and concerns of the Renaissance is clearly reflected in the work of Giovanni Bellini. Although the paintings for the hall of the Great Council in Venice, considered his greatest works, were destroyed by fire in 1577, a large number of altarpieces (such as that in the church of Saints Giovanni e Paolo in Venice) and other extant works show a steady evolution from purely religious, narrative emphasis to a new naturalism of setting and landscape.

Little is known about Bellini's family. His father, Jacopo, a painter, was a pupil of Gentile da Fabriano, one of the leading painters of the early 15th century. Jacopo may have followed him to Florence. In any case, Jacopo introduced the principles of the Florentine Renaissance to Venice before either of his sons. Apart from his sons Gentile and Giovanni, he had at least one daughter, Niccolosa, who married the painter Andrea Mantegna in 1453. Both sons probably began as assistants in their father's workshop.

Giovanni Bellini's earliest independent paintings were influenced by the late Gothic graceful style of his father,

Jacopo, and by the severe manner of the Paduan school, and especially of his brother-in-law, Mantegna. This influence is evident even after Mantegna left for the court of Mantua in 1460. Giovanni's earliest works date from before this period. They include a *Crucifixion*, a *Transfiguration*, and a *Dead Christ Supported by Angels*. Several pictures of the same or earlier date are in the United States, and others are at the Correr Civic Museum in Venice. Four triptychs, sets of three panels used as altarpieces, are still in the Venice Accademia, and two *Pietàs*, both in Milan, are from this early period. His early work is well exemplified in two beautiful paintings, *The Blood of the Redeemer* and *The Agony in the Garden*.

In all his early pictures he worked with tempera, combining the severity and rigidity of the Paduan school with a depth of religious feeling and human pathos all his own. His early Madonnas, following in his father's tradition, are mostly sweet in expression, but he substituted for a mainly decorative richness one drawn more from a sensuous observation of nature. Although the pronounced linear element—i.e., the dominance of line rather than mass as a means of defining form, derived from the Florentine tradition and from the precocious Mantegna—is evident in the paintings, the line is less self-conscious than Mantegna's work, and, from the first, broadly sculptured planes offer their surfaces to the light from a dramatically brilliant sky.

From the beginning Bellini was a painter of natural light, as were Masaccio, the founder of Renaissance painting, and Piero della Francesca, its greatest practitioner at that time. In these earliest pictures the sky is apt to be reflected behind the figures in streaks of water making horizontal lines in a mere strip of landscape. In *The Agony in the Garden* (c. 1465), the horizon moves up, and a deep, wide landscape encloses the figures, to play an equal part in expressing the drama of the scene. As with the dramatis personae, the elaborately linear structure of the landscape provides much of the expression, but an even greater part is played by the colours of the dawn, in their full brilliance and in the reflected light within the shadow. This is the first of a great series of Venetian landscape scenes that was to develop continuously for a century or more. To a city surrounded by water, the emotional value of landscape was now fully revealed. A comparison with Mantegna's treatment of the same subject matter reveals the subtle yet fundamental differences in the styles of the two masters.

The great composite altarpiece with St. Vincent Ferrer, which is still in the church of Saints Giovanni e Paolo in Venice, was painted perhaps 10 years later, toward the mid-1470s. But the principles of composition and the method of painting had not yet changed essentially; they had merely grown stronger in expression. It seems to have been during a voyage down the Adriatic coast, made probably not long afterward, that Bellini encountered the influence that must have helped him most toward his full development: that of Piero della Francesca. Bellini's great *Coronation of the Virgin* at Pesaro, for example, might have reflected some of the compositional elements of Piero's lost *Coronation of the Virgin*, painted as the central panel of a polyptych. Christ's crowning of his mother beneath the effulgence of the Holy Ghost is a solemn act of consecration, and the four saints who stand witness beside the throne are characterized by their deep humanity. Every quality of their forms is fully realized: every aspect of their bodies, the textures of their garments, and the objects that they hold. As with work by Masaccio and Piero della Francesca, the perspective of pavement and throne helps to establish the group in space, and the space is enlarged by the great hills behind and rendered infinite by the luminosity of the sky, which envelops the scene and gathers all the forms together into one.

At this time in his life, Giovanni Bellini also met Antonello da Messina, who traveled to Venice about 1475. The encounter was to prove influential for both painters. The changes in Giovanni's work from his earlier, Mantegnesque style to the more mature, independent, and versatile manner of his later works are already visible in the San Giobbe Altarpiece.

It is the painter's way of using the medium that makes the difference, and that depends upon his intentions and his vision. It was Bellini's richer and broader vision that determined his future development. Unlike tempera paint, which was the medium of Bellini's early career, oil paint is inclined to be the more transparent and fusible and therefore lends itself to richer colour and tone by allowing a further degree of glazing, the laying of one translucent layer of colour over another. This technique and the unprecedented variety with which Bellini handled the oil paint give his fully mature painting the richness associated with the Venetian school.

Giovanni's brother, Gentile, was chosen by the government to continue the painting of great historical scenes in the hall of the Great Council in Venice; but in 1479, when Gentile was sent on a mission to Constantinople, Giovanni took his place. From that time to 1480, much of Giovanni's time and energy was devoted to fulfilling his duties as conservator of the paintings in the hall, as well as painting six or seven new canvases himself. These were his greatest works, but they were destroyed when the huge hall was gutted by fire in 1577. Contemporary students of his work can now gain only an approximate idea of their design from *The Martyrdom of St. Mark* in the Scuola di San Marco in Venice, finished and signed by one of Giovanni's assistants, and of their execution from Giovanni's completion of Gentile's *St. Mark Preaching in Alexandria* after his brother's death in Venice in 1507.

Yet a surprisingly large number of big altarpieces and comparatively portable works have survived and show the steady but adventurous evolution of his work. The principles and the technique of the Pesaro Altarpiece find their full development in the still-larger altarpiece of the Madonna from San Giobbe in the Venice Accademia, where the Virgin enthroned in a great apse and the saints beside her seem ready to melt into the reflected light. This seems to have been painted before the earliest of his dated pictures, the half-length *Madonna degli Alberetti* (1487), also in the Venice Accademia.

While for the first 20 years of Giovanni's career he limited his subject matter mainly to traditional religious subjects (Madonnas, Pietàs, and Crucifixions), toward the end of the century it began to be greatly enriched not so much by the wider choice of subjects as by the development of the mise-en-scène, the physical setting of the picture. He became one of the greatest of landscape painters. His study of outdoor light was such that one can deduce not only the season depicted but almost the hour of the day.

Bellini also excelled as a painter of ideal scenes — i.e., scenes of primeval as opposed to individualized images. For the *St. Francis in Ecstasy* of the Frick Collection or the *St. Jerome at His Meditations*, painted for the high altar of Santa Maria dei Miracoli in Venice, the anatomy of the earth is studied as carefully as those of human figures; but the purpose of this naturalism is to convey idealism through the realistic portrayal of detail. In the landscape *Sacred Allegory*, now in the Uffizi, he created the first of the dreamy enigmatic scenes for which Giorgione, his pupil, was to become famous. The same quality of idealism is to be found in his portraiture. His *Doge Leonardo Loredan* in the National Gallery, London, has all the wise and kindly firmness of the perfect head of state, and his *Portrait of a Young Man* (*c.* 1505; thought to be a likeness of the Venetian writer and humanist Pietro Bembo) in the British royal collection portrays all the sensitivity of a poet.

Both artistically and personally, the career of Giovanni Bellini seems to have been serene and prosperous. He lived to see his own school of painting achieve dominance and acclaim. He saw his influence propagated by a host of pupils, two of whom surpassed their master in world fame: Giorgione, whom he outlived by six years, and Titian.

The only extant description of Giovanni's personality is from the hand of the great German Renaissance artist Albrecht Dürer, who wrote to the German humanist Willibald Pirkheimer from Venice in 1506: "Everyone tells me what an upright man he is, so that I am really fond of him. He is very old, and still he is the best painter of them all."

CARLO CRIVELLI

(b. *c.* 1430/35, Venice [Italy] — d. *c.* 1494/95, Ascoli Piceno, Marche)

Among a number of exceptional 15th-century Venetian painters, Carlo Crivelli was probably the most individual, an artist whose highly personal and mannered style carried Renaissance forms into an unusual expressionism.

Thought to be the son of the painter Jacopo Crivelli, Carlo was probably initially influenced by Jacopo Bellini and by the school of Antonio and Bartolomeo Vivarini, Paduan brothers living in Venice, whose works were characterized by soft, rounded figures, clear modeling and realistic detail, and heavy ornamentation. Carlo Crivelli later came into contact with the linearism of the Paduan tradition and may have seen the works of its most famous artist, Andrea Mantegna, a major 15th-century painter who especially emphasized precise linear definition of form. In 1457 Crivelli served a prison term in Venice for seducing a married woman and then left the city, apparently permanently. Thereafter, he worked mainly in the cities of the Provincia di Ancona, to the south of Venice, coming into little subsequent contact with major artistic trends.

Crivelli's works were exclusively sacred in subject. Although his Classical, realistic figure types and symmetrical compositions follow the conventions of Renaissance painting, his unusual overall treatment transforms these conventions into a personal expression that is both highly sensuous and strongly Gothic in spirit. Crivelli's figures, clad in richly patterned brocades that are painted with an almost incredible attention to detail, are closely crowded together in sumptuously ornamental settings to produce flat, hieratic compositions that are devotional and removed from the world of the viewer. His unique use of sharp outlines surrounding every form and the excessive pallor and flawlessness of complexion in his figures give his scenes the quality of shallow sculptured relief. There is an exaggerated expression of feeling in the faces of his figures, usually pensive and dreamy but sometimes distorted with grief, and in the mannered gestures of their slender hands and spidery fingers; this expression is closer to the religious intensity of Gothic art than to the calm rationalism of the Renaissance. Some of Crivelli's more important works are *Madonna della Passione* (c. 1457), in which his individuality is only slightly apparent; a *Pietà* (1485); The *Virgin Enthroned with Child and Saints* (1491), the masterpiece of his mature style; and the eccentric and powerful late masterpiece *Coronation of the Virgin* (1493).

Crivelli was knighted in 1490 by Ferdinand II of Naples. He had no direct followers of note.

DESIDERIO DA SETTIGNANO

(b. *c.* 1430, Settignano, Republic of Florence [Italy]—d. January 1464, Florence)

The Florentine sculptor Desiderio da Settignano created a number of works, particularly marble low reliefs, that were unrivaled in the 15th century for subtlety and technical accomplishment. He is perhaps best known for carving the funerary monument for the humanist Carlo Marsuppini.

Desiderio was raised in a family of stone masons and entered the Stone and Wood Carvers' Guild of Florence in 1453. Little is known about his education, although he was influenced by the Italian sculptor Donatello, particularly in his low reliefs. In his youth he worked with his brother Geri in a workshop near the Ponte Santa Trinita; his fame seems to have lasted during his lifetime and until soon after his death.

Desiderio's delicate, sensitive, highly original style is perhaps most exquisitely manifest in his sensuous portrait busts of women and children. These lyrical pieces convey a wide range of moods and emotions, from joy and charm to melancholy and pensiveness. His sense of design and highly refined skill as a marble cutter established him as a master of low reliefs. Some of the most notable are his studies of the Madonna and Child, St. John, and Christ as an infant.

Sometime after 1453 Desiderio designed and carved the monument of Marsuppini in Santa Croce in Florence. This monument was inspired by Bernardo Rossellino's funerary monument to Leonardo Bruni in the same church. Desiderio borrowed heavily from Rossellino's design, so the two monuments are strikingly similar. Both feature an arch, an effigy of the entombed man, a relief of the Virgin and Child, and a depiction of angels carrying a garland. With its rich architectural detail and its admirable effigy, Marsuppini's tomb is exceptionally important in the history of Florentine wall monument. Desiderio also carved the tondi for Filippo Brunelleschi's Pazzi Chapel in Florence sometime after 1451 and completed the marble Altar of the Sacrament in San Lorenzo, Florence (1461), which is considered to be one of the decorative masterpieces of the 15th century.

Desiderio masterfully employed the technique of *rilievo stiacciato* (low, or flattened, relief) in a style related to that of Donatello. The delicacy of contrast in his carvings gives his surfaces a glowing, ethereal quality, as seen in his *Angel from the Altar of the Sacrament* (1458–61) and many of his busts of women.

NUNO GONÇALVES

(flourished 1450–72)

The Portuguese painter Nuno Gonçalves is credited with introducing the Renaissance style to painting in Portugal and has been recognized as one of the genuine masters of the 15th century. After the discovery in 1882 of the only extant work certain to be his—the altarpiece for the convent of São Vicente—he was, after 400 years of anonymity, finally acknowledged as the founder of the Portuguese school of painting and as an artist of universal importance.

Apparently Gonçalves was appointed court painter to the Portuguese king Afonso V in 1450. Records also indicate that he received payment for painting an altarpiece for the Palácio Real in Sintra (1470) and that he was appointed the official painter for the city of Lisbon (Pintor das Obras da Cidade) in 1471. Other than this information, very little is known about his life and the extent of his work. Francisco de Hallanda, in his *Dialogues on Ancient Painting* (1548), refers to him as one of the "Eagles"—one of the 15th-century masters—but his name and work were lost to history. His altarpiece for the cathedral of Lisbon was destroyed in the earthquake of 1755, and his other altarpiece on the subject of São Vicente, the patron saint of Lisbon and of the royal house of Portugal, disappeared until 1882, when it was discovered in the convent of São Vicente. It was not until 1931, when this masterpiece was displayed in Paris, that Gonçalves began to receive the international recognition that he deserves.

The polyptych for São Vicente consists of six panels, two large and four narrow ones, dominated by the figure of St. Vincent. In the large *Panel of the Infante* the saint is shown being venerated by a group of notables, among them Afonso V. In the other large panel, the *Panel of the Archbishop*, he is surrounded by clergy and knights. This remarkable portrait gallery of figures grouped in a medieval composition is a meditation on the pilgrimage of the souls of Christians on a voyage of discovery around their patron saint.

Scholars have suggested that a panel in Évora, Port., depicting two scenes, *Adoration of the Magi* and *Two Franciscan Saints*, could be the work of Gonçalves, but there is no proof of this beyond stylistic similarities.

Gonçalves's work is that of a master who shows some debts to Italian and Flemish art but who also reveals his own remarkable gifts—an economy of line, brilliant handling, superb characterization, and a mastery of composition, all united and all subordinated to the religious vision of the work.

HANS MEMLING

(b. c. 1430/35, Seligenstadt, near Frankfurt am Main—d. Aug. 11, 1494, Bruges)

A leading Flemish painter of the Bruges school, Hans Memling was widely popular throughout Flanders

and had a number of imitators and followers. His last commission, which has been widely copied, is a Crucifixion
panel from the *Passion Triptych* (1491).

Memling, also spelled Memlinc, was apparently first
schooled in the art of Cologne and then traveled to the
Netherlands (*c.* 1455–60), where he probably trained in
the workshop of the painter Rogier van der Weyden. He
settled in Bruges (Brugge) in 1465; there he established a
large shop and executed numerous altarpieces and portraits. Indeed, he was very successful in Bruges: it is
known that he owned a large stone house and by 1480 was
listed among the wealthiest citizens on the city tax
accounts. Sometime between 1470 and 1480 Memling
married Anna de Valkenaere (died 1487), with whom he
had three children.

A number of Memling's works are signed and dated,
and still others allow art historians to place them easily
into a chronology on the basis of the patron depicted in
them. Otherwise it is very difficult to discern an early,
middle, and late style for the artist. His compositions and
types, once established, were repeated again and again
with few indications of any formal development. His
Madonnas gradually become slenderer and more ethereal
and self-conscious, and a greater use of Italian motifs
such as putti (nude, chubby child figures, often with
wings), garlands, and sculptural detail for the settings
marks the later works. His portraits, too, appear to
develop from a type with a simple neutral background to
those enhanced with a loggia or window view of a landscape, but these, too, may have been less a stylistic
development than an adaptation of his compositions to
suit the tastes of his patrons.

A good example of the difficulties of dating encountered by scholars is the triptych of *The Virgin and Child
with Saints and Donors* that Memling executed for Sir John

Donne, which was once dated very early—about 1468—because it was believed that the patron commissioned the work while visiting Bruges for the wedding of Charles the Bold (duke of Burgundy) to Margaret of York and that he died the following year (1469) in the Battle of Edgecote. It is now known that Sir John lived until 1503 and that it is probably his daughter Anne (born 1470 or later) who is portrayed as the young girl kneeling with her parents in the central panel, thus indicating that the painting was commissioned about 1475.

Memling's art clearly reveals the influence of contemporary Flemish painters. He borrowed, for example, from the compositions of Jan van Eyck, the famed founder of the Bruges school. The influence of Dirck Bouts and Hugo van der Goes can also be discerned in his works—for example, in a number of eye-catching details such as glistening mirrors, tile floors, canopied beds, exotic hangings, and brocaded robes. Above all, Memling's art reveals a thorough knowledge of, and dependence on, compositions and figure types created by Rogier van der Weyden. In Memling's large triptych (a painting in three panels, generally hinged together) of the *Adoration of the Magi*, one of his earliest works, and in the altarpiece of 1479 for Jan Floreins, the influence of van der Weyden's last masterpiece, the Columba Altarpiece (1460–64), is especially noticeable. Some scholars believe that Memling himself may have had a hand in the production of this late work while still in van der Weyden's studio. He also imitated van der Weyden's compositions in numerous representations of the half-length Madonna with the Child, often including a pendant with the donor's portrait (the *Madonna and Martin van Nieuwenhove*). Many devotional diptychs (two-panel paintings) such as this were painted in 15th-century Flanders. They consist of a portrait of the "donor"—or patron—in one panel, reverently gazing at the Madonna and Child in the other. Such paintings were for the donor's personal use in his home or travels.

Most of Memling's patrons were those associated with religious houses, such as the Hospital of St. John in Bruges, and wealthy businessmen, including burghers of Bruges and foreign representatives of the Florentine Medicis and the Hanseatic League (an association of German merchants dealing abroad). For Tommaso Portinari, a Medici agent, and his wife, Memling painted portraits and an unusual altarpiece that depicts more than 22 scenes from the Passion of Christ scattered in miniature in a panoramic landscape encompassing a view of Jerusalem. Such an altarpiece, perhaps created for new devotional practices, became very popular at the end of the 15th century.

His best known work with extensive narration is the sumptuous Shrine of St. Ursula in the Hospital of St. John. It was commissioned by two nuns, Jacosa van Dudzeele and Anna van den Moortele, who are portrayed at one end of the composition kneeling before Mary. This reliquary, completed in 1489, is in the form of a diminutive chapel with six painted panels filling the areas along the sides where stained glass would ordinarily be placed. The narrative, which is the story of Ursula and her 11,000 virgins and their trip from Cologne to Rome and back, unfolds with charm and colourful detail but with little drama or emotion. Other patrons of the same hospital commissioned Memling to paint a large altarpiece of St. John with the mystical marriage of St. Catherine to Christ as the central theme. Elaborate narratives appear behind the patron saints John the Baptist and John the Evangelist painted on the side panels, while the central piece is an impressive elaboration of the enthroned Madonna between angels and saints (including Catherine) that one finds in innumerable other devotional pieces attributed to Memling.

Because Memling's work was so strongly influenced by that of other painters, some 20th-century critics took him to task. Yet in his own lifetime he was acclaimed to the degree that the notary of Bruges, recording his death, described him as "the most skillful painter in the whole of Christendom."

COSMÈ TURA

(b. c. 1430, Ferrara [Italy]—d. 1495, Ferrara)

The painter Cosmè (or Cosimo) Tura was the founder and the first significant figure of the 15th-century school of Ferrara. His well-documented career provides a detailed glimpse of the life of a court painter.

Tura was probably trained in Francesco Squarcione's workshop in Padua and was influenced by Andrea Mantegna and by Piero della Francesca when the latter artist was working in Ferrara (c. 1449–50). Tura had moved to Ferrara by 1456, and by 1457 he was living in Castello and employed by the Renaissance court of the Este dukes at Ferrara. In 1458 he was appointed the official court painter, and he served successively dukes Borso and Ercole I. His first known work was a painting, the *Nativity* (1458) for the Ferrara Cathedral. In addition to the many paintings and altarpieces he executed throughout his career, he was also responsible for tapestry designs, tournament costumes, and other functional items frequently used at court. He also decorated the library of Giovanni Pico della Mirandola. Meticulous records of each of his commissions and the amount of money he was paid for them still remain, so it is possible to trace his career from his years of economic prosperity to the poverty he faced just before his death.

Tura was a master of allegory and a considerable decorative painter. The important part played by him in the

complex and erudite cycle of frescoes in the Schifanoia
Palace at Ferrara (1469–71) can still be seen. Other important works include his *Primavera* (*c.* 1460); the organ doors
showing the *Annunciation* (1469) in Ferrara Cathedral; a
Pietà (*c.* 1472); and the Roverella Altarpiece (*c.* 1472). The
painting on the organ doors in the Ferrara Cathedral, mentioned above, was some of his best, most visually stunning
work. The exterior of the doors was decorated with St.
George and the Dragon while the interior featured the
Annunciation. By the 1470s Tura was increasingly commissioned to paint portraits of the royal family. He painted
three of the infant prince Alfonso I d'Este (1477) and later
one of the betrothed Beatrice d'Este (1485).

Tura remained within the tradition of Squarcione
throughout his life, but within that tradition he developed
his own personal idiom. His work is characterized by a
mannered, nervous, and wiry line and the use of carefully
rendered detail and brilliant colour. His figures are usually
draped in metallic, angular folds.

ANDREA MANTEGNA

(b. 1431, Isola di Cartura [near Vicenza], Republic of Venice
[Italy]—d. Sept. 13, 1506, Mantua)

The painter and engraver Andrea Mantegna was the
first fully Renaissance artist of northern Italy. His
best known surviving work is the Camera degli Sposi
("Room of the Bride and Groom"), or Camera Picta
("Painted Room") (1474), in the Palazzo Ducale of Mantua,
for which he developed a self-consistent illusion of a total
environment. Mantegna's other principal works include
the Ovetari Chapel frescoes (1448–55) in the Eremitani
Church in Padua and the *Triumph of Caesar* (begun *c.* 1486),
the pinnacle of his late style.

FORMATIVE YEARS IN PADUA

Mantegna's extraordinary native abilities were recognized early. He was the second son of a woodworker but was legally adopted by Francesco Squarcione by the time he was 10 years old and possibly even earlier. A teacher of painting and a collector of antiquities in Padua, Squarcione drew the cream of young local talent to his studio, which some of his protégés, such as Mantegna and the painter Marco Zoppo, later had cause to regret. In 1448, at age 17, Mantegna disassociated himself from Squarcione's guardianship to establish his own workshop in Padua, later claiming that Squarcione had profited considerably from his services without giving due recompense. The award to Mantegna of the important commission for an altarpiece for the church of Santa Sofia (1448), now lost, demonstrates his precocity, since it was unusual for so young an artist to receive such a commission. Mantegna himself proudly called attention to his youthful ability in the painting's inscription: "Andrea Mantegna from Padua, aged 17, painted this with his own hand, 1448."

During the following year, Mantegna worked on the fresco decoration of the Ovetari Chapel in the Eremitani Church in Padua. The figures of Saints Peter, Paul, and Christopher in the apse, his earliest frescoes in this chapel, show to what extent he had already absorbed the monumental figure style of Tuscany. In the *St. James Led to Martyrdom* in the lowest row on the left wall, painted sometime between 1453 and 1455, both Mantegna's mastery of *di sotto in su* (from below to above) perspective and his use of archaeologically correct details of Roman architecture are already apparent. The perspective scheme with a viewpoint below the lower frame of the composition exaggerates the apparent height of the scene with respect to the viewer and lends an aspect of grandiose monumentality to the triumphal arch.

In the two scenes from the life of St. Christopher united in a single perspective on the right-hand wall, Mantegna extended his experiments in illusionism to the framing element by painting a highly realistic column on the front plane. The meticulously detailed column divides the scene in two while appearing to exist in a realm totally apart from the pictorial space, a realm shared with the observer. This extension of illusionistic principles to the elements surrounding a picture anticipates Mantegna's San Zeno Altarpiece, where the carved half columns of the frame abut the painted piers (vertical members) on the front plane of the picture space, so that the frame architecture serves as the exterior of the temple-pavilion architecture depicted in the painting. In this way the sphere of intense ideality inhabited by the Virgin Mary is conjoined to the beholder's own space by a brilliant combination of physical and optical devices. Unfortunately, all Mantegna's frescoes in the Ovetari Chapel except *The Assumption* and *The Martyrdom of St. Christopher* were destroyed by a bomb during World War II.

The environment of the city of Padua, where Mantegna lived during the major formative years of his life (from about age 10 to about age 30), exerted a strong influence on his interests, ideas, painting style, and concept of himself. Padua was the first centre of humanism in northern Italy, the home of a great university (founded in 1222), and renowned as a centre for the study of medicine, philosophy, and mathematics. With the influx of scholars from all over Europe and Italy, an atmosphere of internationalism prevailed. From the time of the 14th-century poet Petrarch, Padua had experienced a rapidly growing revival of interest in antiquity, and many eminent humanists and Latin scholars had resided there. Increasing interest in and imitation of the culture of ancient Rome produced a climate in which feverish collecting of antiquities and ancient inscriptions—even if only in fragmentary form—flourished. Mantegna's friendly relations with several humanists, antiquarians, and university professors are a matter of record, and hence he may be seen as one of the earliest Renaissance artists to fraternize from a position of intellectual equality with such men. In this way, Mantegna's lifestyle contributed to the early 16th-century ideal of the artist as one so intimately familiar with antique history, mythology, and literature as to be able to draw easily from these highly respected sources.

The experience of the Paduan milieu was thus decisive for the formation of Mantegna's attitude toward the Classical world, which may perhaps be characterized best as double faceted. On the one hand, Mantegna's search for accurate knowledge of Roman antiquity was reflected both in his depiction of specific monuments of Roman architecture and sculpture and in his creation of a vocabulary of antique forms that became the language of antique revival for more than a generation of northern Italian painters and sculptors after the mid-1450s. On the other hand, through a process of artistic synthesis, Mantegna sensed the forces and significances below the surfaces of Roman grandeur. The architectural backgrounds of pictures in the Ovetari Chapel, such as the *St. James Before Herod* and the *St. James Led to Martyrdom*, as well as of the two paintings of St. Sebastian in Vienna and Paris, were infused with a brooding harshness and severity against which the suffering of the Christian saints took on the added tragic implication of an impending cultural clash that was to separate and alienate the Christian and pagan worlds. In Mantegna's century, overcoming the experience of alienation from antiquity through the study and revitalization of its architectural and sculptural vocabulary was an obsessive theme.

That the Roman world still existed in Italy in ruins only served to increase the sudden sense of cultural loss that struck the 15th century. By his thoroughgoing description of antique forms coupled with an instinctive sense of the political realities that underlay their original creation, Mantegna lent great impetus to the antique revival movement at mid-century.

Mantegna's starting point had been a still earlier form of antique revival—the monumental Tuscan figure style brought to Venice by the Florentine painter Andrea del Castagno in 1442. Mantegna presumably saw Castagno's frescoes of evangelists and saints in the church of San Zaccaria during a visit to Venice in 1447. His Venetian connections were strengthened by his marriage in 1453 to Nicolosia, daughter of Jacopo Bellini and sister of Giovanni and Gentile Bellini, who became the leading family of painters in Venice during the following decade. Jacopo's studies in perspective and drawings of fantastic architectural settings based on antique architecture would have interested his new son-in-law, who very likely had studied such drawings during his earlier visit to Venice.

Though Mantegna might have been expected to join the Bellini studio, he preferred to pursue his independent practice in Padua, where the overwhelming artistic influence on him for the preceding few years had come from the wealth of sculpture produced by the Florentine Donatello for the high altar of San Antonio (finished by 1450). Giovanni Bellini's response to Mantegna's style has been termed a dialogue, but Mantegna's reaction to Donatello's works might more aptly be called a struggle or even a dialectic. The frame and painted architecture of Mantegna's San Zeno Altarpiece (1459) answered the challenge posed by Donatello's Padua altar, for example. Mantegna's art always retained echoes of Donatello's sculpture in its hard, even metallic, surfaces, revealing an essentially sculptural approach that was somewhat softened only in the 1490s.

YEARS AS COURT PAINTER IN MANTUA

Mantegna has been characterized as strongly jealous of his independence. Yet by entering the service of the marchese di Montova (Mantua), Ludovico Gonzaga, in 1459, he was forced to submit to limitations on his freedom of travel and acceptance of commissions from other patrons. Despite such restrictions, Mantegna journeyed to Florence and Pisa in 1466–67, where he renewed contact with works of art by Donatello, Fra Filippo Lippi, Paolo Uccello, and Andrea del Castagno. During this decade (1460–70), Mantegna produced his finest small-scale works, such as *The Circumcision* and the Venice *St. George*.

The Gonzaga patronage provided Mantegna a fixed income (which did not always materialize) and the opportunity to create what became his best-known surviving work, the so-called Camera degli Sposi. Earlier practitioners of 15th-century perspective delimited a rectangular field as a transparent window onto the world and constructed an imaginary space behind its front plane. In the Camera degli Sposi, however, Mantegna constructed a system of homogeneous decoration on all four walls of the room, mainly by means of highly realistic painted architectural elements on walls and ceilings, which from ground level convincingly imitate three-dimensionally extended shapes. Though the ceiling is flat, it appears concave. Mantegna transformed the small interior room into an elegant open-air pavilion, to which the room's real and fictive occupants (actually one and the same, since the beholders must have been members of that very court) were transported from deep within an essentially medieval urban castle.

Directly above the centre of the room is a painted oculus, or circular opening to the sky, with putti (nude, chubby child figures, often with wings) and women around a balustrade in dramatically foreshortened perspective. The strong vertical axis created by the oculus locates the spectator at a single point in the centre of the room, the point from which the observer's space blends with that of the frescoed figures.

The realism of the perspective handling of the oculus made it the most influential illusionistic *di sotto in su* ceiling decoration of the early Renaissance. Its implications for the future of ceiling decoration were largely unrealized, however, until the time of Correggio, a major northern Italian painter of the early 16th century, who employed the same type of illusionism in a series of domes in Parma (Italy). Furthermore, the idea of total spatial illusion generated by Mantegna was not fully exploited until inventors of ingenious schemes of ceiling decoration in the Baroque era (the 17th century), such as Giovanni Lanfranco and Andrea Pozzo, utilized a basically identical concept of total illusion dependent upon the location of a hypothetical viewer standing at a single point in the room.

While at the Gonzaga court, Mantegna attained a position of great respect. His close relations with his patron Ludovico were a unique phenomenon at such an early date. As one might expect, the signatures of Mantegna's paintings reveal intense pride in his accomplishments as a painter. Other than that there are only a few legal records of disputes with his neighbours (from which Ludovico had to rescue him) to provide tentative evidence for the painter's irascible and contentious personality during his later years. An empathetic viewer may draw many subjective conclusions as to Mantegna's thoughts and emotions by looking carefully at his paintings.

Ludovico died in 1478, followed soon after by Mantegna's son Bernardino, who had been expected to carry on his father's studio. Mantegna's financial situation was so bad that, in 1484, he was forced to ask for help from the powerful Florentine merchant prince Lorenzo de' Medici and even contemplated moving to Florence. But Ludovico's son Federico outlived his father by only a few years, and, with the accession of young Francesco II in 1484, the financial conditions of patronage improved.

Though many of Mantegna's works for the Gonzaga family were subsequently lost, the remains of nine canvases depicting a Roman triumphal procession, the *Triumph of Caesar*, begun about 1486 and worked on for several years, still exist. In these paintings, reflecting the Classical tastes of his new patron, Francesco, Mantegna reached the peak of his late style. Perhaps it was this new imaginative synthesis of the colour, splendour, and ritualistic power of ancient Rome that brought about Pope Innocent VIII's commission to decorate his private chapel in the Belvedere Palace in Rome (destroyed 1780), which Mantegna carried out in 1488–90.

Notwithstanding ill health and advanced age, Mantegna worked intensively during the remaining years of his life. In 1495 Francesco ordered the *Madonna of the Victory* (1496) to commemorate his supposed victory at the Battle of Fornovo. In the last years of his life, Mantegna painted the *Parnassus* (1497), a picture celebrating the marriage of Isabella d'Este to Francesco Gonzaga in 1490, and *Wisdom Overcoming the Vices* (1502) for Isabella's *studiolo* (a small room in the Gonzaga palace at Mantua embellished with fine paintings and carvings of mythological subjects intended to display the erudition and advanced taste of

Madonna of the Victory, *altarpiece by Andrea Mantegna, 1496; in the Louvre, Paris.* Giraudon/Art Resource, New York

its patron). A third canvas intended for this program, with the legend of the god Comus, was unfinished when Mantegna died and was completed by his successor at the Gonzaga court, Lorenzo Costa.

A funerary chapel in the church of St. Andrea at Mantua was dedicated to Mantegna's memory. Decorated with frescoes, including a dome painted (possibly by Correggio) with paradise symbols related to Mantegna's *Madonna of the Victory*, it was finished in 1516. No other 15th-century artist was dignified by having a funerary chapel dedicated to him in the major church of the city where he worked, which attests to the high stature Mantegna came to enjoy in his adopted city.

ASSESSMENT

Mantegna's art and his attitude toward Classical antiquity provided a model for other artists, among them Giovanni Bellini in Venice and Albrecht Dürer in Germany. By placing the Virgin and saints of the St. Zeno Altarpiece in a unified space continuous with its frame, Mantegna introduced new principles of illusionism into *sacra conversazione* paintings (i.e., paintings of the Madonna and Child with saints).

Perhaps of even greater significance were his achievements in the field of fresco painting. Mantegna's invention of total spatial illusionism by the manipulation of perspective and foreshortening began a tradition of ceiling decoration that was followed for three centuries. Mantegna's portraits of the Gonzaga family in their palace at Mantua (1474) glorified living subjects by conferring upon them the over-life-size stature, sculptural volume, and studied gravity of movement and gesture normally reserved for saints and heroes of myth and history.

Ludovico Gonzaga, His Family and Court, *detail of a fresco by Andrea Mantegna, 1474; in the Camera degli Sposi, Palazzo Ducale, Mantua, Italy.* SCALA/Art Resource, New York

POLLAIUOLO BROTHERS

(Antonio del Pollaiuolo: b. Jan. 17, 1413/21, Florence [Italy]—d.
1496, Rome) and (Piero del Pollaiuolo: b. 1443, Florence [Italy]—d.
1496, Rome)

The Pollaiuolo brothers were sculptors, painters, engravers, and goldsmiths who produced myriad works together under a combined signature. Together Antonio di Jacopo d'Antonio Benci had a significant influence on the development of Florentine art. Their workshop is regarded as one of the most important in Florence during the late 15th century.

The brothers received the name of Pollaiuolo because their father was alleged to have been a poulterer (from *pollaio*, meaning "hen coop"). Antonio learned goldsmithing and metalworking from either Vittore Ghiberti (son of Lorenzo) or Andrea del Castagno. Piero probably learned painting from Andrea del Castagno and became his brother's associate in goldsmithing, painting, sculpture, and engraving.

After 1460 the two collaborated consistently, and the individual contributions of each are frequently difficult to determine. Their Florentine commissions included the altarpiece in the Chapel of the Cardinal of Portugal in San Miniato al Monte (1466) and the *Martyrdom of St. Sebastian* (1475) for the Pucci Chapel in the church of Santissima Annunziata. In 1484 they went to Rome, where their works included the tomb of Pope Sixtus IV (1484–93) in the Vatican Grottoes of St. Peter's and, in the final years of their lives, the tomb of Pope Innocent VIII (1493–97), also in St. Peter's. When Old St. Peter's was demolished (1506), these were the only tombs to be transferred into the new building.

Antonio Pollaiuolo is recognized individually as a superb draftsman whose mastery of line is best exemplified in his renderings of the human figure in motion; he

Portrait of a Woman, *tempera on wood by Antonio del Pollaiuolo, c. 1475; in the Uffizi Gallery, Florence.* © Photos.com/Jupiterimages was among the first artists to practice anatomical dissection in the study of the human form. His contributions to landscape representation were also significant. His notable works include the engraving *Battle of the Nudes* (*c.* 1470) and the bronze statuette *Hercules and Antaeus* (*c.* 1475).

In general, however, the individual works of Piero are regarded as less artistically significant than those of his brother. His principal works were his *Coronation of the Virgin*, an altarpiece painted in 1483 (in the choir of the cathedral at San Gimignano); his *Three Saints* (1467–68), an altarpiece; and *Prudence* (1469–70), one of six Virtues he painted for the Mercanzia (Merchants' Court).

MICHAEL PACHER

(b. *c.* 1435, County of Tirol—d. August 1498, Salzburg?, Archbishopric of Salzburg)

The late Gothic painter and wood-carver Michael Pacher was one of the first artists to introduce the principles of Renaissance painting into Germany.

Little is known of Pacher's early life, but he is thought to have gone to Italy, where he was much impressed by the experiments in perspective of two eminent northern Italian artists of the Renaissance, Jacopo Bellini and Andrea Mantegna. That trip must have occurred sometime before Pacher began work on the St. Wolfgang Altarpiece of the Pilgrimage Church of St. Wolfgang in Upper Austria (centre completed in 1479; wings completed in 1481). The large figures placed close to the picture plane and seen from a low viewpoint, the deep architectural perspective, and the dramatic foreshortening in such scenes as the *Expulsion of the Money Changers from the Temple* and the *Nativity* betray knowledge of Mantegna's frescoes in the Church of the Eremitani in Padua. Pacher, however, rejected Mantegna's statuesque compositions in favour of a dynamic sense of movement. In contrast to the painted wings, the carved and painted centre of the altarpiece, showing the *Coronation of the Virgin*, exhibits no Italian characteristics. Instead, its intricate carving that accentuates minute detail, the bright polychrome and sweeping draperies are wholly northern in spirit.

In the Altarpiece of the Church Fathers (*c.* 1483), Pacher uses direct and reflected light to create a convincing spatial ambience within a shallow depth. His narrow niches are dominated by the four monumental figures of the Fathers of the Church. The back of the altarpiece exhibits scenes from the life of St. Wolfgang and is notable for its attenuated male nude, whose idealized form and sharp outline again reflect Pacher's knowledge of Mantegna's art. Such late works as the *Betrothal of the Virgin* and the *Flagellation* (both 1484) repudiate his early dynamic compositions and introduce a new, static serenity. The faces and drapery are more idealized and more monumental than in his early works, and the figures are emphasized at the expense of the architectural background.

ANDREA DEL VERROCCHIO

(b. 1435, Florence [Italy]—d. 1488, Venice)

The 15th-century Florentine sculptor and painter Andrea del Verrocchio is perhaps best known as the teacher of Leonardo da Vinci. His equestrian statue of Bartolomeo Colleoni, erected in Venice in 1496, is particularly important.

EARLY LIFE

Little accurate biographical information is known about Verrocchio. He was the son of Michele di Francesco Cioni, a maker of bricks and tiles who later became a tax collector.

Financial security always seemed to be a family problem. Verrocchio had to support several of his brothers and sisters. Never marrying, he later provided for the education and dowries of the daughters of his younger brother Tommaso.

Initially he was trained as a goldsmith. His master has traditionally been recorded as a supposed goldsmith, Giuliano Verrocchi, whose last name Andrea apparently took as his own. Another questionable biographical tradition is that of his apprenticeship under Donatello, the greatest Italian sculptor of the early Renaissance. Since the stylistic affinity of Verrocchio's early sculpture is with the work of Antonio Rossellino rather than Donatello, this liaison seems doubtful.

Verrocchio's first studies in painting date possibly from the mid-1460s. He is said to have been a pupil of the Florentine artist Alessio Baldovinetti. But it is assumed that he and Sandro Botticelli worked together under the early Renaissance master Fra Filippo Lippi in Prato, a city near Florence, where Lippi had been commissioned to execute a series of murals for the cathedral.

MEDICI PATRONAGE

Verrocchio's most important works were executed in the last two decades of his life. His rise to artistic prominence, which he owed chiefly to encouragement by Piero de' Medici and his son Lorenzo, the leading art patrons of Florence, evidently began only after the death, in 1466, of Donatello, who had been the Medici favourite. Besides the paintings and sculptures Verrocchio produced for the Medici, he designed costumes and decorative armour for their festivals, tournaments, and solemn receptions. Made curator of the collection of antiquities in the Medici palace, he restored many pieces of ancient Roman sculpture, especially portrait busts.

It appears that Verrocchio produced few works for patrons outside of Florence. Though he is said to have worked in Rome for Pope Sixtus IV, among others, there is no documentary trace that he ever left the area around Florence until the early 1480s, when he moved to Venice, where he died within a few years. Even while he was in Venice his Florentine workshop was maintained and directed by his favourite student, Lorenzo di Credi. Di Credi was also the administrator and principal heir of Verrocchio's estate.

Verrocchio's reputation was widespread in the second half of the 15th century and many well-known artists of the Italian Renaissance studied painting and sculpture at his Florentine studio. The most important of his students were Leonardo da Vinci and Perugino, the latter Raphael's teacher. The mural painter Domenico Ghirlandaio, Michelangelo's master, was temporarily in close contact with Verrocchio. Sandro Botticelli, the major Florentine painter of the late 15th century, and Francesco di Giorgio, the important Sienese artist, clearly oriented themselves toward Verrocchio's art in certain phases of their development, as did the prominent Florentine sculptors Benedetto da Maiano and Andrea Sansovino.

THE PAINTINGS AND SCULPTURES

The only surviving painting that, according to documentary proof, should be by Verrocchio, an altarpiece of the *Madonna and Child with Saints* in the Donato de' Medici Chapel of the cathedral at Pistoia, was not completed by the master himself. Largely executed by his pupil Lorenzo di Credi, its handling is inconsistent with that of the *Baptism of Christ* (c. 1470–75), which has been attributed to Verrocchio ever since it was first mentioned in 1550 by Giorgio Vasari in his *Lives of the Most Eminent Painters,*

Sculptors, and Architects. One of the two angels and part of the distant landscape in the *Baptism*, however, were certainly painted by his apprentice, the young Leonardo da Vinci. Other paintings ascribed to Verrocchio are a Madonna, a *Tobias and the Angel*, and the altarpiece in Argiano, with Christ on the Cross between St. Jerome and St. Anthony. After the mid-1470s Verrocchio dedicated himself principally to sculpture, in which he manifested strong personal convictions and an inventive ability.

The sculptural works either recorded to be by Verrocchio or actually extant are few in number. According to his brother Tommaso, Verrocchio was responsible for an inlaid slab (1467) in the Florentine church of San Lorenzo recording the burial place of Cosimo de' Medici, who died in 1464. In 1468 Verrocchio is known to have executed a bronze candlestick for the Palazzo della Signoria in Florence. This work was followed by his first major commission, the tomb of Piero and Giovanni de' Medici in the Old Sacristy of San Lorenzo. Completed in 1472, this sarcophagus, set in an archway, is impressive for its originality of composition and its inspired use of coloured marble and porphyry in conjunction with rich bronze ornamentation.

Verrocchio's earliest surviving example of figurative sculpture is a small bronze statue of David, which is generally dated before 1476. A second bronze figure, the *Putto with Dolphin*, is important in the development of freestanding Renaissance sculpture for its spiral design, which represents a successful effort to evolve a pose in which all views are of equal significance. It was originally commissioned for a fountain in the Medici villa in Careggi, near Florence.

Verrocchio's reputation as one of the great relief sculptors of the 15th century was clearly established with his cenotaph, or memorial, in the cathedral at Pistoia, to a

Tuscan ecclesiastical dignitary, Cardinal Niccolò Forteguerri. Ordered in 1476, the cenotaph was still unfinished when Verrocchio died. Though its effect was altered by changes and additions foreign to Verrocchio's original design, the Forteguerri cenotaph contains some of the artist's most important relief sculpture. Its scenographic arrangement of the figures into a dramatically unified composition anticipates the theatrical effect of the dynamically composed wall reliefs executed by Baroque sculptors of the 17th century. Another relief dates from 1478/79, when it was decided to extend the silver altar in the baptistery of the cathedral of Florence, and one of the four supplementary scenes was allotted to Verrocchio. Depicting the *Beheading of St. John the Baptist*, this work was delivered in 1480. Dating from about 1477/78 is a terracotta relief of the Madonna from the Florentine hospital of Santa Maria Nuova.

In the late 1470s Verrocchio produced two portrait sculptures. A penetrating realism distinguishes his terracotta bust of Giuliano de' Medici from the idealization of the individual that characterizes his marble bust known as *Lady with Primroses*. The latter work created a new type of Renaissance bust, in which the arms of the sitter are included in the manner of ancient Roman models. This compositional device allows the hands, as well as the face, to express the character and mood of the sitter.

Perhaps the most important work Verrocchio executed in Florence was a bronze group of *Christ and St. Thomas* commissioned for a niche in the east exterior wall of the Or San Michele in Florence. Executed between 1467 and 1483, the work is remarkable for its technical perfection, highly intellectual sense of compositional design, and understanding of the subtle emotional nature of the subject. In 1483 Verrocchio was commissioned by the Venetian government to undertake a second major work in bronze, a commemorative statue of Bartolomeo Colleoni, a condottiere, or professional soldier, who had been employed by the Venetian republic. At Verrocchio's death the model was not yet cast, and the work of casting and chasing, or polishing, was entrusted to the Venetian sculptor Alessandro Leopardi. It was erected in 1496 in the Campo di Santi Giovanni e Paolo in Venice. The movement of the horse and commanding forward gaze of Colleoni gives the impression that the warrior is riding into battle at the head of his troops, who press behind. This innovative scenographic conception was influential in the development of the equestrian figures executed from the Baroque period of the 17th century to those produced in the 19th century by sculptors of the Romantic style. Besides Donatello's monument to the condottiere Gattamelata (*c.* 1447–53) at Padua, Verrocchio's Colleoni monument is aesthetically the most important equestrian statue of the Renaissance. Contrived with great technical assurance and modeled with power and sensitivity, it forms a fitting climax to Verrocchio's sculptural career.

MELOZZO DA FORLÌ

(b. 1438, Forlì, near Ravenna [Italy]—d. Nov. 8, 1494, Forlì)

A Renaissance painter of the Umbrian school, Melozzo da Forlì was one of the great fresco artists of the 15th century. He is mentioned in Forlì in 1460 and 1464 and between 1465 and 1475 probably was active at Urbino, where he came into contact with Piero della Francesca (the main source of his pictorial style), the architect Donato Bramante, and the Flemish and Spanish painters employed by Federico da Montefeltro. Melozzo may have worked with Justus of Ghent and Pedro Berruguete on the decorations of the *studiolo* of the ducal palace at Urbino.

About 1475 Melozzo moved from Urbino to Rome, where he may also have worked temporarily somewhat earlier. His first major work in Rome (completed 1477) was a fresco showing the investiture of Platina as librarian to the Pope, painted in the library of Sixtus IV in the Vatican. Records of payments of 1480 and 1481 relate to subsidiary frescoes and decorative paintings in the library. In 1478 Melozzo became a member of the Guild of St. Luke and about 1480 completed one of his most important works, a fresco of *The Ascension* in the Santissima Apostoli. The athletic figures in this work amply account for the reputation Melozzo enjoyed among Giovanni Santi and other contemporary writers as an exponent of perspective and foreshortening (contracting a figure in the direction of depth to obtain an illusion of projection or extension in space).

Melozzo seems to have left Rome in 1484, on the death of Pope Sixtus IV, after completing the decoration of a chapel (destroyed) in St. Maria in Trastevere, and returned there in 1489. Probably during this second Roman period he prepared cartoons for mosaics in St. Croce in Gerusalemme. In 1493 he was painting in the Palazzo Comunale at Ancona and later in the year returned to Forlì. Little of his work has been preserved, and none of his great decorative schemes survives intact.

BARTOLOMÉ BERMEJO

(b. c. 1440, Córdoba [Spain]—d. c. 1495, Zaragoza?)

The painter Bartolomé Bermejo, who cultivated the Flemish style, was considered the finest painter in Spain before El Greco. Bermejo helped introduce Renaissance style to Spain, and his work was emulated by many painters of his era.

Little is known of Bermejo's early activity. By the late 1460s he was living in Valencia. His earliest surviving work is an altarpiece painting of *St. Michael* commissioned for the parish church of Tous (1468). He worked for three years (between 1474 and 1477) in Aragon, where he had been commissioned to paint the altarpiece of *Santo Domingo de Silos* for the church in Daroca. Although Bermejo's contract stipulated that he would face excommunication if he did not complete the work on time, he arranged an appendix to the contract that would allow another artist to finish it for him. He then renegotiated the contract in 1477 and completed the work himself.

The finished panel, which depicted the enthroned figure of Santo Domingo, contained Gothic elements. Under the influence of the Flemish masters, these elements gradually disappeared as he became more skilled in the use of foreshortening, in depiction of details, and in the resolution of difficult problems in perspective. Bermejo moved to Barcelona in the mid-1480s, where he collaborated with Jaime Huguet, the principal master of Catalan Gothic painting.

The work that demonstrates most clearly Bermejo's mastery of Renaissance techniques is the *Pietà* of 1490 in the Barcelona Cathedral. It is widely considered his finest work. The painting lacks gold in the background (present in earlier works). Instead, a landscape under a stormy sky is painted very much in the manner of the Flemish master Rogier van der Weyden; it is rich in detail, colour, and life and features the small intricate figures of butterflies, birds, and lizards. The figure of the donor (Luis Desplá, canon of Barcelona Cathedral), who is seen kneeling to the left of the central group in this picture, is considered one of the finest portraits painted in Europe in this period. Some scholars have attributed the uniqueness of the painting to the influence of Desplá, a humanist.

HUGO VAN DER GOES

(b. *c.* 1440 — d. 1482, Roode Kloster, near Brussels [now in Belgium])

One of the greatest Flemish painters of the second half of the 15th century, Hugo van der Goes expressed his strange, melancholy genius in religious works of profound but often disturbing spirituality.

Early sources disagree about van der Goes's birthplace, with Ghent, Antwerp, Bruges, and Leiden mentioned as potential candidates. Nothing is known of his life before 1467, when he was accepted as a master in the painters' guild in Ghent. From then until 1475 he received many commissions from the town of Ghent and provided decorations (heraldic shields, processional banners, etc.) for such occasions as the marriage of Charles the Bold in Bruges (1468) and the transference of the remains of Philip the Good to Dijon (1473). In 1474 he was elected dean of the guild, but the following year—when he was at the climax of his career—he decided to enter Roode Kloster, a priory near Brussels, as a lay brother. There he continued to paint and received distinguished visitors; he also undertook journeys. In 1481 a tendency to acute depression culminated in a mental breakdown during which he tried to kill himself. An account of the artist's last years at Roode Kloster, written by a monk, Gaspar Ofhuys (who apparently resented some of van der Goes's privileges), has survived.

Van der Goes's masterpiece, and his only securely documented work, is the large triptych usually known as the Portinari Altarpiece (*c.* 1474–76) with a scene called *The Adoration of the Shepherds* on the centre panel. It was commissioned by Tommaso Portinari, agent for the Medici in Bruges, who is portrayed with his family on the wings. One of the greatest of the early examples of northern realism, it yet subordinates this quality to spiritual content, uses still-life detail with symbolic intent, and shows unprecedented psychological insight in portraiture, especially in the faces of the awe-struck shepherds and the Portinari children. It achieves an emotional intensity unprecedented in Flemish painting. Soon after its completion it was taken to Florence, where its rich colours and careful attention to detail impressed many Italian artists.

Van der Goes's earlier and more tentative style shows that he had studied the leading Netherlandish masters of the first half of the 15th century. A diptych begun about 1467 reflects his awareness of the Ghent Altarpiece of Jan van Eyck in the *Fall of Man*, while the *Lamentation* is reminiscent of Rogier van der Weyden. A comparison between the large *Adoration of the Magi* and the *Nativity* reveals the direction in which van der Goes's later works were to evolve. The *Adoration* is spatially rational, compositionally tranquil, and harmonious in colour. By contrast, the *Nativity* (also called *Adoration of the Shepherds*), a later work painted on a curiously elongated panel, is disturbing even in its format—an emotionally charged supernatural drama on an uncomfortably low stage revealed by the drawing of curtains. This exploitation of space and colour for emotional potentiality rather than rational effect characterizes van der Goes's later works. It appears in the *Holy Trinity Adored by Sir Edward Bonkil* and *The Royal Family of Scotland*, panels that were probably designed as organ shutters (*c.* 1478–79), and culminates in the *Death of the Virgin*, executed not long before van der Goes's death. The unearthly colours of this work are particularly disturbing, and its poignancy is intensified by the controlled grief seen in the faces of the Apostles, who are placed in irrationally conceived space. Van der Goes's art, with its affinities to Mannerism, and his tortured personality found a particularly sympathetic response in the 20th century.

SANDRO BOTTICELLI

(b. 1445, Florence [Italy]—d. May 17, 1510, Florence)

Sandro Botticelli, creator of *The Birth of Venus* and *Primavera*, is one of the greatest painters of the Florentine Renaissance. His works are often said to epitomize for modern viewers the spirit of the Renaissance.

EARLY LIFE AND CAREER

Botticelli was born Alessandro di Mariano Filipepi. The name by which he is best known was derived from that of his elder brother Giovanni, a pawnbroker who was called Botticello ("The Little Barrel"). As is often the case with Renaissance artists, most of the modern information about Botticelli's life and character derives from Giorgio Vasari's *Lives of the Most Eminent Painters, Sculptors, and Architects*, as supplemented and corrected from documents. Botticelli's father was a tanner who apprenticed Sandro to a goldsmith after his schooling was finished. Because Sandro preferred painting, his father then placed him under Filippo Lippi, who was one of the most admired Florentine masters.

Lippi's painterly style, which was formed in the early Florentine Renaissance, was fundamental to Botticelli's own artistic formation, and his influence is evident even in his pupil's late works. Lippi taught Botticelli the techniques of panel painting and fresco and gave him an assured control of linear perspective. Stylistically, Botticelli acquired from Lippi a repertory of types and compositions, a certain graceful fancifulness in costuming, a linear sense of form, and a partiality to certain paler hues that is still visible even after Botticelli had developed his own strong and resonant colour schemes.

After Lippi left Florence for Spoleto, Botticelli worked to improve the comparatively soft, frail figural style he had learned from his teacher. To this end he studied the sculptural style of Antonio Pollaiuolo and Andrea del Verrocchio, the leading Florentine painters of the 1460s, and under their influence Botticelli produced figures of sculptural roundness and strength. He also replaced Lippi's delicate approach with a robust and vigorous naturalism, shaped always by conceptions of ideal beauty. Already by 1470 Botticelli was established in Florence as an independent master with his own workshop. Absorbed in his art, he never married, and he lived with his family.

These transitions in Botticelli's style can be seen in the small panels of Judith (*The Return of Judith*) and Holofernes (*The Discovery of the Body of Holofernes*), both c. 1470, and in his first dated work, *Fortitude* (1470). Botticelli's art from that time shows a use of ochre in the shadowed areas of flesh tones that gives a brown warmth very different from Lippi's pallor. The forms in his paintings are defined with a line that is at once incisive and flowing, and there is a growing ability to suggest the character and even the mood of the figures by action, pose, and facial expression.

About 1478–81 Botticelli entered his artistic maturity; all tentativeness in his work disappeared and was replaced by a consummate mastery. He was able to integrate figure and setting into harmonious compositions and to draw the human form with a compelling vitality. He would later display unequaled skill at rendering narrative texts, whether biographies of saints or stories from Boccaccio's *Decameron* or Dante's *Divine Comedy*, into a pictorial form that is at once exact, economical, and eloquent.

DEVOTIONAL PAINTINGS

Botticelli worked in all the current genres of Florentine art. He painted altarpieces in fresco and on panel, tondi (round paintings), small panel pictures, and small devotional

Virgin and Child, *painting on poplar wood by Sandro Botticelli, date unknown; in the Musée du Petit Palais, Avignon, France.* © Photos.com/ Jupiterimages

triptychs. His altarpieces include narrow vertical panels such as the *St. Sebastian* (1474); small oblong panels such as the famous *Adoration of the Magi* (c. 1476) from the Church of Santa Maria Novella; medium-sized altarpieces, of which the finest is the beautiful Bardi Altarpiece (1484–85); and large-scale works such as the St. Barnabas Altarpiece (c. 1488) and the *Coronation of the Virgin* (c. 1490). His early mastery of fresco is clearly visible in his *St. Augustine* (1480) in the Church of Ognissanti, in which the saint's cogent energy and vigour express both intellectual power and spiritual devotion. Three of Botticelli's finest religious frescoes (completed 1482) were part of the decorations of the Sistine Chapel undertaken by a team of Florentine and Umbrian

Madonna of the Magnificat, *tempera on wood by Sandro Botticelli, 1482; in the Uffizi Gallery, Florence.* © Photos.com/Jupiterimages

artists who had been summoned to Rome in July 1481. The theological themes of the frescoes were chosen to illustrate papal supremacy over the church; Botticelli's are remarkable for their brilliant fusion of sequences of symbolic episodes into unitary compositions.

Florentine tondi were often large, richly framed paintings, and Botticelli produced major works in this format, beginning with the *Adoration of the Magi* (c. 1473) that he painted for Antonio Pucci. Before Botticelli, tondi had been conceived essentially as oblong scenes, but Botticelli suppressed all superfluity of detail in them and became adept at harmonizing his figures with the circular form. His complete mastery of the tondo format is evident in

The Virgin and Child with St. John and an Angel, *tempera on wood by the workshop of Sandro Botticelli, c. 1490; in the National Gallery, London.* © Photos.com/Jupiterimages

two of his most beautiful paintings, *The Madonna of the Magnificat* (1482) and *The Madonna of the Pomegranate* (*c.* 1487). Botticelli also painted a few small oblong Madonnas, notably the *Madonna of the Book* (*c.* 1480), but he mostly left the painting of Madonnas and other devotional subjects to his workshop, which produced them in great numbers. In his art the Virgin Mary is always a tall, queenly figure wearing the conventional red robe and blue cloak, but enriched in his autograph works by sensitively rendered accessories. She often has an inner pensiveness of expression, the same inwardness of mood that is communicated by Botticelli's saints.

SECULAR PATRONAGE AND WORKS

Botticelli is the earliest European artist whose paintings of secular historical subjects survive in some number and are equal or superior in importance to his religious paintings. Nevertheless, much of his secular work is lost; from a working life of some 40 years, only eight examples by him survive in an already well-established genre, the portrait. One of these, the portrait of a young man holding a medal of Cosimo de' Medici (*c.* 1474), is especially significant because in it Botticelli copied the Flemish painter Hans Memling's recently invented device of setting the figure before a landscape seen from a high vantage point. This is the earliest instance of the influence on Botticelli of contemporary Flemish landscape art, which is clearly visible in a number of his landscape settings.

Perhaps it was Botticelli's skill in portraiture that gained him the patronage of the Medici family, in particular of Lorenzo de' Medici and his brother Giuliano, who then dominated Florence. Botticelli painted a portrait of Giuliano and posthumous portraits of his grandfather Cosimo and father Piero. Portraits of all four Medici appear as the Three

La Bella Simonetta, *oil on wood by Sandro Botticelli, 1475; in the Palatine Gallery, Pitti Palace, Florence.* © Photos.com/Jupiterimages

Magi and an attendant figure in the *Adoration of the Magi* from Santa Maria Novella. Botticelli is also known to have painted (1475) for Giuliano a banner of Pallas trampling on the flames of love and Cupid bound to an olive tree. This work, though lost, is important as a key to Botticelli's use of Classical mythology to illustrate the sentiment of medieval courtly love in his great mythological paintings.

After Giuliano de' Medici's assassination in the Pazzi conspiracy of 1478, it was Botticelli who painted the defamatory fresco of the hanged conspirators on a wall of the Palazzo Vecchio. The frescoes were destroyed after the expulsion of the Medici in 1494. Lorenzo certainly always favoured Botticelli, as Vasari claims, but even more significant in the painter's career was the lasting friendship and patronage of Lorenzo di Pierfrancesco de' Medici, head of the junior Medici line and from 1494 an open opponent of the senior line. Tommaso Soderini, who secured for Botticelli in 1470 the commission for the *Fortitude*, and Antonio Pucci, for whom he painted his earliest surviving tondo, were both prominent Medicean partisans, as was Giovanni Tornabuoni, who about 1486–87 commissioned Botticelli's most important surviving secular frescoes.

MYTHOLOGICAL PAINTINGS

Many of the commissions given to Botticelli by these rich patrons were linked to Florentine customs on the occasion of a marriage, which was by far the most important family ceremony of that time. A chamber was usually prepared for the newly married couple in the family palace of the groom, and paintings were mounted within it. The themes of such paintings were either romantic, exalting love and lovers, or exemplary, depicting heroines of virtuous fame. Botticelli's earliest known work of this kind was commissioned by Lorenzo de' Medici for the marriage of Antonio Pucci's son Giannozzo in 1483. The set of four panels— *The Story of Nastagio degli Onesti*—narrates a story from Boccaccio. Mythological figures had been used in earlier Renaissance secular art, but the complex culture of late Medicean Florence, which was simultaneously infused with the romantic sentiment of courtly love and with the humanist interest for Classical antiquity and its vanished artistic traditions, employed these mythological figures more fully and in more correctly antiquarian fashion. A new mythological language became current, inspired partly by Classical literature and sculpture and by descriptions of lost ancient paintings and partly by the Renaissance search for the full physical realization of the ideal human figure.

Among the greatest examples of this novel fashion in secular painting are four of Botticelli's most famous works: *Primavera* (c. 1477–82), *Pallas and the Centaur* (c. 1485), *Venus and Mars* (c. 1485), and *The Birth of Venus* (c. 1485). The *Primavera*, or *Allegory of Spring*, and *The Birth of Venus* were painted for the home of Lorenzo di Pierfrancesco de' Medici. All four of these panel paintings have been variously interpreted by modern scholarship. The figures certainly do not enact a known myth but rather are used allegorically to illustrate various aspects of love: in *Primavera*, its kindling and its fruition in marriage; in *Pallas*, the subjugation of male lust by female chastity; in *Venus and Mars*, a celebration of woman's calm triumph after man's sexual exhaustion; and in *The Birth of Venus*, the birth of love in the world. The *Primavera* and *The Birth of Venus* contain some of the most sensuously beautiful nudes and semi-nudes painted during the Renaissance. The four paintings' settings, which are partly mythological—that of the *Primavera* is the Garden of the Hesperides—and partly symbolic, are pastoral and idyllic in sentiment.

Botticelli's frescoes from a chamber in the Villa Lemmi, celebrating the marriage of Lorenzo Tornabuoni and Giovanna degli Albizzi in 1486, also draw on Classical mythology for their subject matter. In these frescoes, real personages mingle with mythological figures: Venus, attended by her Graces, gives flowers to Giovanna degli Albizzi, while Lorenzo Tornabuoni, who is called to a mercantile life, is brought before Prudentia and the Liberal Arts.

The influence of the Renaissance humanist Leon Battista Alberti's art theories is apparent in Botticelli's Classical borrowings and his meticulous use of linear perspective. The work that best illustrates Botticelli's interest in reviving the glories of Classical antiquity is the *Calumny of Apelles* (c. 1495), a subject recommended by Alberti, who took it from a description of a work by the ancient Greek

Calumny of Apelles, *tempera on panel by Sandro Botticelli, 1490s; in the Uffizi Gallery, Florence.* © Photos.com/Jupiterimages

painter Apelles. Botticelli also drew inspiration from Classical art more directly. While in Rome in 1481–82, for example, he reproduced that city's Arch of Constantine in one of his Sistine frescoes. Three of the figures in *Primavera* are taken from a Classical statue of the Three Graces, while the figure of Venus in *The Birth of Venus* derives from an ancient statue of *Venus Pudica*.

LATE WORKS

An incipient mannerism appears in Botticelli's late works of the 1480s and in works such as the magnificent Cestello *Annunciation* (1490) and the small *Pietà* (late 1490s) now in the Poldi-Pezzoli Museum. After the early 1490s his style

Three Miracles of Saint Zenobius, *tempera on wood by Sandro Botticelli, 1500–10; in the Metropolitan Museum of Art, New York.* © Photos.com/ Jupiterimages

changed markedly. The paintings are smaller in scale, the figures in them are now slender to the point of idiosyncrasy, and the painter, by accentuating their gestures and expressions, concentrates attention on their passionate urgency of action. This mysterious retreat from the idealizing naturalism of the 1480s perhaps resulted from Botticelli's involvement with the fiery reformist preacher Girolamo Savonarola in the 1490s.

The years from 1494 were dramatic ones in Florence. The city's Medici rulers fell, and a republican government under Savonarola's dominance was installed. Savonarola was an ascetic idealist who attacked the church's corruption and prophesied its future renewal. According to Vasari, Botticelli was a devoted follower of Savonarola, even after the friar was executed in 1498. The spiritual tensions of these years are reflected in two religious paintings, the apocalyptic *Mystic Crucifixion* (1497) and the *Mystic Nativity* (1501), which expresses Botticelli's own faith in the renewal of the church. *The Tragedy of Lucretia* (c. 1499) and *The Story of Virginia Romana* (1499) appear to condemn the Medici's tyranny and to celebrate republicanism.

Botticelli, according to Vasari, took an enduring interest in the study and interpretation of Dante's *Divine Comedy*. He made some designs to illustrate the first printed edition of 1481 and worked intermittently over the following years on an uncompleted set of large drawings that matched each canto with a complete visual commentary. He was also much in demand by engravers, embroiderers, and tapestry workers as a designer; among his few surviving drawings are some that can be associated with these techniques.

Although Vasari describes Botticelli as impoverished and disabled in his last years, other evidence suggests that he and his family remained fairly prosperous. He received commissions throughout the 1490s and was still paying his dues, if belatedly, to the Company of Saint Luke, the Florentine painters' guild, in 1505. But the absence of any further commissions and the tentativeness of the very last Dante drawings suggest that he was perhaps overtaken by ill health. Upon his death in 1510 he was buried in the Church of Ognissanti. About 50 paintings survive that are either wholly or partly from his own hand. The Uffizi Gallery's magnificent collection of his works includes many of his masterpieces.

MARTIN SCHONGAUER

(b. 1445/50, Colmar, Alsace [now in France]—d. Feb. 2, 1491, Breisach, Baden [now in Germany])

The finest German engraver before Albrecht Dürer was the painter and printmaker Martin Schongauer, who was the son of Caspar Schongauer, a goldsmith of Augsburg. In 1465, Martin Schongauer registered at the University of Leipzig but apparently remained there only for a short time. It is not clear whether he was there as a student or as a visiting artist enjoying the university's protection from interference by the local painters' guild. No work of his has ever been discovered that could with certainty be dated earlier than 1469, and the wide distribution of his work did not get under way until the late 1470s. In 1469 his name is mentioned for the first time in the Colmar register of property. The same date appears also on three of his early drawings, but these dates and signatures were added by Albrecht Dürer, who may have received them from Schongauer's brothers.

According to contemporary sources, Schongauer was a prolific painter whose panels were sought in many countries. Few paintings by his hand survive. Among these, the *Madonna in a Rose Garden* (1473), altarpiece of the Church of Saint-Martin in Colmar, ranks first in importance. This work combines monumentality with tenderness, approaching the manner of the great Flemish painter Rogier van der Weyden, by whom Schongauer was profoundly influenced. Other paintings by Schongauer include two wings of the Orliac altar; six small panels among which the *Nativity* and the *Holy Family* are the most mature; and finally the murals of the *Last Judgment* in the cathedral of Breisach, probably his last work (uncovered in 1932).

It is as an engraver that Schongauer stands without rival in northern Europe in his time. He was influenced by and may have studied with the master engraver who signed his work simply "E.S." Schongauer's engraved work, consisting of about 115 plates, all signed with his monogram, is a final, highly refined and sensitive manifestation of the late Gothic spirit. Technically he brought the art of engraving to maturity by expanding its range of contrasts and textures, thus introducing a painter's viewpoint into an art that had been primarily the domain of the goldsmith. The larger and more elaborate engravings, such as the *Temptation of St. Anthony* or the *Death of the Virgin*, belong to his earlier period.

In his later years he preferred smaller plates, even for such subjects as the *Passion of Christ*, a set of 12 engravings. Some of his most eloquent plates are single figures, such as the *Madonna in a Courtyard* and *St. Sebastian*. Within the diversity of trends in German art in this period, Schongauer represents the most idealistic and aristocratic element, devoting his art mainly to Christian subjects and shunning the crude and often humorous realism of some of his fellow engravers. The grace of his work became proverbial even in his lifetime and gave rise to such names as "Hübsch ["charming"] Martin" and "Schön Martin" ("Bel Martino" in Italian), whereby the

German adjective *schön* ("beautiful") often became confused with the artist's family name.

In 1488 Schongauer left Colmar and moved to Breisach, in Baden, where he died.

LUCA SIGNORELLI

(b. 1445/50, Cortona, Republic of Florence [Italy]—d. Oct. 16, 1523, Cortona)

The Renaissance painter Luca Signorelli, also called Luca da Cortona, is best known for his nudes as well as for his novel compositional devices.

Born Luca d'Egidio di Ventura de' Signorelli, he likely was a pupil of Piero della Francesca in the 1460s. The first

The Condemned in Hell, *fresco by Luca Signorelli, 1500–02; in the chapel of S. Brizio, Orvieto, Italy.* SCALA/Art Resource, New York

certain surviving work by him, a fragmentary fresco (1474) now in the museum at Città di Castello, shows a strong influence from Piero. His first signed work was a processional banner with a Madonna on one side and a Flagellation on the other. They still show links with the style of Piero, but in these pictures the dominant influence is that of Florence and especially the scientific naturalism of the Pollaiuolo brothers, which suggests that Signorelli visited Florence in the 1470s. In 1479 he was elected to the Council of 18 in his native Cortona, and for the rest of his life he was active in politics.

About 1483 he went to Rome, where the *Testament of Moses* fresco in the Sistine Chapel is unanimously attributed to him. By that date his style had become fixed, his interest in dramatic action and the expression of great muscular effort marking him as an essentially Florentine naturalist. The St. Onofrio Altarpiece (1484) for Perugia Cathedral shows the same qualities. Between 1497 and 1498 he was at work on a fresco cycle of scenes from the life of St. Benedict in the monastery at Monteoliveto Maggiore, near Siena.

His masterpiece, the frescoes of *The End of the World* and the *Last Judgment* (1499–1502), is in the chapel of St. Brizio in Orvieto Cathedral. Those frescoes, which greatly influenced Michelangelo, are crowded with powerful nudes painted in many postures that accentuate their musculature. Signorelli had little sense of colour, but here his greenish and purple devils add to the horror induced by the strained poses and the anatomical details in the decayed bodies.

When commissions in Rome and Florence became infrequent, Signorelli returned to his less sophisticated Umbrian clientele. Most of his later works betray the hands of his numerous assistants.

DOMENICO GHIRLANDAIO

(b. 1449, Florence [Italy]—d. Jan. 11, 1494, Florence)

The detailed narrative frescoes of the Florentine painter Domenico Ghirlandaio are remarkable for several reasons, among which there are many portraits of leading citizens in contemporary dress.

Domenico di Tommaso Bigordi was the son of a goldsmith, and his nickname, "Ghirlandaio," was derived from his father's skill in making garlands for the hair of Florentine women. Domenico probably began as an apprentice in his father's shop, but almost nothing is known about his training as a painter or the beginnings of his career. The earliest works attributed to him, dating from the early 1470s, show strong influences from the frescoes of Andrea del Castagno, who died when Ghirlandaio was about eight years old. The Italian painter, architect, and biographer Giorgio Vasari recorded in his *Lives of the Most Eminent Painters, Sculptors, and Architects* (1550) that Ghirlandaio was a pupil of the Florentine painter Alessio Baldovinetti, even though Baldovinetti was only four or five years older than Ghirlandaio himself. Ghirlandaio preferred to work in fresco on large wall surfaces, but he used smaller-scale paintings executed on wood panels for the altarpieces of the chapels that housed his fresco cycles. He never experimented with oil painting, although most Florentine painters of his generation began to use it exclusively in the last quarter of the 15th century.

The village church of Cercina, near Florence, has a fresco of three saints, now thought to be Ghirlandaio's earliest work, but there is general agreement that some frescoes in the Church of Ognissanti in Florence, almost certainly dating from around 1472–73, show his style at its

The Birth of the Virgin, *fresco by Domenico Ghirlandaio, 1486–90; in the choir of Santa Maria Novella, Florence.* SCALA/Art Resource, New York

earliest developed stage. One of them, the *Pietà*, depicts several members of the Vespucci family as mourners, thus already introducing Ghirlandaio's characteristic combination of portrait figures in contemporary dress with religious subjects. Something of the passion for minute detail shown by the early Flemish painters can be found in Ghirlandaio's work of this period; his fresco *St. Jerome in His Study* (1480), also in Ognissanti, may even be an enlarged version in fresco of an oil painting by the Flemish painter Jan van Eyck, which had found its way to Florence. The St. Jerome fresco is particularly important because it is a companion piece to one of St. Augustine by Ghirlandaio's Florentine contemporary Sandro Botticelli.

The Last Supper, *fresco by Domenico Ghirlandaio, 1480; in the Church of Ognissanti, Florence.* SCALA/Art Resource, New York

Ghirlandaio's first major commissioned works were the two frescoes depicting scenes from the life of St. Fina, painted in 1475 in the Chapel of Santa Fina in the Collegiata at San Gimignano, near Florence. Both works derive from Fra Filippo Lippi's slightly earlier fresco cycle in the cathedral at Prato and contain a number of portrait heads arranged, rather stiffly, in the symmetrical type of composition that was to become increasingly identified with Ghirlandaio. Even then he was already employing assistants; in his later works he clearly could only complete large commissions in the comparatively short time allotted by the extensive use of highly trained assistants working simultaneously on different parts of the frescoes.

In 1481–82 Ghirlandaio received an important commission in the Vatican for a fresco, representing the calling of the first Apostles, Peter and Andrew, in the Sistine Chapel. Its style is reminiscent of the frescoes by Masaccio of about 1427, which had been the great innovating works of the early 15th century in Florence. The principal feature of this fresco is the group of portraits of the Florentine colony in Rome, who are represented as witnesses of the biblical event. It has been suggested that the inclusion of these Florentines in a fresco painted for the Vatican had political significance, since the Florentine government had recently accused Pope Sixtus IV of complicity in the Pazzi conspiracy. The Pazzi, a powerful Tuscan banking family, had attempted to murder the leading members of the Florentine Medici family, Giuliano and Lorenzo de' Medici (1478). Giuliano had been killed in the attempt while Lorenzo escaped with few wounds.

Ghirlandaio must have used his stay in Rome to study Roman antiquities at first hand, for many details of triumphal arches, ancient sarcophagi, and similar antique elements occur in his works throughout the rest of his career. A sketchbook filled with drawings of such antiquities seems to be the work of a member of his shop.

Late in his short life, Ghirlandaio and his assistants, including his brothers Davide and Benedetto and his brother-in-law Sebastiano Mainardi, produced two major fresco cycles. The earlier was executed for the Sassetti Chapel in Santa Trinita in Florence. Commissioned by Francesco Sassetti, an agent of the Medici bank, they were painted between about 1482 and 1485. The six main frescoes represent scenes from the life of St. Francis of Assisi, Sassetti's patron saint. Once more, the frescoes contain many details of the buildings and customs of the period—for example, the Piazza della Signoria with the Loggia dei Lanzi—and, in particular, there are numerous portraits of members of the Sassetti family shown together with some of the leading members of the Medici family, and of leading members of the Florentine mercantile aristocracy. The altarpiece, dated 1485, contains further evidence of Ghirlandaio's interest in Classical antiquity, for it shows the *Adoration of the Shepherds* with a Roman triumphal arch in the background and a Roman sarcophagus in place of the traditional manger. This painting in tempera has several direct references to contemporary Flemish paintings, especially the enormous Portinari Altarpiece painted in oil by Hugo van der Goes, which had been commissioned in Flanders by Tommaso Portinari, another agent of the Medici bank, and which arrived in Florence in the late 1470s.

Ghirlandaio's last and greatest fresco cycle was painted for another Medici banker, Giovanni Tornabuoni, and represents scenes from the life of the Virgin and of St. John the Baptist, the patron saint of Florence. Ghirlandaio signed the contract on Sept. 1, 1485, for these large frescoes on the walls of the choir of Santa Maria Novella in Florence. Ghirlandaio and his assistants, among whom was probably the young Michelangelo, completed the frescoes by about 1490. The front panel of the altarpiece was completed by assistants according to Ghirlandaio's design soon after his death in 1494. Even more than in the Sassetti Chapel, these narrative scenes contain a wealth of detail showing patrician interiors and contemporary dress; as a result they are one of the most important sources for current knowledge of the furnishings of a late 15th-century Florentine palace.

The frescoes in Santa Maria Novella are overcrowded with detail, so that the compositions fail to make their full impact. Some of Ghirlandaio's smaller panel paintings, particularly the portrait of Giovanna Tornabuoni (1488), have a simplicity that makes them far more striking than the frescoes of Santa Maria Novella. The portrait representing an old man with his grandchild (*c.* 1480–90) is perhaps Ghirlandaio's finest painting, notable for its tenderness and humanity, as well as a simplicity and directness of handling.

Ghirlandaio was considered by his contemporaries to be one of the best painters of his generation. In the 19th century, however, the degree of realism in his work was decried by critics, who appreciated him only for his decorative qualities. His work has been reevaluated since the 1960s, and he is now regarded as one of the most eloquent and elegant narrators of Florentine society at the end of the 15th century.

Ghirlandaio's son, Ridolfo, was also a noted painter and a friend of Vasari. Among his best-known works are a pair representing scenes from the life of St. Zenobius (1517).

HIËRONYMUS BOSCH

(b. *c.* 1450, 's-Hertogenbosch, Brabant [now in the Netherlands]— d. Aug. 9, 1516, 's-Hertogenbosch)

Hiëronymus Bosch was a brilliant and original northern European painter whose work reveals an unusual iconography of a complex and individual style. Although at first recognized as a highly imaginative "creator of devils" and a powerful inventor of seeming nonsense full of satirical meaning, Bosch demonstrated insight into the depths of the mind and an ability to depict symbols of life and creation.

Bosch was a pessimistic and stern moralist who had neither illusions about the rationality of human nature nor confidence in the kindness of a world that had been corrupted by human presence in it. His paintings are sermons, addressed often to initiates and consequently difficult to translate. Unable to unlock the mystery of the artist's works, critics at first believed that he must have been affiliated with secret sects. Although the themes of his work were religious, his choice of symbols to represent the temptation and eventual ensnarement of human beings in earthly evils caused many critics to view Bosch as a practitioner of the occult arts. Later scholarship views Bosch as a talented artist who possessed deep insight into human character and as one of the first artists to represent abstract concepts in his work. A number of exhaustive interpretations of Bosch's work were put forth in the late 20th century, but there remain many obscure details.

An exact chronology of Bosch's surviving work is difficult because, of the approximately 35 to 40 paintings attributed to him, only 7 are signed and none are dated. There exists little documentary information on the early life of the artist, other than the fact that he was the son and grandson of accomplished painters. His name does appear on the register of the Brotherhood of Our Lady, located in the city of his birth, and there is mention of him in official records from 1486 until the year of his death, when he was acclaimed an *Insignis pictor* ("distinguished painter"). In addition to painting he undertook decorative works and altarpieces and executed designs for stained glass.

He was born Jerome van Aeken, also called Jeroen Anthoniszoon. His original last name is also spelled Aquen, or Aken, and the pseudonym he adopted is also spelled Jheronimus Bos. Works attributed to his youthful period show an awkwardness in drawing and composition and brushwork somewhat limited in its scope. Such paintings as *The Cure of Folly, Crucifixion, The Adoration of the Magi, The Seven Deadly Sins, The Marriage at Cana, Ecce Homo,* and *The Conjurer* are representative of this period. The presence of certain motifs, expanded in the more sophisticated works of the artist's middle period, and a limited technique, unsure yet bold, provide a beginning from which to view Bosch's artistic origins. Between the first painting in this early group, *The Cure of Folly*, and the last, *The Conjurer*, a steady development can be seen. The iconography of the latter is more complex, and the characteristic themes that received their fullest expression in the great masterpieces of his late period have begun to emerge.

In these early paintings Bosch had begun to depict humanity's vulnerability to the temptation of evil, the deceptive allure of sin, and the obsessive attraction of lust, heresy, and obscenity. In calm and prosaic settings, groups of people exemplify the credulity, ignorance, and absurdities of the human race. However, the imagery of the early works is still relatively conventional, with only an occasional intrusion of the bizarre in the form of a lurking demon or a strangely dressed magician.

To Bosch's fruitful middle period belong the great panoramic triptychs such as the *Hay Wain*, *The Temptation of St. Anthony*, and the *Garden of Earthly Delights*. His figures are graceful and his colours subtle and sure, and all is in motion in these ambitious and extremely complex works. These paintings are marked by an eruption of fantasy, expressed in monstrous, apocalyptic scenes of chaos and nightmare that are contrasted and juxtaposed with idyllic portrayals of mankind in the age of innocence. During this period Bosch elaborated on his early ideas, and the few paintings that survive establish the evolution of his thought. Bosch's disconcerting mixture of fantasy and reality is further developed in the *Hay Wain*, the outside wings, or cover panels, of which recall the scenes of *The Seven Deadly Sins*. The cursive style that he worked out for the triptych resembles that of watercolour. In the central panel, a rendition of the Flemish proverb "The world is a haystack from which each takes what he can," Bosch shows the trickery of the demon who guides the procession of people from the earthly paradise depicted on the left wing to the horrors of hell shown on the right one.

Bosch's *The Temptation of St. Anthony* displays his ascent to stylistic maturity. The brushstrokes are sharper and terser, with much more command than before. The composition becomes more fluid, and space is regulated by the incidents and creatures that the viewer's attention is focused on. His mastery of fine brush-point calligraphy, permitting subtle nuances of contour and movement, is fully evident. Bosch portrays the struggle against temptation, as well as the omnipresence of the Devil, in his *St. Anthony*, one of the best keys to the artist's personal iconography. The hermit saint in this work is cast as the heroic symbol of man. In the central panel St. Anthony is beset by an array of grotesque demons, their horrible bodies being brilliantly visualized amalgamations of human, animal, vegetable, and inanimate parts. In the background is a hellish, fantastically bizarre landscape painted with the most exquisite detail. Bosch's development of the theme of the charlatan deceiving man and taking away his salvation receives its fullest exposition in the *St. Anthony*, with its condemnation of heresy and the seductions of false doctrines.

The Garden of Earthly Delights, representative of Bosch at his mature best, shows the earthly paradise with the creation of woman, the first temptation, and the fall. The painting's beautiful and unsettling images of sensuality and of the dreams that afflict the people who live in a pleasure-seeking world express Bosch's iconographic originality with tremendous force. The chief characteristic of this work is perhaps its dreamlike quality; multitudes of nude human figures, giant birds, and horses cavort and frolic in a delightfully implausible, otherworldly landscape, and all the elements come together to produce a perfect, harmonious whole.

Bosch's late works are fundamentally different. The scale changes radically, and, instead of meadows or hellish landscapes inhabited by hundreds of tiny beings, he painted densely compacted groups of half-length figures pressed tight against the picture plane. In these dramatic close-ups, of which *The Crowning with Thorns* and the *Carrying of the Cross* are representative, the spectator is so near the event portrayed that he seems to participate in it physically as well as psychologically. The most peaceful and untroubled of Bosch's mature works depict various saints in contemplation or repose. Among these works are *St. John the Evangelist in Patmos* and *St. Jerome in Prayer*.

Bosch's preoccupation in much of his work with the evils of the world did not preclude his vision of a world full of beauty. His adeptness at handling colour harmonies and at creating deeply felt works of the imagination is readily apparent. Though a spate of imitators tried to appropriate his visual style, its uniqueness prevented his having any real followers.

PERUGINO

(b. *c.* 1450, Città della Pieve, near Perugia, Romagna [Italy]—d. Feb./ March 1523, Fontignano, near Perugia)

Pietro di Cristoforo Vannucci, better known by the name Perugino, was an Italian Renaissance painter of the Umbria school and the teacher of Raphael. His work (e.g., *Giving of the Keys to St. Peter*, 1481–82, a fresco in the Sistine Chapel in Rome) anticipated High Renaissance ideals in its compositional clarity, sense of spaciousness, and economy of formal elements.

EARLY WORK

Nothing is known for certain of Perugino's early training, but he may have been a pupil of Fiorenzo di Lorenzo (*c.* 1440–1525), a minor painter in Perugia, and of the renowned Umbrian Piero della Francesca (*c.* 1420–92) in Arezzo, in which case he would have been a fellow pupil of one of his most famous contemporaries, Luca Signorelli. The two men were acquainted, and an occasional influence from Signorelli is visible in Perugino's work, notably in the direction of an increased hardness of drawing (e.g., *Crucifixion and Saints*, c. 1480–1500). In Florence, where he is first recorded in 1472, he almost certainly worked in the shop of the painter and sculptor Andrea del Verrocchio, where the young Leonardo da Vinci was apprenticed.

The first certain work by Perugino is a *Saint Sebastian*, at Cerqueto, near Perugia. This fresco (a mural painted on wet plaster with water-soluble pigments) dates from 1478 and is typical of Perugino's style. He must have attained a considerable reputation by this time, since he probably worked for Pope Sixtus IV in Rome, 1478–79, on frescoes now lost. Sixtus IV also employed him to paint a number of the frescoes in the Sistine Chapel in the Vatican Palace. Completed between 1481 and 1482, three narrative scenes behind the altar were destroyed by Michelangelo in 1535–36 in order to use the space for his fresco of the *Last Judgment*. Of the scenes completely by Perugino's own hand, only the fresco *Giving of the Keys to St. Peter* has survived. The simple and lucid arrangement of the composition reveals the centre of narrative action, unlike the frescoes in the same series by the Florentine painter Sandro Botticelli, which, in comparison, appear overcrowded and confused in their narrative focus. After completing his work in the Sistine Chapel, Perugino returned to Florence, where he was commissioned to work in the Palazzo della Signoria. In 1491 he was invited to sit on the committee concerned with finishing the Florence Cathedral.

MATURE WORK

From approximately 1490 to 1500, Perugino was at his most productive and at the artistic summit of his career.

Adoration of the Magi, *oil on wood by Perugino, c. 1496–98; in the Musée des Beaux-Arts, Rouen, France.* © Photos.com/Jupiterimages

Among the finest of his works executed during this time are the *Vision of St. Bernard*, the *Madonna and Saints*, the *Pietà*, and the fresco of the *Crucifixion* for the Florentine convent of St. Maria Maddalena dei Pazzi. These works are characterized by ample sculptural figures gracefully posed in simple Renaissance architectural settings, which act as a frame to the images and the narrative. The harmonious space is tightly controlled in the foreground and middle ground, while the background effect is conversely one of infinite space. During this period he painted his best known portrait, a likeness of Francesco delle Opere. Perugino must have been well acquainted with the late

Resurrection of Christ, *oil on wood by Perugino, c. 1496–98.* © Photos.com/Jupiterimages

15th-century portraiture of Flanders, since the influence of the Flemish painter Hans Memling is unmistakable.

Commissioned by the guild of bankers of Perugia, Perugino painted a fresco cycle in their Sala dell'Udienza that is believed to have been completed during or shortly after 1500, the date that appears opposite Perugino's self-portrait in one of the scenes. The importance of these frescoes lies less in their artistic merit than in the fact that the young Raphael, Perugino's pupil about 1500, probably was an assistant learning the technique of fresco painting. An allegorical figure of Fortitude from this series is often attributed to Raphael.

Late Work

After 1500 Perugino's art began to decline, and he frequently repeated his earlier compositions in a routine manner. The 16th-century biographer and artist Giorgio Vasari wrote that the critical Florentines began to lampoon him, and Perugino replied that they had once praised his work, and, if he now gave the same designs, they had no right to blame him. It is certainly true that the *Combat of Love and Chastity* was commissioned in 1503 by Isabella d'Este and was delivered only in 1505, after a great many letters had passed between all concerned, at which time Isabella expressed herself as satisfied but only moderately so. Perugino left Florence about 1505 and began to work

Combat of Love and Chastity, *oil on canvas by Perugino, 1505; in the Louvre, Paris.* © Photos.com/Jupiterimages

principally for the citizens of Umbria, who were less inclined to be critical.

In 1508 he made a temporary comeback by painting roundels on the ceiling of the Stanza dell'Incendio in the Vatican. The commission for the frescoes on the walls of the room went to his pupil Raphael, who, in the few years after leaving Perugino's studio, proved himself the greater artist.

One of Perugino's last commissions was the completion in 1521 of some frescoes in St. Severo, Perugia, which had been begun by Raphael. He was still painting in February or March 1523 when he died of the plague. The fresco of the *Nativity* comes from Fontignano and is generally supposed to be Perugino's last work.

ERCOLE DE' ROBERTI

(b. *c.* 1450, Ferrara, Papal States — d. 1496, Ferrara)

The work of Ercole de' Roberti, an Italian painter of the Ferrarese school, is characterized by a highly personal style of sensibility and deep pathos. Roberti is believed to have studied with Cosmè Tura, a court painter to the Este family of Ferrara, and he is known to have studied with Tura's student Francesco del Cossa. Although his early paintings are influenced by the styles of both Tura and Cossa, he distinguished his work by exaggerating the emotional quality of his painting, at times at the expense of naturalism. Later works show Roberti to have achieved seriousness and intensity of emotion without sacrificing technique.

In 1470 Roberti worked with Cossa on a series of frescoes at the Palazzo Schifanoia in Ferrara. Scholars also believe he assisted Cossa in painting altarpieces in the Church of San Petronio in Bologna. During that five-year period, Roberti is believed to have worked on a predella and on the side panels of a large altarpiece now dismantled.

Roberti worked in Cossa's workshop until the master's death in 1478. From 1479 to 1486 he ran his own workshop in Ferrara, but he left the city to complete works begun by Cossa and to execute new commissions in other cities. About 1480 Roberti painted the famous profile portrait of *Ginevra Bentivoglio*. The large church work thought to have been executed solely by Roberti, *The Madonna and Child with Saints* (1481), is now known as the Ravenna Altarpiece.

Roberti was appointed by Duke Ercole I to replace Tura as court painter in 1486. His ability as a portraitist is evident thereafter in the many paintings of the members of this family that he completed. A predella, with scenes of the Passion, for the altar of the church of San Giovanni in Monte, Bologna, is also thought by most critics to be by Roberti; three of its panels remain: the *Pietà*, the *Harvest of the Manna*, and the *Way of the Cross*.

Roberti's work is characterized by bright, metallic colours, sinuous lines, and an open conception of space. His dynamic figurative compositions are marked by an exceptional intensity of feeling.

LEONARDO DA VINCI

(b. April 15, 1452, Anchiano, near Vinci, Republic of Florence [Italy]—d. May 2, 1519, Cloux [now Clos-Lucé], France)

The Italian painter, draftsman, sculptor, architect, and engineer Leonardo da Vinci perhaps more than any other individual, epitomized the Renaissance humanist ideal. His *Last Supper* (1495–98) and *Mona Lisa* (c. 1503–06) are among the most widely popular and influential paintings of the Renaissance.

Early Period: Florence

Leonardo's parents were unmarried at the time of his birth. His father, Ser Piero, was a Florentine notary and landlord, and his mother, Caterina, was a young peasant woman who shortly thereafter married an artisan. Leonardo grew up on his father's family's estate, where he was treated as a "legitimate" son and received the usual elementary education of that day: reading, writing, and arithmetic. Leonardo did not seriously study Latin, the key language of traditional learning, until much later, when he acquired a working knowledge of it on his own. He also did not apply himself to higher mathematics—advanced geometry and arithmetic—until he was 30 years old, when he began to study it with diligent tenacity.

When Leonardo was about 15, his father apprenticed him to artist Andrea del Verrocchio. In Verrocchio's renowned workshop Leonardo received a multifaceted training that included painting and sculpture as well as the technical-mechanical arts. He also worked in the next-door workshop of artist Antonio Pollaiuolo. In 1472 Leonardo was accepted into the painters' guild of Florence.

First Milanese Period (1482–99)

In 1482 Leonardo moved to Milan to work in the service of Duke Ludovico Sforza. He spent 17 years in Milan, until the duke fell from power in 1499. Leonardo was listed in the register of the royal household as *pictor et ingeniarius ducalis* ("painter and engineer of the duke"). His gracious but reserved personality and elegant bearing were well-received in court circles. Highly esteemed, he was constantly kept busy as a painter and sculptor and as a designer of court festivals. He was also frequently consulted as a technical adviser in the fields of architecture, fortifications, and military matters, and he served as a hydraulic and mechanical engineer.

As a painter, Leonardo completed six works in the 17 years in Milan, including one of his most famous works, the monumental wall painting *The Last Supper* (1495–98), in the refectory of the monastery of Santa Maria delle Grazie. During this period Leonardo worked on a grandiose sculptural project that seems to have been the real reason he was invited to Milan: a monumental equestrian statue in bronze to be erected in honour of Francesco Sforza, the founder of the Sforza dynasty. Leonardo devoted 12 years—with interruptions—to this task, envisioning a colossal figure that was to be 16 feet (5 metres) high. Ultimately, the plan was not realized.

SECOND FLORENTINE PERIOD (1500–08)

In December 1499 or, at the latest, January 1500—shortly after the victorious entry of the French into Milan—Leonardo left that city in the company of mathematician Lucas Pacioli. After visiting Mantua in February 1500, in March he proceeded to Venice, where the Signoria (governing council) sought his advice on how to ward off a threatened Turkish incursion in Friuli. Leonardo recommended that they prepare to flood the menaced region. From Venice he returned to Florence, where, after a long absence, he was received with acclaim and honoured as a renowned native son.

In the summer of 1502 Leonardo entered the service of Cesare Borgia as "senior military architect and general engineer," but he returned to Florence in the spring of 1503, to work on another engineering project. That year he also received a prized commission to paint a mural for the council hall in Florence's Palazzo Vecchio, a monumental mural (had it been realized it would have been twice as large as *The Last Supper*); it remained unfinished. During these same years Leonardo painted the *Mona Lisa* (*c.* 1503–06). The second Florentine period was also a time of intensive scientific study. Among other activities, Leonardo did dissections in the hospital of Santa Maria Nuova and broadened his anatomical work into a comprehensive study of the structure and function of the human organism.

SECOND MILANESE PERIOD (1508–13)

Leonardo returned to settle in Milan in 1508. Honoured and admired by his generous patrons there, Charles d'Amboise and King Louis XII, he enjoyed his duties, which were limited largely to advice in architectural matters. He created very little as a painter. As he had during his first residence in Milan, he again gathered pupils around him. Of his older disciples, Bernardino de' Conti and Salaì (Gian Giacomo Caprotti) were again in his studio; new students came, among them Bernardino Luini and the young nobleman Francesco Melzi, Leonardo's most faithful friend and companion until the artist's death.

Leonardo's scientific activity flourished during this period. His studies in anatomy achieved a new dimension in his collaboration with Marcantonio della Torre, a famous anatomist from Pavia. Leonardo outlined a plan for an overall work that would include not only exact, detailed reproductions of the human body and its organs but would also include comparative anatomy and the whole field of physiology. His scientific investigations became increasingly driven by a central idea: the conviction that force and motion as basic mechanical functions produce all outward forms in organic and inorganic nature and give them their shape. Furthermore, he believed that these functioning forces operate in accordance with orderly, harmonious laws.

LAST YEARS (1513–19)

In 1513 political events caused the now 60-year-old Leonardo to move again. At the end of the year he went to Rome, accompanied by his pupils Melzi and Salaì as well as by two studio assistants, hoping to find employment there through his patron, Giuliano de' Medici, brother of the new pope, Leo X. Giuliano gave him a suite of rooms in his residence, the Belvedere, in the Vatican. He also gave Leonardo a considerable monthly stipend, but no large commissions followed. For three years Leonardo remained in Rome at a time of great artistic activity: Donato Bramante was building St. Peter's, Raphael was painting the last rooms of the pope's new apartments, Michelangelo was struggling to complete the tomb of Pope Julius, and many younger artists such as Timoteo Viti and Sodoma were also active. Drafts of embittered letters betray the disappointment of the aging master, who kept a low profile while he worked in his studio on mathematical studies and technical experiments or surveyed ancient monuments as he strolled through the city.

Perhaps stifled by this scene, at age 65 Leonardo accepted the invitation of the young king Francis I to enter his service in France. At the end of 1516 he left Italy forever, together with Melzi, his most devoted pupil. Leonardo spent the last three years of his life in the small residence of Cloux (later called Clos-Lucé), near the king's summer palace at Amboise on the Loire. He proudly bore the title *Premier peintre, architecte et méchanicien du Roi* ("First painter, architect, and engineer to the King"). For the king, Leonardo drew up plans for the palace and garden of Romorantin, which was destined to be the widow's residence of the Queen Mother. But the carefully worked-out project, combining the best features of Italian-French traditions in palace and landscape architecture, had to be halted because the region was threatened with malaria.

Leonardo did little painting while in France, spending most of his time arranging and editing his scientific studies, his treatise on painting, and a few pages of his anatomy treatise. In the so-called *Visions of the End of the World*, or *Deluge*, series (*c.* 1514–15), he depicted with overpowering imagination the primal forces that rule nature, while also perhaps betraying his growing pessimism.

Leonardo died at Cloux and was buried in the palace church of Saint-Florentin. The church was devastated during the French Revolution and completely torn down at the beginning of the 19th century; his grave can no longer be located. Melzi was heir to Leonardo's artistic and scientific estate.

ARTISTIC ACCOMPLISHMENT

Only 17 of the paintings that have survived can be definitely attributed to Leonardo, and several of them are unfinished. Two of his most important works—the *Battle of Anghiari* and the *Leda*, neither of them completed—have survived only in copies. Yet these few creations have established the unique fame of a man whom Giorgio Vasari, in his seminal *Lives of the Most Eminent Painters, Sculptors, and Architects* (1550, 2nd ed., 1568), described as the founder of the High Renaissance. Leonardo's works, unaffected by the vicissitudes of aesthetic doctrines in subsequent centuries, have stood out in all subsequent periods and all countries as consummate masterpieces of painting.

In the *Benois Madonna* (1475–78) Leonardo succeeded in giving a traditional type of picture a new, unusually charming, and expressive mood by showing the child Jesus

Linear perspective study for The Adoration of the Magi, *silverpoint, pen, and bistre heightened with white on prepared ground by Leonardo da Vinci, c. 1481; in the Uffizi Gallery, Florence.* Alinari/Art Resource, New York

reaching, in a sweet and tender manner, for the flower in Mary's hand. In his *Portrait of Ginevra de' Benci* (c. 1480) Leonardo opened new paths for portrait painting with his singular linking of nearness and distance and his brilliant rendering of light and texture. He presented the emaciated body of his *St. Jerome* (unfinished; begun 1480) in a sobering light, imbuing it with a realism that stemmed from his keen knowledge of anatomy; Leonardo's mastery of gesture and facial expression gave his Jerome an unrivalled expression of transfigured sorrow.

The interplay of masterful technique and affective gesture—"physical and spiritual motion," in Leonardo's words—is also the chief concern of his first large creation containing many figures, *The Adoration of the Magi* (begun 1481). Never finished, the painting nonetheless affords rich insight into the master's subtle methods. The various aspects of the scene are built up from the base with very delicate, paper-thin layers of paint in sfumato (the smooth transition from light to shadow) relief. The main treatment of the Virgin and Child group and the secondary treatment of the surrounding groups are clearly set apart with a masterful sense of composition—the pyramid of the Virgin Mary and Magi is demarcated from the arc of the adoring followers. Yet thematically they are closely interconnected: the bearing and expression of the figures—most striking in the group of praying shepherds—depict many levels of profound amazement.

The Virgin of the Rocks in its first version (1483–86) is the work that reveals Leonardo's painting at its purest. It depicts the apocryphal legend of the meeting in the wilderness between the young John the Baptist and Jesus returning home from Egypt. The secret of the picture's effect lies in Leonardo's use of every means at his disposal to emphasize the visionary nature of the scene.

THE LAST SUPPER

Leonardo's *Last Supper* (1495–98) is among the most famous paintings in the world. In its monumental simplicity, the composition of the scene is masterful; the power of its effect comes from the striking contrast in the attitudes of the 12 disciples as counterposed to Christ. Leonardo portrayed a moment of high tension when, surrounded by the Apostles as they share Passover, Jesus says, "One of you will betray me." All the Apostles—as human beings who do not understand what is about to occur—are agitated, whereas Christ alone, conscious of his divine mission, sits in lonely, transfigured serenity. Only one other being shares the secret knowledge: Judas, who is both part of and yet excluded from the movement of his companions. In this isolation he becomes the second lonely figure—the guilty one—of the company.

Technical deficiencies in the execution of the work have not lessened its fame. Leonardo bypassed traditional fresco painting, which, because it is executed on fresh plaster, demands quick and uninterrupted painting, in favour of another technique he had developed: tempera on a base, which he mixed himself, on the stone wall. The base soon began to loosen from the wall. A major restoration campaign begun in 1980 and completed in 1999 restored the work to brilliance but also revealed that very little of the original paint remains.

Mona Lisa

Leonardo's *Mona Lisa* set the standard for all future portraits. The painting presents a woman revealed in the 21st century to have been Lisa del Giocondo, the wife of the Florentine merchant Francesco del Giocondo, hence, the alternative title to the work, *La Gioconda*. The picture presents a half-body portrait of the subject, with a distant landscape visible as a backdrop. Although utilizing a seemingly simple formula for portraiture, the expressive synthesis that Leonardo achieved between sitter and landscape has placed this work in the canon of the most popular and most analyzed paintings of all time. The sensuous curves of the woman's hair and clothing, created through sfumato, are echoed in the undulating valleys and rivers behind her. The sense of overall harmony achieved in the painting—especially apparent in the sitter's faint smile—reflects Leonardo's idea of the cosmic link connecting humanity and nature, making this painting an enduring record of Leonardo's vision and genius. The young Raphael sketched the work in progress, and it served as a model for his *Portrait of Maddalena Doni* (c. 1506).

VITTORE CARPACCIO

(b. *c.* 1460, Venice [Italy] — d. 1525/26, Venice)

The greatest early Renaissance narrative painter of the Venetian school was Vittore Carpaccio, whose incorporation of realistic figures into an orderly and coherent perspectival space made him a predecessor of the Venetian painters of *vedute* (townscapes).

Carpaccio may have been a pupil of Lazzaro Bastiani, but the dominant influences on his early work were those of Gentile Bellini and Antonello da Messina. The style of his work suggests he might also have visited Rome as a young man. He probably painted *Salvator Mundi with Four Apostles* before 1490. Other works from this early period are sometimes attributed to Carpaccio, although, because he did not sign and date his early works, there is often little proof he painted them. About 1490 he began painting a cycle of scenes from the legend of St. Ursula for the Scuola di Santa Orsola, now in the Galleries of the Academy of Venice. In these works he emerged as a mature artist of originality, revealing a gift for organization, narrative skill, and a command of light. The genre scene of the *Dream of St. Ursula* has been especially praised for its wealth of naturalistic detail.

Carpaccio's later career can be charted in terms of three further narrative cycles. The first of these survives intact in the Scuola di San Giorgio degli Schiavoni, in Venice, and involves scenes from the life of St. Jerome; dating from 1502, these paintings represent the climax of Carpaccio's art. A cycle of scenes from the life of the Virgin, executed after 1504 for the Scuola degli Albanesi, is now scattered. Also dispersed is the cycle of scenes from the life of St. Stephen, painted between 1511 and 1520, that is stylistically reminiscent of his earlier works. Carpaccio completed three notable altarpieces for Venetian churches — *St. Thomas Aquinas Enthroned* (1507), *Presentation in the Temple* (1510), and *Martyrdom of the Ten Thousand* (1515). His last dated works are two organ shutters for the Duomo at Capodistria (1523).

Carpaccio's precise rendering of architecture and the luminous atmosphere of his paintings were praised by the 19th-century English critic John Ruskin. Carpaccio's panoramic depictions of pageants, processions, and other public gatherings are notable for their wealth of realistic detail, sunny colouring, and dramatic narratives.

GERARD DAVID

(b. *c.* 1460, Oudewater, Neth. — d. Aug. 13, 1523, Bruges [now in Belgium])

The last great master of the Bruges school was the Flemish painter Gerard David. Very little is known about David's early life, during which time his work reflects the influence of Jacob Jansz, Dirck Bouts, and Geertgen tot Sint Jans. He went to Bruges, presumably from Haarlem, where it is believed he formed his early style under the instruction of A. van Ouwater. He joined the guild of St. Luke at Bruges in 1484 and became dean in 1501.

In his early work, such as *Christ Nailed to the Cross* (*c.* 1480) and the *Nativity*, he followed the Haarlem tradition as represented by Ouwater and Geertgen but already gave evidence of his superior power as a colourist. In Bruges he studied masterpieces by Hubert and Jan van Eyck, Rogier van der Weyden, and Hugo van der Goes, and he came under the influence of Hans Memling. To this period belong the *Madonna Triptych* (*c.* 1495–98) and the *Enthroned*

Virgin and Child with Saints and Donor, *panel painting by Gerard David, c. 1505; in the National Gallery, London.* Courtesy of the trustees of the National Gallery, London; photograph, J.R. Freeman & Co. Ltd.

Madonna with Angels. But the works on which David's fame rests most securely are his great altarpieces—the *Judgment of Cambyses* (two panels, 1498) and the triptych of the *Baptism of Christ* (c. 1502–07) at Bruges; the *Virgin and Child with Saints and Donor* (c. 1505); the *Annunciation* on two panels; and, above all, the documented altarpiece of the *Madonna with Angels and Saints* (1509). These are mature works—severe yet richly coloured, showing a masterful handling of light, volume, and space. The *Judgment* panels are especially notable for being among the earliest Flemish paintings to employ such Italian Renaissance devices as putti (nude, chubby child figures, often with wings) and garlands.

In Antwerp David became impressed by the life and movement in the work of Quentin Massys, who had introduced a more intimate and more human conception of sacred themes. David's *Deposition* (*c.* 1515) and the *Crucifixion* (*c.* 1510–15) were painted under this influence and are remarkable for their dramatic movement.

Authorities disagree about the intent of David's eclectic, deliberately archaic manner. Some feel that he drew on earlier masters in an effort, doomed by lack of imagination, to revive the fading art of Bruges. Others see David as a progressive artist who sought to base his innovations on the achievements of the founders of the Netherlandish school.

PIERO DI COSIMO

(b. 1462, Florence [Italy]—d. 1521, Florence)

Piero di Cosimo, born Piero di Lorenzo, was an Italian Renaissance painter noted for his eccentric character and his fanciful mythological paintings.

His name derives from that of his master, Cosimo Rosselli, whom he assisted (1481) in the frescoes *Crossing of the Red Sea* and *Sermon on the Mount* in the Sistine Chapel in the Vatican. There he saw the frescoes of Sandro Botticelli and Domenico Ghirlandaio, whose styles dominate his early *Story of Jason* (1486). In *The Visitation with Two Saints* (*c.* 1487), the permanent influence of the enamel-like colours of Hugo van der Goes's Portinari Altarpiece is first visible.

Piero's mature style is exemplified by his mythological paintings, which exhibit a bizarre, romantic fantasy. Many are based on Vitruvius' account of the evolution of man. They are filled with fantastic hybrid forms of men and animals engaged in revels (*The Discovery of Wine*, *c.* 1500) or in fighting (*Battle of the Centaurs and the Lapiths*, 1486). Others show early man learning to use fire (*A Forest Fire*, *c.* 1487) and tools (*Vulcan and Aeolus*, *c.* 1486). The multitude of firm, glossy-skinned nudes in these paintings show Piero's interest in Luca Signorelli's work. But, while *The Discovery of Honey* (*c.* 1500) retains Signorelli's figure types, its forms are more softly modeled, and its light is warmer, showing Piero's mastery of the new technique of oil painting. In the *Rescue of Andromeda* (*c.* 1515), Piero adopts Leonardo da Vinci's sfumato (shading that softens the transitions between areas of light and dark) to achieve a new lush, atmospheric effect.

Piero painted several portraits, of which the best known is the memorial bust of Simonetta Vespucci (*c.* 1498), mistress of Giuliano de' Medici. Simonetta is partly nude, and her rhythmic profile is accentuated by the black cloud placed behind it. She wears a gold necklace, around which two snakes coil, possibly an allusion to her death from consumption. The transience of youth and beauty is the theme of the famous *Death of Procris* (*c.* 1490–1500). The softly undulating form of the accidentally slain Procris lies in a meadow bathed in a golden light while a curious satyr kneels beside her, and her faithful dog—considered the first humanized dog in art—mourns at her feet.

Piero's art reflects his bizarre, misanthropic personality. He belonged to no school of painting and operated outside the official artistic milieu. Instead, he borrowed from many artists, incorporating elements of their style into his own idiosyncratic manner. He painted many works to please only himself (an unusual practice for the time) and declared that he often found inspiration for his paintings in the stains on walls.

QUENTIN MASSYS

(b. 1465/66, Leuven, Brabant [now in Belgium]—d. 1530, Antwerp)

The first important painter of the Antwerp school was Quentin Massys, a Flemish artist. His given name is

The Money Changer and His Wife, *painting by Quentin Massys, 1514; in the Louvre, Paris.* Lauros—Giraudon/Art Resource, New York

also spelled Matsys, Metsys, or Messys. Trained as a blacksmith in his native Leuven, Massys is said to have studied painting after falling in love with an artist's daughter. In 1491 he went to Antwerp and was admitted into the painters' guild.

Among Massys's early works are two pictures of the Virgin and Child. His most celebrated paintings are two large triptych altarpieces, *The Holy Kinship*, or St. Anne Altarpiece, ordered for the Church of Saint-Pieter in Leuven (1507–09), and *The Entombment of the Lord* (c. 1508–11), both of which exhibit strong religious feeling and precision of detail. His tendency to accentuate individual expression is demonstrated in such pictures as *The*

Old Man and the Courtesan and *The Money Changer and His Wife*. *Christus Salvator Mundi* and *The Virgin in Prayer* display serene dignity. Pictures with figures on a smaller scale are a polyptych, the scattered parts of which have been reassembled, and a later *Virgin and Child*. His landscape backgrounds are in the style of one of his contemporaries, the Flemish artist Joachim Patinir; the landscape depicted in Massys's *The Crucifixion* is believed to be the work of Patinir. Massys painted many notable portraits, including one of his friend Erasmus.

Although his portraiture is more subjective and personal than that of Albrecht Dürer or Hans Holbein, Massys's painting may have been influenced by both German masters. Massys's lost *St. Jerome in His Study*, of which a copy survives in Vienna, is indebted to Dürer's *St. Jerome*, now in Lisbon. Some Italian influence may also be detected, as in *Virgin and Child*, in which the figures are obviously copied from Leonardo da Vinci's *Virgin of the Rocks*.

Massys's two sons were artists. Jan (1509–75), who became a master in the guild of Antwerp in 1531, was banished in 1543 for his heretical opinions, spent 15 years in Italy or France, and returned to Antwerp in 1558. His early pictures were imitations of his father's work, but a half-length *Judith with the Head of Holofernes* of a later date shows Italian or French influence, as does *Lot and His Daughters* (1563). Cornelis Massys (1513–79), Quentin's second son, became a master painter in 1531, painting landscapes in his father's style and also executing engravings.

ANDREA SANSOVINO

(b. *c.* 1467, Monte San Savino, Republic of Florence [Italy] — d. 1529, Monte San Savino)

The works of Italian architect and sculptor Andrea Sansovino, born Andrea Contucci, reflect the transition from early to High Renaissance. Their elegant and graceful style offered a model different from that of Michelangelo.

Sansovino's earliest great work was the marble Altar of the Sacrament in St. Spirito, Florence, executed for the Corbinelli family between 1485 and 1490; the fineness of detail, high emotional pitch, and lively narrative quality seen in the altar are typical of his early style. After several years in Portugal, according to Giorgio Vasari, the 16th-century biographer of Italian artists, Sansovino was again in Florence in 1502, when he began the marble group of the *Baptism of Christ*, now above the central door of the baptistery. The calm and dignified poses, the strong but controlled emotion, and the generalized beauty of the bodies mark this as one of the first works in the style of the High Renaissance.

In 1505 Sansovino went to Rome and was commissioned by Pope Julius II to execute the almost identical tombs of cardinals Ascanio Sforza and Girolamo Basso della Rovere in St. Maria del Popolo. These tombs, completed by 1509, were the most influential of all Sansovino's innovations, with their adaptation of the triumphal-arch form and the novel sleeping attitude of the deceased cardinals. Sansovino's last great charge was to supervise both the decoration of the Santa Casa (Holy House of the Virgin) and the construction of several buildings at Loreto. His marble relief of the *Annunciation* on the shrine there is a composition of great richness that still has some of the narrative charm of his very early work.

The influence of Sansovino's suave and graceful style acted as a counterbalance to Michelangelo's titanic and muscular sculpture throughout the 16th century. His most important follower was Jacopo Tatti, called Sansovino after his master.

ALBRECHT DÜRER

(b. May 21, 1471, Imperial Free City of Nürnberg [Germany]—d.
April 6, 1528, Nürnberg)

The greatest German Renaissance artist is generally considered to be the painter and printmaker Albrecht Dürer. His vast body of work includes altarpieces and religious works, numerous portraits and self-portraits, and copper engravings. His woodcuts, such as the *Apocalypse* series (1498), retain a more Gothic flavour than the rest of his work.

EDUCATION AND EARLY CAREER

Dürer was the second son of the goldsmith Albrecht Dürer the Elder, who had left Hungary to settle in Nürnberg in 1455, and of Barbara Holper, who had been born there. Dürer began his training as a draughtsman in the goldsmith's workshop of his father. His precocious skill is evidenced by a remarkable self-portrait done in 1484, when he was 13 years old, and by a *Madonna with Musical Angels*, done in 1485, which is already a finished work of art in the late Gothic style. In 1486 Dürer's father arranged for his apprenticeship to the painter and woodcut illustrator Michael Wohlgemuth, whose portrait Dürer would paint in 1516. After three years in Wohlgemuth's workshop, he left for a period of travel. In 1490 Dürer completed his earliest known painting, a portrait of his father that heralds the familiar characteristic style of the mature master.

Dürer's years as a journeyman probably took the young artist to the Netherlands, to Alsace, and to Basel, Switz., where he completed his first authenticated woodcut, a picture of *St. Jerome Curing the Lion*. During 1493 or 1494 Dürer was in Strasbourg for a short time, returning again

Self-Portrait in Furred Coat, *oil on wood panel by Albrecht Dürer, 1500; in the Alte Pinakothek, Munich.* Alte Pinakothek, Munich; photograph, Blauel/Gnamm—Artothek

to Basel to design several book illustrations. An early masterpiece from this period is a self-portrait with a thistle painted on parchment in 1493.

FIRST JOURNEY TO ITALY

At the end of May 1494, Dürer returned to Nürnberg, where he soon married Agnes Frey, the daughter of a merchant. In the autumn of 1494 Dürer seems to have undertaken his first journey to Italy, where he remained until the spring of 1495. A number of bold landscape watercolours dealing with subjects from the Alps of the southern Tirol were made on this journey and are among Dürer's most beautiful creations. Depicting segments of landscape scenery cleverly chosen for their compositional values, they are painted with broad strokes, in places roughly sketched in, with an amazing harmonization of detail. Dürer used predominantly unmixed, cool, sombre colours, which, despite his failure to contrast light and dark adequately, still suggest depth and atmosphere.

The trip to Italy had a strong effect on Dürer; direct and indirect echoes of Italian art are apparent in most of his drawings, paintings, and graphics of the following decade. While in Venice and perhaps also before he went to Italy, Dürer saw engravings by masters from central Italy. He was most influenced by the Florentine Antonio Pollaiuolo, with his sinuous, energetic line studies of the human body in motion, and by the Venetian Andrea Mantegna, an artist greatly preoccupied with Classical themes and with precise linear articulation of the human figure.

Dürer's secular, allegorical, and frequently self-enamoured paintings of this period are often either adaptations of Italian models or entirely independent creations that breathe the free spirit of the new age of the Renaissance. Dürer adapted the figure of Hercules from

Pollaiuolo's *The Rape of Deianira* for a painting of *Hercules and the Birds of Stymphalis*. A purely mythological painting in the Renaissance tradition, the *Hercules* is exceptional among Dürer's works. The centre panel from the Dresden Altarpiece, which Dürer painted in about 1498, is stylistically similar to the *Hercules* and betrays influences of Mantegna. In most of Dürer's free adaptations the additional influence of the more lyrical, older painter Giovanni Bellini, with whom Dürer had become acquainted in Venice, can be seen.

The most striking painting illustrating Dürer's growth toward the Renaissance spirit is a self-portrait, painted in 1498. Here Dürer sought to convey, in the representation of his own person, the aristocratic ideal of the Renaissance. He liked the way he looked as a handsome, fashionably attired young man, confronting life rather conceitedly. In place of the conventional, neutral, monochromatic background, he depicts an interior, with a window opening on the right. Through the window can be seen a tiny landscape of mountains and a distant sea, a detail that is distinctly reminiscent of contemporary Venetian and Florentine paintings. The focus on his own figure in the interior distinguishes his world from the vast perspective of the distant scene, another world to which the artist feels himself linked.

Italian influences were slower to take hold in Dürer's graphics than in his drawings and paintings. Strong late Gothic elements dominate the visionary woodcuts of his *Apocalypse* series (the Revelation of St. John), published in 1498. The woodcuts in this series display emphatic expression, rich emotion, and crowded, frequently overcrowded, compositions. The same tradition influences the earliest woodcuts of Dürer's *Great Passion* series, also from about 1498. Nevertheless, the fact that Dürer was adopting a more modern conception, a conception inspired by Classicism and humanism, is indicative of his basically

Italian orientation. The woodcuts *Samson and the Lion* (*c.* 1497) and *Hercules Conquering Cacus* and many prints from the woodcut series *The Life of the Virgin* (*c.* 1500–10) have a distinct Italian flavour. Many of Dürer's copper engravings are in the same Italian mode. Some examples of them that may be cited are *Fortune* (*c.* 1496), *The Four Witches* (1497), *The Sea Monster* (*c.* 1498), *Adam and Eve* (1504), and *The Large Horse* (1505).

Dürer's graphics eventually influenced the art of the Italian Renaissance that had originally inspired his own efforts. His painterly style, however, continued to vacillate between Gothic and Italian Renaissance until about 1500. Then his restless striving finally found definite direction. He seems clearly to be on firm ground in the penetrating half-length portraits of Oswolt Krel, in the portraits of three members of the aristocratic Tucher family of Nürnberg—all dated 1499—and in the *Portrait of a Young Man* of 1500. In 1500 Dürer painted another self-portrait that is a flattering, Christlike portrayal.

During this period of consolidation in Dürer's style, the Italian elements of his art were strengthened by his contact with Jacopo de' Barbari, a minor Venetian painter and graphic artist who was seeking a geometric solution to the rendering of human proportions. It is perhaps due to his influence that Dürer began, around 1500, to grapple with the problem of human proportions in true Renaissance fashion. Initially, the most concentrated result of his efforts was the great engraving *Adam and Eve* (1504) in which he sought to bring the mystery of human beauty to an intellectually calculated ideal form.

In all aspects Dürer's art was becoming strongly Classical. One of his most significant Classical endeavours is his painting *Altar of the Three Kings* (1504), which was executed with the help of pupils. Although the composition, with its five separate pictures, has an Italian character,

Dürer's intellect and imagination went beyond direct dependence on Italian art. From this maturity of style comes the bold, natural, relaxed conception of the centre panel, *The Adoration of the Magi*, and the ingenious and unconventional realism of the side panels, one of which depicts the *Drummer and Piper* and the other *Job and His Wife*.

SECOND JOURNEY TO ITALY

In the autumn of 1505, Dürer made a second journey to Italy, where he remained until the winter of 1507. Once again he spent most of his time in Venice. Of the Venetian artists, Dürer now most admired Giovanni Bellini, the leading master of Venetian early Renaissance painting, who, in his later works, completed the transition to the High Renaissance. Dürer's pictures of men and women from this Venetian period reflect the sweet, soft portrait types especially favoured by Bellini. One of Dürer's most impressive small paintings of this period, a compressed half-length composition of the *Young Jesus with the Doctors* of 1506, harks back to Bellini's free adaptation of Mantegna's *Presentation in the Temple*. Dürer's work is a virtuoso performance that shows mastery and close attention to detail. In the painting the inscription on the scrap of paper out of the book held by the old man in the foreground reads, "Opus quinque dierum" ("the work of five days"). Dürer thus must have executed this painstaking display of artistry, which required detailed drawings, in no more than five days. Of even greater artistic merit than this quickly executed work are the half-length portraits of young men and women painted between 1505 and 1507, which seem to be entirely in the style of Bellini. In these paintings there is a flexibility of the subject, combined with a warmth and liveliness of expression and a genuinely artistic technique, that Dürer otherwise rarely attained.

In 1506, in Venice, Dürer completed his great altarpiece *The Feast of the Rose Garlands* for the funeral chapel of the Germans in the church of St. Bartholomew. Later that same year Dürer made a brief visit to Bologna before returning to Venice for a final three months. The extent to which Dürer considered Italy to be his artistic and personal home is revealed by the frequently quoted words found in his last letter from Venice (dated October 1506) to Willibald Pirkheimer, his long-time humanist friend, anticipating his imminent return to Germany: "O, how cold I will be away from the sun; here I am a gentleman, at home a parasite."

DEVELOPMENT AFTER THE SECOND ITALIAN TRIP

By February 1507 at the latest, Dürer was back in Nürnberg, where two years later he acquired an impressive house, which still stands and is preserved as a museum. It is clear that the artistic impressions gained from his Italian trips continued to influence Dürer to employ Classical principles in creating largely original compositions. Among the paintings belonging to the period after his second return from Italy are *Martyrdom of the Ten Thousand* (1508) and *Adoration of the Trinity* (1511), which are both crowd scenes. Drawings from this period recall Mantegna and betray Dürer's striving for Classical perfection of form through sweeping lines of firmly modeled and simple drapery. Even greater simplicity and grandeur characterize the diptych of *Adam and Eve* (1507), in which the two figures stand calmly in relaxed Classical poses against dark, almost bare, backgrounds.

Between 1507 and 1513 Dürer completed a *Passion* series in copperplate engravings, and between 1509 and 1511 he produced the *Small Passion* in woodcuts. Both of these works are characterized by their tendency toward spaciousness and serenity. During 1513 and 1514 Dürer created the greatest of his copperplate engravings: the *Knight, Death, and Devil*, *St. Jerome in His Study*, and *Melencolia I* — all of approximately the same size, about 24.5 by 19.1 cm (9.5 by 7.5 inches). The extensive, complex, and often contradictory literature concerning these three engravings deals largely with their enigmatic, allusive, iconographic details. Although repeatedly contested, it probably must be accepted that the engravings were intended to be interpreted together. There is general agreement, however, that Dürer, in these three master engravings, wished to raise his artistic intensity to the highest level, which he succeeded in doing. Finished form and richness of conception and mood merge into a whole of Classical perfection. To the same period belongs Dürer's most expressive portrait drawing—one of his mother.

SERVICE TO MAXIMILIAN I

While in Nürnberg in 1512, the Holy Roman emperor Maximilian I enlisted Dürer into his service, and Dürer continued to work mainly for the emperor until 1519. He collaborated with several of the greatest German artists of the day on a set of marginal drawings for the emperor's prayer book. He also completed a number of etchings in iron (between 1515 and 1518) that demonstrate his mastery of the medium and his freedom of imagination. In contrast to these pleasing improvisations are the monumental woodcuts, overloaded with panegyrics, made for Maximilian. In these somewhat stupendous, ornate woodcuts, Dürer had to strain to adapt his creative imagination to his client's mentality, which was foreign to him.

Besides a number of formal show pieces—a painting entitled *Lucretia* (1518), and two portraits of the emperor (*c.* 1519)—during this decade Dürer produced a number of more informal paintings of considerably greater charm. He also traveled. In the fall of 1517 he stayed in Bamberg. In the summer of 1518 he went to Augsburg where he met Martin Luther, who had in the previous year circulated his Ninety-five Theses denouncing the sale of papal indulgences. Dürer later became a devoted follower of Luther. Dürer had achieved an international reputation as an artist by 1515, when he exchanged works with the illustrious High Renaissance painter Raphael.

FINAL JOURNEY TO THE NETHERLANDS

In July 1520 Dürer embarked with his wife on a journey through the Netherlands. In Aachen, at the October 23 coronation of the emperor Charles V, successor to Maximilian I (who had died in 1519), Dürer met and presented several etchings to the mystical and dramatic Matthias Grünewald, who stood second only to Dürer in contemporary German art. Dürer returned to Antwerp by way of Nijmegen and Cologne, remaining there until the summer of 1521. He had maintained close relations with the leaders of the Netherlands school of painting. In December 1520 Dürer visited Zeeland and in April 1521 traveled to Bruges and Ghent, where he saw the works of the 15th-century Flemish masters Jan and Hubert van Eyck, Rogier van der Weyden, and Hugo van der Goes, as well as the Michelangelo Madonna. Dürer's sketchbook of the Netherlands journey contains immensely detailed and realistic drawings. Some paintings that were created either during the journey or about the same time seem spiritually akin to the Netherlands school—for example, the portrait of Anna Selbdritt, a half-length picture of St. Jerome (1521), and the small portrait of Bernhard von Resten, previously Bernard van Orley.

FINAL WORKS

By July, the travelers were back in Nürnberg, but Dürer's health had started to decline. He devoted his remaining years mostly to theoretical and scientific writings and illustrations, although several well-known character portraits and some important portrait engravings and woodcuts also date from this period. One of Dürer's greatest paintings, the so-called *Four Apostles* (St. John, St. Peter, St. Paul, and St. Mark), was done in 1526. This work marks his final and certainly highest achievement as a painter. His delight in his own virtuosity no longer stifled the ideal of a spaciousness that is simple, yet deeply expressive.

Dürer died in 1528 and was buried in the churchyard of Johanniskirchhof in Nürnberg. That he was one of his country's most influential artists is manifest in the impressive number of pupils and imitators that he had. Even Dutch and Italian artists did not disdain to imitate Dürer's graphics occasionally. The extent to which Dürer was internationally celebrated is apparent in the literary testimony of the Florentine artist Giorgio Vasari (1511–74), in whose *Lives of the Most Eminent Painters, Sculptors, and Architects* the importance of Albrecht Dürer, the "truly great painter and creator of the most beautiful copper engravings," is repeatedly stressed. Like most notable Italian artists, Dürer probably felt himself to be an "artist-prince," and his self-portraits seem incontestably to show a man sure of his own genius.

FRA BARTOLOMMEO

(b. March 28, 1472, Florence [Italy] — d. Oct. 31, 1517, Florence)

A prominent exponent of the High Renaissance style in early 16th-century Florence was the painter Fra Bartolommeo (Bartolomeo), also called Bartolomeo della Porta, or Baccio della Porta. Bartolommeo served as an apprentice in the workshop of Cosimo Rosselli and then formed a workshop with the painter Mariotto Albertinelli.

Bartolommeo's early works, such as the *Annunciation* (1497), were influenced by the balanced compositions of the Umbrian painter Perugino and by the sfumato of Leonardo da Vinci. In 1499 Bartolommeo was commissioned to paint a large-scale fresco, *The Last Judgment*, for one of the cemetery chapels in Santa Maria Nuova. Influenced by the preaching of the Florentine Dominican religious reformer Girolamo Savonarola, Bartolommeo joined a convent in 1500, and in 1501 he gave up painting and joined the Dominican order. He began painting again in 1504, producing devotional paintings mostly at the service of his order. His *Vision of St. Bernard* (completed 1507) shows him achieving the transition from the subtle grace of late Quattrocento painting to the monumentality of the High Renaissance style.

In 1508 Bartolommeo visited Venice, where he assimilated the Venetian painters' use of richer colour harmonies. Back in Florence soon afterward, he painted a number of calm and simple religious pictures in which monumental figures are grouped in balanced compositions and portrayed with a dense and somewhat shadowy atmospheric treatment. Among such works are his *God the Father with SS. Catherine of Siena and Mary Magdalene* (1509) and the *Mystic Marriage of St. Catherine* (1512).

Bartolommeo visited Rome in 1514, where he saw Raphael's mature work and Michelangelo's frescoes on the ceiling of the Sistine Chapel. In response Bartolommeo's art took on a greater power of dramatic expression, as in the *Madonna della Misericordia* (1515) and the *Pietà* (c. 1515). Also in this vein were his large frescoes of *St. Mark* and *St. Sebastian* on the wall at San Marco in Florence. The *St. Sebastian*, an ornamental pendant, was later purchased by King Henry I of France. Despite Bartolommeo's assimilation of the progressive currents of his time, his art is restrained, conservative, and somewhat severe, and he painted religious subjects almost exclusively. His production of drawings and preparatory sketches shows a delicate sensitivity and technical superiority. His landscapes are among the most notable of his time.

LUCAS CRANACH THE ELDER

(b. 1472, Cranach, Bishopric of Bamberg [now Kronach, Germany]—d. Oct. 16, 1553, Weimar, Saxe-Weimar)

Lucas Cranach the Elder was a leading painter of Saxony and one of the most important and influential artists in 16th-century German art. Among his vast output of paintings and woodcuts, the most important are altarpieces, court portraits and portraits of the Protestant Reformers, and innumerable pictures of women—elongated female nudes and fashionably dressed ladies with titles from the Bible or mythology.

LIFE AND CAREER

Lucas Müller was born in a village approximately 55 miles (90 km) north of Nürnberg. Although only a year younger, he survived Albrecht Dürer, the great genius of German art, by 25 years and, in fact, outlived all the significant German artists of his time. Lucas's teacher was his father, the painter Hans Müller, with whom he worked from 1495 to 1498. He is known to have been in Coburg in 1501, but the earliest of his works that have been preserved date from about 1502, when he was already 30 and living in Vienna. It was in that city that he dropped the surname of Müller, calling himself Cranach after his hometown, which is now spelled Kronach.

In Vienna, Cranach made an important contribution to the painting and illustrations of the Danube school, the art of the Austrian Danubian region around Vienna and other towns. He also came in contact with the humanists teaching at the university, and did portraits of the scholars Johannes Stephan Reuss (1503) and Johannes Cuspinian (c. 1502–03).

Presumably while Cranach was still in Vienna, he received news of his appointment as court painter to the elector Frederick the Wise of Saxony. Cranach must already have been a famous artist, for he was given two and a half times the salary paid to his predecessor. In spring 1505 he arrived in Wittenberg, a university town on the Elbe River and seat of the electors, where he remained for 45 years, until 1550, as court painter. He became a prominent citizen, serving as a member of the town council in 1519–20 and as burgomaster three times in the years 1537–44. Through Cranach, who received important commissions from three successive electors and caused many young artists to come to Wittenberg, the town became an art centre.

The Protestant Reformation had begun in 1517 in Wittenberg with Martin Luther's Ninety-five Theses. Cranach was on friendly terms with Luther, who had been a teacher at the University of Wittenberg since 1508. Cranach painted portraits of Luther, his wife, Katherina von Bora, and his parents. Through these and other portraits, he helped form today's image of Luther's circle. Indeed, apart from his other duties as court artist, Cranach became the chief pictorial propagandist of the Protestant cause in Germany, multiplying the images of the Reformers and the Protestant princes in innumerable painted, engraved, and woodcut portraits. The scope of this activity is indicated by a single payment in the electoral accounts (1533) for "sixty pairs of small paintings of the late Electors." Cranach also did altarpieces and paintings for Lutheran churches. His works were sought after by Protestant and Roman Catholic patrons alike, and hundreds of pictures now in museums and private collections testify to his exceptional productivity. Aside from his paintings, there are more than 100 separate woodcuts by him.

PAINTINGS

Cranach did not sign his works with his full name. The early ones, before 1504, were unsigned; from 1504 to 1506 his signature consisted of an entwined "LC"; from 1506 to 1509, it consisted of the separated initials "LC"; from 1509 to 1514, it consisted of these spaced initials and his coat of arms, the winged serpent, which became his sole signature in 1515. All works, even those that had issued from his large workshop or studio (in which he often employed 10 or more assistants), henceforth carried this device, which was also used by his son Lucas the Younger, until the latter's death in 1586. This gave rise to many problems of attribution that still remain unsolved. The fact that so few works bear any date further complicates the establishment of a Cranach chronology.

It is certain, however, that Cranach's style was fully formed and underwent little development after about 1515, and the highly finished, mass-produced paintings after that date suffer by comparison with the more individual works he painted in early adulthood. The paintings the 30-year-old artist did in Vienna were of a profoundly devotional kind set in the wild landscapes of the Alpine foothills, with ruins and windswept trees. These pictures show Cranach as an avant-garde artist of considerable emotional force, and one of the initiators of the Danube school. Notable among them are a *Crucifixion* (*c.* 1500) and *St. Jerome in Penitence* (1502).

The first decade of Cranach's stay at Wittenberg was marked by a series of experiments in which he adapted his style to suit the demands of the Saxon court. The right wing of the St. Catherine Altarpiece (1506) already shows a radical break with his earlier style; there is exquisite detail in the realistic portrait heads, but courtly decorum has purged the scene of all emotion and given it a decorative bias, with strong emphasis on the patterns of dress. Following his visit to the Netherlands in 1508, Cranach experimented with Italo-Netherlandish ideas of spatial construction and with monumental nudes, but his true talent lay elsewhere, as is shown by the splendid full-length portraits of *Duke Henry the Pious* and *Duchess Katharina von Mecklenburg* (1514), which mark the establishment of his official portrait style. Here, space and volume are annihilated; magnificent clothes, set off by a featureless backdrop, are topped by faces reduced to their essential, typical features.

Cranach was a pioneer of the frigid state portraiture of the 16th century, but he fell short of the icy reserve of his successors—Hans Holbein the Younger and Bronzino— because his abiding Gothic taste invariably led him to exaggerate a feature or elaborate a beard or dress for the sake of linear rhythms or calligraphic effects. With male sitters his method sometimes yields an image of startling power—e.g., the *Portrait of Dr. J. Scheyring* (1529). His female portraits are uniformly vapid, however.

The resurgence of Gothic linear rhythms is fundamental for the whole of Cranach's later work, in which the border- line between sacred and mundane art is blurred. He represented female saints as beautiful and elegant ladies in fashionable dress and covered with jewelry. His *Reclining River Nymph at the Fountain* (1518) shows with what assurance he translated a Renaissance model—Giorgione's *Venus*— into his personal language of linear arabesque. This work inaugurated a long series of paintings of Venus, Lucretia, the Graces, the judgment of Paris, and other subjects that serve as pretexts for the sensuous female nude, in which Cranach appears as a kind of 16th-century François Boucher. The naive elegance of these ladies, whose slender, sinuous bodies defy basic principles of anatomy, were clearly to the taste of the German courts and have an enduring charm. But in conception and style they look back to the International Gothic style of a century before. Thus from a historical viewpoint Cranach's work was a backwater in European art of the 16th century. Though he was the dominant figure in the painting of northeastern Germany during his lifetime, his influence was confined to his immediate circle.

Cranach is called *Pictor celerrimus* ("swiftest of painters") on his tombstone, and his contemporaries never ceased to marvel at the speed with which he worked. But this very speed also suggested the limitations of his art, for his strength lay not in reflection, composition, and construction but in an impulsive creativity that was nourished by his imagination and fancy, particularly in unheroic and idyllic scenes. His art was especially popular in that period of great political upheavals, perhaps because his contemporaries, who in public life were the protagonists of embattled ideologies, yearned for beauty in man and in nature and for a peaceful refuge from the world's turmoil.

Both of Cranach's sons were members of his studio. The elder, Hans Cranach, who died in 1537, left a few signed works that are indistinguishable in style from those of his father. Lucas Cranach the Younger (1515–86), whose part in the joint production of the studio became important from about 1545, continued to work in the family style long after his father's death in 1553.

MICHELANGELO

(b. March 6, 1475, Caprese, Republic of Florence [Italy] — d. Feb. 18, 1564, Rome, Papal States)

The influence of Italian Renaissance sculptor, painter, architect, and poet Michelangelo on the development of Western art is unparalleled. Michelangelo was considered the greatest living artist in his lifetime, and ever since then he has been held to be one of the greatest artists of all time. A number of his works in painting, sculpture, and architecture rank among the most famous in existence. Although the frescoes on the ceiling of the Sistine Chapel are probably the best known of his works today, the artist thought of himself primarily as a sculptor. His practice of several arts, however, was not unusual in his time, when all of them were thought of as based on design, or drawing. Michelangelo worked in marble sculpture all his life and in the other arts only during certain periods.

A side effect of Michelangelo's fame in his lifetime was that his career was more fully documented than that of any artist of the time or earlier. He was the first Western artist whose biography was published while he was alive—in fact, there were two rival biographies. The first was the final chapter in the series of artists' lives (1550) by the painter and architect Giorgio Vasari. It was the only chapter on a living artist and explicitly presented Michelangelo's works as the culminating perfection of art, surpassing the efforts of all those before him. Despite such an encomium, Michelangelo was not entirely pleased and arranged for his assistant Ascanio Condivi to write a brief separate book (1553); probably based on the artist's own spoken comments, this account shows him as he wished to appear. After Michelangelo's death, Vasari in a second edition (1568) offered a rebuttal. While scholars have often preferred the authority of Condivi, Vasari's lively writing, the importance of his book as a whole, and its frequent reprinting in many languages have made it the most usual basis of popular ideas on Michelangelo and other Renaissance artists.

EARLY LIFE AND WORKS

Michelangelo di Lodovico Buonarroti was born to a family that had for several generations belonged to minor nobility in Florence but had, by the time the artist was born, lost its patrimony and status. Nevertheless, it was something of a downward social step to become an artist, and Michelangelo became an apprentice relatively late, at 13, perhaps after overcoming his father's objections. He was apprenticed to the city's most prominent painter, Domenico Ghirlandaio, for a three-year term, but he left after one year, having (Condivi recounts) nothing more to learn. Several drawings, copies of figures by Ghirlandaio and older great painters of Florence, Giotto and Masaccio, survive from this stage; such copying was standard for apprentices, but few examples are known to survive.

Obviously talented, he was taken under the wing of the ruler of the city, Lorenzo de' Medici, known as the Magnificent. This good fortune gave him access not only to leading poets and intellectuals but to the Medici art collection. The bronze sculptor Bertoldo di Giovanni, a Medici friend who was in charge of the collection, was the nearest he had to a teacher of sculpture, but Michelangelo did not follow his medium or in any major way his approach. Still, one of the two marble works that survive from the artist's first years is a variation on the composition of an ancient Roman sarcophagus, and Bertoldo had produced a similar one in bronze. This lively and powerful composition is the *Battle of the Centaurs* (*c.* 1492).

Florence was at this time regarded as the leading centre of art, producing the best painters and sculptors in Europe, but many of the leading Florentine-born artists, such as Leonardo da Vinci and Leonardo's teacher, Andrea del Verrocchio, had moved away for better opportunities in other cities. The Medici were overthrown in 1494, and even before the end of the political turmoil Michelangelo had left.

In Bologna he was hired to carve the last small figures required to complete a grand project, the tomb and shrine

Pietà, *marble sculpture by Michelangelo, 1499; in St. Peter's Basilica, Rome.*
SCALA/Art Resource, New York

of St. Dominic (1494–95). The three marble figures are original and expressive. His first surviving large statue was the *Bacchus*, produced in Rome (1496–97) following a brief return to Florence. It relies on ancient Roman nude figures as a point of departure, but it is much more mobile and more complex in outline. The conscious instability evokes the god of wine and Dionysian revels with extraordinary virtuosity. Made for a garden, it is also unique among Michelangelo's works in calling for observation from all sides rather than primarily from the front.

The *Bacchus* led at once to the commission (1498) for the *Pietà*, now in St. Peter's Basilica. The name refers not (as is often presumed) to this specific work but to a common traditional type of devotional image, this work being today the most famous example. Extracted from narrative scenes of the lamentation after Christ's death, the concentrated group of two is designed to evoke the observer's repentant prayers for sins that required Christ's sacrificial death. The patron was a French cardinal, and the type was earlier more common in northern Europe than in Italy. The complex problem for the designer was to extract two figures from one marble block, an unusual undertaking in all periods. Michelangelo treated the group as one dense and compact mass as before so that it has an imposing impact, yet he underlined the many contrasts present—of male and female, vertical and horizontal, clothed and naked, dead and alive—to clarify the two components.

The artist's prominence, established by this work, was reinforced at once by the commission (1501) of the *David* for the cathedral of Florence. For this huge statue, an exceptionally large commission in that city, Michelangelo reused a block left unfinished about 40 years before. The modeling is especially close to the formulas of Classical antiquity, with a simplified geometry suitable to the huge scale yet with a mild assertion of organic life in its asymmetry. It has continued to serve as the prime statement of the Renaissance ideal of perfect humanity.

On the side Michelangelo produced in the same years (1501–04) several Madonnas for private houses, the staple of artists' work at the time. These include one small statue, two circular reliefs that are similar to paintings in suggesting varied levels of spatial depth, and the artist's only easel painting. While the statue (*Madonna and Child*) is blocky and immobile, the painting (*Holy Family*) and one of the reliefs (*Madonna and Child with the Infant St. John*) are full of motion; they show arms and legs of figures interweaving in actions that imply movement through time. The forms carry symbolic references to Christ's future death, common in images of the Christ Child at the time.

They also betray the artist's fascination with the work of Leonardo. Michelangelo regularly denied that anyone influenced him, and his statements have usually been accepted without demur. But Leonardo's return to Florence in 1500 after nearly 20 years was exciting to younger artists there, and late 20th-century scholars generally agreed that Michelangelo was among those affected. Leonardo's works were probably the most powerful and lasting outside influence to modify his work, and he was able to blend this artist's ability to show momentary processes with his own to show weight and strength. The resulting images, of massive bodies in forceful action, are those special creations that constitute the larger part of his most admired major works.

The *Holy Family*, probably commissioned for the birth of the first child of Agnolo and Maddalena Doni, was a particularly innovative painting that would later be influential in the development of early Florentine Mannerism. Its spiraling composition and cold, brilliant colour scheme underline the sculptural intensity of the figures and create a dynamic and expressive effect.

THE MIDDLE YEARS

After the success of the *David* in 1504, Michelangelo's work consisted almost entirely of vast projects. He was attracted to these ambitious tasks while at the same time rejecting the use of assistants, so that most of these projects were impractical and remained unfinished. In 1504 he agreed to paint a huge fresco for the Sala del Gran Consiglio of the Florence city hall to form a pair with another just begun by Leonardo da Vinci. Both murals recorded military victories by the city (Michelangelo's was the *Battle of Cascina*), but each also gave testimony to the special skills of the city's much vaunted artists. Leonardo's design shows galloping horses, Michelangelo's active nudes—soldiers stop swimming and climb out of a river to answer an alarm. Both works survive only in copies and partial preparatory sketches.

In 1505 Michelangelo began work on a planned set of 12 marble Apostles for the Florence Cathedral, of which only one, the *St. Matthew*, was even begun. Its writhing ecstatic motion shows the full blend of Leonardo's fluid organic movement with Michelangelo's own monumental power. This is also the first of his unfinished works to fascinate later observers. His figures seem to suggest that they are fighting to emerge from the stone. This would imply that their incomplete state was intentional, yet he undoubtedly did want to complete all of the statues. He did, however, write a sonnet about how hard it is for the sculptor to bring the perfect figure out of the block in which it is potentially present. Thus, even if the works remained unfinished due only to lack of time and other external reasons, their condition, nonetheless, reflects the artist's intense feeling of the stresses inherent in the creative process.

Pope Julius II's call to Michelangelo to come to Rome spelled an end to both of these Florentine projects. The

David, *marble sculpture by Michelangelo, 1501–04; in the Accademia, Florence.* Alinari/Art Resource, New York

pope sought a tomb for which Michelangelo was to carve 40 large statues. Recent tombs had been increasingly grand, including those of two popes by the Florentine sculptor Antonio Pollaiuolo, those of the doges of Venice, and the one then in work for Holy Roman emperor Maximilian I. Pope Julius had an ambitious imagination, parallel to Michelangelo's, but because of other projects, such as the new building of St. Peter's and his military campaigns, he evidently became disturbed soon by the cost. Michelangelo believed that Bramante, the equally prestigious architect at St. Peter's, had influenced the pope to cut off his funds.

Michelangelo left Rome, but the pope brought pressure on the city authorities of Florence to send him back. He was put to work on a colossal bronze statue of the pope in his newly conquered city of Bologna, which the citizens pulled down soon after when they drove out the papal army. Then he began work on a less expensive project—painting the ceiling of the Sistine Chapel (1508–12).

THE SISTINE CHAPEL

The Sistine Chapel had great symbolic meaning for the papacy as the chief consecrated space in the Vatican, used for great ceremonies such as electing and inaugurating new popes. It already contained distinguished wall paintings, and Michelangelo was asked to add works for the relatively unimportant ceiling. The Twelve Apostles was planned as the theme—ceilings normally showed only individual figures, not dramatic scenes. Traces of this project are seen in the 12 large figures that Michelangelo produced: seven prophets and five sibyls, or female prophets found in Classical myths. The inclusion of female figures was very unusual, though not totally unprecedented. Michelangelo placed these figures around the edges of the ceiling and filled the central spine of the long curved surface with nine scenes from Genesis: three of them depicting the Creation of the World, three the stories of Adam and Eve, and three the stories of Noah. These are naturally followed, below the prophets and sibyls, by small figures of the 40 generations of Christ's ancestors, starting with Abraham. The vast project was completed in less than four years; there was an interruption perhaps of a year in 1510–11 when no payment was made.

Michelangelo began by painting figures and scenes that allowed him to reuse devices from his earlier works, such as the *Pietà*. These first figures are relatively stable, and the scenes are on a relatively small scale. As he proceeded, he quickly grew in confidence. Indeed, recent investigations of the technical processes used show that he worked more and more rapidly, reducing and finally eliminating such preparatory helps as complete drawings and incisions on the plaster surface. The same growing boldness appears in the free, complex movements of the figures and in their complex expressiveness. While remaining always imposing and monumental, they are more and more imbued with suggestions of stress and grief.

He got about halfway through before his work was interrupted. When he painted the second half, he seemed to repeat the same evolution from quiet stability to intricacy and stress. Thus, Michelangelo worked his way from the quietly monumental and harmonious scene of the creation of Adam to the acute, twisted pressures of the prophet Jonah. Yet, in this second phase he shows greater inward expressiveness, giving a more meditative restraint to the earlier pure physical mass.

OTHER PROJECTS

As soon as the ceiling was finished, Michelangelo reverted to his preferred task, the tomb of Pope Julius. In about

1513–15 he carved the *Moses*, which may be regarded as the realization in sculpture of the approach to great figures used for the prophets on the Sistine ceiling. The control of cubic density in stone evokes great reserves of strength; there is richer surface detail and modeling than before, with bulging projections sharply cut. The surface textures also have more variety than the earlier sculptures, the artist by now having found how to enrich detail without sacrificing massiveness.

Of about the same date are two sculptures of bound prisoners or slaves, also part of the tomb project but never used for it, since in a subsequent revised design they were of the wrong scale. Michelangelo kept them until old age, when he gave them to a family that had helped him during an illness; these sculptures are now in the Louvre. Here again he realized, in stone, types painted in many variants on the ceiling, such as the pairs of nudes that hold wreaths above the prophets' thrones. The complexity of their stances, expressive of strong feeling, was unprecedented in monumental marble sculpture of the Renaissance.

Julius II's death in 1513 cut off most of the funds for his tomb. Pope Leo X, his successor, a son of Lorenzo the Magnificent, had known Michelangelo since their boyhoods. He chiefly employed Michelangelo in Florence on projects linked to the glory of the Medici family rather than of the papacy. The city was under the rule of Leo's cousin Cardinal Giulio de' Medici, who was to be Pope Clement VII from 1523 to 1534, and Michelangelo worked with him closely in both reigns. The cardinal took an active interest in Michelangelo's works. He made detailed suggestions, but he also gave the artist much room for decision. Michelangelo was moving into architectural design with a small remodeling project at the Medici mansion and a large one at their parish church, San Lorenzo. The larger project never materialized, but Michelangelo and the cardinal did better with a more modest related effort, the new chapel attached to the same church for tombs of the Medici family.

THE MEDICI CHAPEL

The immediate occasion for the chapel was the deaths of the two young family heirs (named Giuliano and Lorenzo after their forebears) in 1516 and 1519. Up until 1527, Michelangelo gave his chief attention to the marble interior of this chapel, both the very original wall design and the carved figures on the tombs. The latter are an extension, in organic form, of the dynamic shapes of the wall details. The result is the fullest existing presentation of Michelangelo's intentions. Windows, cornices, and the like have strange proportions and thicknesses, suggesting an irrational, willful revision of traditional classical forms in buildings.

Abutting these active surfaces, the two tombs on opposite walls of the room are also very original, starting with their curved tops. A male and a female figure sit on each of these curved bases; these are personifications of Day and Night on one tomb, according to the artist's own statement, and, on the other, Dawn and Dusk, according to early reports. Such types had never appeared on tombs before, and they refer, again according to Michelangelo, to the inevitable movement of time, which is circular and leads to death.

The figures are among the artist's most famous and accomplished creations. The immensely massive *Day* and *Dusk* are relatively tranquil in their mountainous grandeur, though *Day* perhaps implies inner fire. Both female figures have the tall, slim proportions and small feet considered beautiful at the time, but otherwise they form a contrast: *Dawn*, a virginal figure, strains upward along her curve as if trying to emerge into life; *Night* is asleep, but in a posture suggesting stressful dreams. These four figures are naturally noticed more immediately than the effigies of the two Medici buried there, placed higher and farther back in wall niches.

THE LAURENTIAN LIBRARY AND FORTIFICATIONS

During the same years, Michelangelo designed another annex to that church, the Laurentian Library. The library was required to receive the books bequeathed by Pope Leo; it was traditional in Florence and elsewhere that libraries were housed in convents. It contains Michelangelo's most famous and original wall designs. The library is also notable for its bold and free rearrangement of traditional building components. These characteristics have led to the work's being cited frequently as the first and a chief instance of Mannerism as an architectural style.

The sack of Rome in 1527 saw Pope Clement ignominiously in flight, and Florence revolted against the Medici, restoring the traditional republic. It was soon besieged and defeated, and Medici rule permanently reinstalled, in 1530. During the siege Michelangelo was the designer of fortifications.

OTHER PROJECTS AND WRITING

When the Medici returned in 1530, Michelangelo returned to work on their family tombs. Two separate projects of statues of this date are the *Apollo* or *David* (its identity is problematic), used as a gift to a newly powerful political figure, and the *Victory*, a figure trampling on a defeated enemy, an old man. It was probably meant for the never-forgotten tomb of Pope Julius, because the motif had been present in the plans for that tomb. Victor and loser both have intensely complicated poses; the loser seems packed in a block, the victor—like the *Apollo*—forms a lithe spiral. The *Victory* group became a favourite model for younger sculptors of the Mannerist group, who applied the formula to many allegorical subjects.

In 1534 Michelangelo left Florence for the last time, though he always hoped to return to finish the projects he had left incomplete. He passed the rest of his life in Rome, working on projects in some cases equally grand but in most cases of quite new kinds. From this time on, a large number of his letters to his family in Florence were preserved; many of them concentrated on plans for his nephew's marriage, essential to preserve the family name. Michelangelo's father had died in 1531 and his favourite brother at about the same time. He himself showed increasing anxiety about his age and death.

It was at this time that the nearly 60-year-old artist wrote letters expressing strong feelings of attachment to young men, chiefly to the talented aristocrat Tommaso Cavalieri, later active in Roman civic affairs. These have naturally been interpreted as indications that Michelangelo was homosexual, but this interpretation seems implausible when one considers that no similar indications had emerged when the artist was younger. The correlation of these letters with other events seems consistent instead with the view that he was seeking a surrogate son, choosing for the purpose a younger man who was admirable in every way and would welcome the role.

In 1534 Michelangelo returned after a quarter century to fresco painting, executing for the new pope, Paul III, the huge *Last Judgment* for the end wall of the Sistine Chapel. The work is in a painting style noticeably different from that of 25 years earlier. The colour scheme is simpler than that of the ceiling: brownish flesh tones against a stark blue sky. The figures have less energy and their forms are less articulate, the torsos tending to be

The Last Judgement, *fresco by Michelangelo, 1533–41; in the Sistine Chapel, the Vatican.* SCALA/Art Resource, New York

single fleshy masses without waistlines. The *Last Judgment*, conceived as a single, unified, grandiose scene without architectural elements to divide and define its space, is permeated by a sense of dynamic intensity derived from the emotional gestures and expressions of the judged.

THE LAST DECADES

In his late years Michelangelo was less involved with sculpture and, along with painting and poetry, more with architecture, an area that did not require much physical labour. He was sought after to design imposing monuments for the new and modern Rome that were to enunciate architecturally the city's position as a world centre. Two of these monuments, the Capitoline Square and the dome of St. Peter's, are still among the city's most notable visual images. He did not finish either, but after his death both were continued in ways that probably did not depart much from his plans.

While remaining head architect of St. Peter's, Michelangelo worked on many smaller building projects in Rome. He completed the main unit of the Palazzo Farnese, the residence of Pope Paul III's family. The top story wall of its courtyard is a rare example of an architectural unit fully finished under his eye.

His last paintings were the frescoes of the Pauline Chapel in the Vatican, which still is basically inaccessible to the public. Unlike his other frescoes, they are in the position normal for narrative painting, on a wall and not exceptionally high up. They consistently treat spatial depth and narrative drama in a way that brings them closer to other paintings of the age than to the artist's previous paintings. Among the artists Michelangelo came to know and admire was Titian, who visited Rome during the period of this project (1542–50), and the frescoes seem to betray his influence in colour. There are only two late sculptures, which Michelangelo did for himself, both presenting the dead Christ being mourned, neither one finished.

ASSESSMENT AND INFLUENCE

For posterity, Michelangelo has always remained one of the small group of the most exalted artists who have been felt to express, like Shakespeare or Beethoven, the tragic experience of humanity with the greatest depth and universal scope. In contrast to the great fame of the artist's works, their visual influence on later art is relatively limited. This cannot be explained by hesitation to imitate an art simply because it appeared so great, for artists such as Raphael were considered equally great but were used as sources to a much greater degree. It may be instead that the particular type of expression associated with Michelangelo, of an almost cosmic grandeur, was inhibiting.

The limited influence of his work includes a few cases of almost total dependence. The most talented artist who worked in this way was Daniele da Volterra. Otherwise, Michelangelo was treated as a model for specific limited aspects of his work. In the 17th century, he was regarded as supreme in anatomical drawing but less praised for broader elements of his art. While the Mannerists utilized the spatial compression seen in a few of his works, and later the serpentine poses of his sculpture of *Victory*, the 19th-century master Auguste Rodin exploited the effect of unfinished marble blocks. Certain 17th-century masters of the Baroque perhaps show the fullest reference to him, but in ways that have been transformed to exclude any literal similarity. Besides Gian Lorenzo Bernini, the painter Peter Paul Rubens may best show the usability of Michelangelo's creations for a later great artist.

GIORGIONE

(b. *c.* 1477/78, Castelfranco Veneto, Republic of Venice [Italy] — d. before Nov. 7, 1510, Venice)

Giorgione was an extremely influential Italian painter and one of the initiators of a High Renaissance style in Venetian art. His qualities of mood and mystery were epitomized in *The Tempest* (*c.* 1505), an evocative pastoral scene that was among the first of its genre in Venetian painting.

LIFE

Nothing is really known about Giorgione's personal life, except for the legends reported by the biographer and Mannerist artist Giorgio Vasari in the two editions (1550 and 1568) of his *Lives of the Most Eminent Painters, Sculptors, and Architects*. Giorgione's name is given in two surviving documents of 1507 and 1508 as Zorzi da Castelfranco (in Venetian dialect); i.e., Giorgio of Castelfranco. The form Giorgione (or Zorzon), which is customarily used today, first appears in the 1528 inventory of the Grimani Collection. His name means "tall George," or "big George," implying that he was a large man. Tradition holds that he was handsome and amorous. Correspondence dated Oct. 25, 1510, between the celebrated Renaissance patron of the arts Isabella d'Este of Mantua and her agent Taddeo Albano at Venice mentions Giorgione's death as having occurred recently, probably caused by the plague that was raging in Venice at that time. Vasari's biography is the earliest. It emphasizes the artist's humble origin, his elevated mind, and his personal charm, but this characterization undoubtedly was a product of Vasari's imagination, based upon the poetic quality of Giorgione's paintings.

That the young painter went to Venice to study about 1490 under Giovanni Bellini, the greatest Venetian master of the day, is undeniable. The technique, colour, and mood of Giorgione's pictures are clearly related to Bellini's late style.

WORKS

The commission of 1507 for a painting or paintings to be placed in the Audience Hall of the Ducal Palace at Venice was perhaps never completed, since no further notice of the work is recorded. Giorgione's principal public commission was the execution of frescoes on the exterior of the Fondaco dei Tedeschi (the German Exchange), where he painted the figures on the facade over the canal. The frescoes over the street were carried out by the young Titian, perhaps under Giorgione's direction. These works, documented in 1508, are lost, except for fragments that contain faint outlines of figures.

Aside from the works mentioned in specific documents, the notes on the art collections of Venice (*Notizie d'opere del disegno*), written between 1520 and 1543 by the Venetian patrician Marcantonio Michiel, contain references to pictures by Giorgione. This information occurs so shortly after the master's death that it is considered generally reliable. Of the 12 paintings and 1 drawing listed, 5 works have survived: *The Tempest*, *The Three Philosophers*, *Sleeping Venus*, *Boy with an Arrow*, and *Shepherd with a Flute*.

The Tempest is a milestone in Renaissance landscape painting, with its dramatization of a storm about to break. Here is the kind of poetic interpretation of nature that the Renaissance writers Pietro Bembo and Jacopo Sannazzaro evoked. This feeling for nature is probably also intimately

The Tempest, *oil on canvas by Giorgione, c. 1505; in the Galleria dell'Accademia, Venice.* SCALA/Art Resource, New York

related to, though not directly derived from, the philosophical "naturalism" of the contemporary Venetian and Paduan humanists grouped around the important Renaissance philosopher Pietro Pomponazzi. The meaning of the two people seated in the foreground of *The Tempest* has been the subject of numerous interpretations, none of them definitive. Michiel called them a soldier and a Gypsy. Some literary source of a romantic, Arcadian nature is generally assumed, since no Renaissance artist would include two mysterious figures devoid of meaning. The same kind of literary theme is evoked in the *Pastoral Concert* (c. 1510), the attribution of which is much debated.

Sleeping Venus, *oil on canvas by Giorgione, c. 1510, landscape background by Titian; in the Gemäldegalerie Alte Meister, Dresden, Ger.* Sachsische Landesbibliothek/Abteilung Deutsche Fotothek; photograph, B. Walther

The *Sleeping Venus* (*c.* 1510) was left unfinished at Giorgione's death. Michiel stated that the task of adding the landscape background fell to Titian. The picture itself validates this statement, for the landscape, with buildings in the right distance, is repeated in other works by Titian. Giorgione's *Sleeping Venus* inaugurates a long series of paintings of the goddess of love in Venetian art, particularly those of Titian. None, however, achieved so fully the expression of remoteness and unself-conscious beauty as this majestic and ideally conceived figure. *Judith* (*c.* 1505), though undocumented, evokes the same concept of universal beauty; she is more goddess than avenger of her people.

Few religious paintings are mentioned in the early documentary sources on Giorgione. The panels representing the *Trial of Moses* and the *Judgment of Solomon* are generally agreed to number among the artist's first works (*c.* 1495–1500). Although the figures look slightly archaic, the beauty of the landscape setting, with its soft melting distances, unmistakably reveals the hand of the painter of *The Tempest*. Most celebrated of his religious pictures is the Castelfranco Altarpiece (*c.* 1504). The composition of this painting forms an equilateral triangle in conformance with the search for geometric solutions characteristic of the Renaissance mind. Thoroughly in the spirit of the master are the landscape and the dreamy mood of the figures, who seem lost in reverie. *The Holy Family* (*c.* 1500) and the

The Holy Family, *oil on panel transferred to hardboard, by Giorgione, c. 1500; in the National Gallery of Art, Washington, D.C.* Courtesy of the National Gallery of Art, Washington, D.C., Samuel H. Kress Collection

Adoration of the Shepherds (1505/1510) are of equally fine quality. The latter is particularly noteworthy for its exquisite use of colour.

The Three Philosophers (*c.* 1510) is one of the works Michiel saw and specifically identified as being by Giorgione. He stated, however, that it was completed by the Venetian painter Sebastiano del Piombo after the master's death. The composition and colour are so fully Giorgione's that Sebastiano could only have added a few finishing touches. In addition, the dreamy melancholy of the three men—who represent youth, maturity, and old age—embodies the spirit of the master. Though the notion of three ages of man is surely implied, little agreement

Adoration of the Shepherds, *oil on panel by Giorgione, 1505/1510; in the National Gallery of Art, Washington, D.C.* Courtesy of the National Gallery of Art, Washington, D.C., Samuel H. Kress Collection

prevails among critics as to whether the three magi, three philosophers, or a literary source in ancient Roman legend is really intended.

The *Christ Carrying the Cross* is widely disputed even today. Nevertheless, Vasari in 1568 specifically stated that the painter was Titian, correcting an error that he had committed in the edition of 1550 in attributing the picture to Giorgione. The canvas, much restored and repainted, possesses no more than archaeological interest. Other questioned paintings that seem to a number of contemporary critics to be the works of Giorgione rather than Titian are *The Adulteress Brought Before Christ* (*c.* 1500), the *Madonna and Child with SS. Roch and Anthony of Padua* (*c.* 1505), and the *Madonna and Child in a Landscape* (*c.* 1504).

INFLUENCE AND SIGNIFICANCE

In portraiture Giorgione made a most profound and far-reaching impression. Venetian painters such as Titian, Palma Vecchio, and Lorenzo Lotto so closely imitated him in the early 16th century that it is at times virtually impossible to distinguish between them. Nevertheless, the portrait of a *Youth* (*c.* 1504) is universally considered to be by Giorgione. The indescribably subtle expression of serenity and the immobile features, added to the chiseled effect of the silhouette and modeling, combine to make the *Youth* an unforgettable expression of Renaissance man. The same sort of exquisite refinement and sensibility characterizes the disputed portrait supposedly of the poet *Antonio Broccardo* (*c.* 1506). Accepted by all critics is the portrait of the so-called *Laura*, on the back of which is an inscription giving the date as June 1, 1506, and naming Zorzi of Castelfranco as the painter.

Giorgione's *Self-Portrait as David* (*c.* 1510), recorded in an engraving of 1650 by the well-known German engraver

Wenzel Hollar, can safely be considered a much-damaged original that has been drastically cut down in size. The artist gave his own portrait more dramatic force by the frown upon his face and by turning the body inward at an angle to the parapet. Titian adopted the same arrangement in his portrait of a gentleman in blue (*c.* 1512), where the initials TV (Tiziano Vecellio) establish him as the painter rather than Giorgione, as was formerly believed.

Despite considerable recent research, the short-lived master from Castelfranco still remains one of the most enigmatic of Renaissance painters. Yet the quality and charm of his paintings have made him as highly esteemed today as he was in his own time—a Venetian master of poetic mood created through idealized form, colour, and light.

IL SODOMA

(b. 1477, Vercelli, duchy of Savoy [Italy]—d. Feb. 14/15, 1549, Siena, Republic of Siena)

The paintings of Il Sodoma (the sobriquet of Giovanni Antonio Bazzi) reflect the transition from High Renaissance to Mannerist style. Sodoma had a peculiar gift for suggesting the sensuous beauty of the human form and an exaggerated, almost mystical, emotionalism that anticipates one aspect of the Baroque.

Sodoma was the son of a shoemaker. From 1490 to 1497 he was apprenticed to G.M. Spanzotti, a minor Piedmontese artist, but he was afterward much influenced by Leonardo da Vinci and later by Raphael, who was particularly decisive in determining his mature style. Sodoma was invited to Siena in 1501 and subsequently spent the bulk of his working life there. From 1503 to 1504 he painted multiple panels of frescoes in the convent of Saint Anna in Camprena, including *Miracle of the Loaves and Fishes* and scenes from the life of St. Anna. Thereafter he worked on a series of more than two dozen scenes from the life of St. Benedict, a series begun by Luca Signorelli for the Olivetans in the Monte Oliveto Maggiore monastery, near Siena.

In 1508 Sodoma was invited to Rome by the celebrated Sienese banker Agostino Chigi and was employed by Pope Julius II in the Stanza della Segnatura in the Vatican. Although Raphael worked on the same ceiling in 1509, he left some of Sodoma's ceiling decoration, including mythological figures and Roman military scenes, intact. About 1510 Sodoma again utilized mythological figures for ceiling decoration in Via del Casato, a palace belonging to Chigi. One of his most successful frescoes, the *Marriage of Alexander and Roxane* (*c.* 1516) in the Villa Farnesina, Rome, is often

Marriage of Alexander and Roxane, *fresco by Sodoma, c. 1511–12; in the Villa Farnesina, Rome.* SCALA/Art Resource, New York

considered a rival as a decorative achievement to the frescoes by the school of Raphael in the same villa. Later in his career Sodoma also painted frescoes for San Domenico in Siena, including *Vision of St. Catherine of Siena* and *Execution of Nicolò di Tuldo*, that were considered some of his best work. That same year he was also commissioned to paint frescoes in the town hall (Palazzo Pubblico) in Siena. Although he continued to paint until his death, much that he produced in his later years is considered unimpressive.

Sodoma gained a wide reputation during his lifetime as a homosexual; the historian Giorgio Vasari, who disliked him, made the most of the byname Il Sodoma ("the Sodomite"), by which he was known from 1512 onward. It has been claimed that the nickname is likely to have been the result of a joke, but it was adopted by the artist himself and is the name by which he is now generally known.

JAN GOSSART

(b. *c.* 1478, Maubeuge?, France—d. Oct. 1, 1532, Antwerp?)

The Flemish painter Jan Gossart (Gossaert), often called Jan Mabuse, was one of the first artists to introduce the style of the Italian Renaissance into the Low Countries.

Gossart is most likely to be identified with Jennyn van Hennegouwe, who is registered as a master in the Guild of St. Luke at Antwerp in 1503. His most important early extant work is the *Adoration of the Kings*, which is painted in the ornate style of the Antwerp school. Other early works, such as *Jesus, the Virgin, and the Baptist*, reflect his interest in the works of Jan van Eyck and Albrecht Dürer. Another early work, famous for its sense of mood, is the *Agony in the Garden*.

In 1508 Gossart accompanied his employer, Philip of Burgundy, to Italy, where he was strongly impressed by

The Descent from the Cross, *oil on canvas by Jan Gossart, c. 1520; in the State Hermitage Museum, St. Petersburg.* © Photos.com/Jupiterimages

the art of the High Renaissance. After his return from Italy in 1509, he continued to study Italian art through the engravings of Marcantonio Raimondi and Jacopo de' Barbari. Gossart's subsequent work shows a continuous effort to develop a fully Italianate style. This is evident in such works as the *Neptune and Amphitrite* (1516) and the *Hercules and Deianira* (1517), in which his early, complex designs have given way to a comparatively simple and direct conception.

Sculpturesque nudes become common in Gossart's later paintings, but they seldom avoid the stiff quality of his earlier figures. In his *Danae*, Gossart employs an

Danae, *oil on panel by Jan Gossart, 1527; in the Alte Pinakothek, Munich.*
Courtesy of the Alte Pinakothek, Munich

elaborate architectural setting as a foil for the seminude figure, a device he frequently used. Throughout his life, he retained the lapidary technique and careful observation that were traditional in Netherlandish art.

Gossart was also a renowned portrait painter. His portraits, such as the *Charles de Bourgogne, Eleanor of Austria* (*c.* 1525), and *Jean Carondelet* (1517), reveal his facility for psychological perception and are particularly notable for their expressive depiction of hands.

ALBRECHT ALTDORFER

(b. *c.* 1480 — d. Feb. 12, 1538, Regensburg [Germany])

The German painter, printmaker, and draftsman Albrecht Altdorfer was a leading member of a group of 16th-century German artists known as the Danube school and one of the founders of landscape painting. He was the guiding spirit of the Danube school of painting.

Altdorfer spent most of his life in Regensburg, becoming a citizen in 1505 and, in later years, serving as official architect of the city and a member of its inner council. His early figure paintings show a growing preoccupation with landscape, until in *St. George and the Dragon* (1510) the knight is practically overwhelmed by the primeval forest in which he performs his feat. With the *Regensburg Landscape* (*c.* 1522–25) and other works, Altdorfer painted the first pure landscapes—i.e., landscape scenes containing no human figures whatsoever—since antiquity. His favourite subject was the leafy and impenetrable forests of Germany and Austria. He was also among the first to depict sunset lighting and picturesque ruins in twilight. Several of his altar panels in the Church of St. Florian near Linz, completed in 1518, depicting the Passion of Christ and the martyrdom of St. Sebastian, are night scenes in which he exploited the possibilities of torch light, star light, or twilight with unusual brilliance. Altdorfer's masterpiece, the *Battle of Alexander at Issus* (1529), is both a battle scene of incredible detail and a highly dramatic and expressive landscape.

The fantastic element that pervaded Altdorfer's paintings was also prominent in his drawings, most of which were done in black with white highlights on brown or blue-gray paper. His engravings and woodcuts, usually miniatures, are distinguished by their playful inventiveness. Late in his career he used the new medium of etching to produce a series of landscapes.

MATTHIAS GRÜNEWALD

(b. *c.* 1480, Würzburg, Bishopric of Würzburg [Germany]—d. August 1528, Halle, Archbishopric of Magdeburg)

Matthias Grünewald, one of the greatest German painters of his age, painted works on religious themes that achieve a visionary expressiveness through intense colour and agitated line. The wings of the altarpiece of the Antonite monastery at Isenheim, in southern Alsace (dated 1515), are considered to be his masterpiece.

Although it is commonly agreed that "Master Mathis" was born in the German city of Würzburg, the date of his birth remains problematic. The first securely dated work by Grünewald (a name fabricated by a biographer in the 17th century; his actual surname was Gothardt), the *Mocking of Christ* of 1503, seems to be that of a young man just become a master. Grünewald appears first in documents of about 1500 either in the town of Seligenstadt am Main or Aschaffenburg. By about 1509 Grünewald had become court painter and later the leading art official (his title was supervisor or clerk of the works) to the elector of Mainz, the archbishop Uriel von Gemmingen.

About 1510 Grünewald received a commission from the Frankfurt merchant Jacob Heller to add two fixed wings to the altarpiece of the *Assumption of the Virgin* recently completed by the painter Albrecht Dürer. These wings depicting four saints are painted in grisaille (shades of gray) and already show the artist at the height of his powers. Like Grünewald's drawings, which are done primarily in black chalk with some yellow or white highlighting, the Heller wings convey colouristic effects without the use of colour. Expressive hands and active draperies help blur the boundaries between cold stone and living form.

About 1515 Grünewald was entrusted with the largest and most important commission of his career. Guido Guersi, an Italian preceptor, or knight, who led the religious community of the Antonite monastery at Isenheim (in southern Alsace), asked the artist to paint a series of wings for the shrine of the high altar that had been carved in about 1505 by Niclaus Hagnower of Strasbourg. The subject matter of the wings of the Isenheim Altarpiece provided Grünewald's genius with its fullest expression and was based largely on the text of the popular, mystical *Revelations* of St. Bridget of Sweden (written about 1370).

The Isenheim Altarpiece consists of a carved wooden shrine with one pair of fixed and two pairs of movable wings flanking it. Grünewald's paintings on these large wing panels consist of the following. The first set of panels depicts the *Crucifixion*, the *Lamentation*, and portraits of *SS. Sebastian and Anthony*. The second set focuses on the Virgin Mary, with scenes of the *Annunciation* and a *Concert of Angels*, a *Nativity*, and the *Resurrection*. The third set of wings focuses on St. Anthony, with *St. Anthony and St. Paul in the Desert* and the *Temptation of St. Anthony*.

The altarpiece's figures are given uniquely determined gestures, their limbs are distended for expressive effect, and their draperies (a trademark of Grünewald's that expand and contract in accordion pleats) mirror the passions of the soul. The colours used are simultaneously biting and brooding. The Isenheim Altarpiece expresses deep spiritual mysteries. The *Concert of Angels*, for instance, depicts an exotic angel choir housed within an elaborate baldachin. At one opening of the baldachin a small, glowing female form, the eternal and immaculate Virgin, kneels in adoration of her own earthly manifestation at the right. And at the far left of the same scene under the baldachin, a feathered creature, probably the evil archangel Lucifer, adds his demonic notes to the serenade.

Other details in the altarpiece, including the horribly wounded body of Christ in the *Crucifixion*, may refer to the role of the monastery as a hospital for victims of the plague and St. Anthony's fire. The colour red takes on unusual power and poignancy in the altarpiece, first in the *Crucifixion*, then in the *Annunciation* and *Nativity*, and finally on Christ's shroud in the *Resurrection*, which is at first lifeless in the cold tomb but which then smolders and bursts into white-hot flame as Christ ascends, displaying his tiny purified red wounds. Such transformations of light and colour are perhaps the most spectacular found in German art until the late 19th century. And through all this drama, Grünewald never misses the telling picturesque detail: a botanical specimen, a string of prayer beads, or a crystal carafe.

Another important clerical commission came from a canon in Aschaffenburg, Heinrich Reitzmann. As early as 1513 he had asked Grünewald to paint an altar for the Mariaschnee Chapel in the Church of Saints Peter and Alexander in Aschaffenburg. The artist painted this work in the years 1517–19. Grünewald apparently married about 1519, but the marriage does not appear to have brought him much happiness (at least, that is the tradition recorded in the 17th century). Grünewald occasionally added his wife's surname, Neithardt, to his own, thereby accounting for several documentary references to him as Mathis Neithardt or Mathis Gothardt Neithardt.

In 1514 Uriel von Gemmingen had died, and Albrecht von Brandenburg had become the elector of Mainz. For Albrecht, Grünewald executed one of his most luxurious works, portraying *The Meeting of SS. Erasmus and Maurice* (Erasmus is actually a portrait of Albrecht). This work exhibits the theme of religious discussion or debate, so important to this period of German art and history. In this painting, as well as in the late, two-sided panel known as the Tauberbischofsheim Altarpiece, Grünewald's forms become more massive and compact, his colours restrained but still vivid.

Apparently because of his sympathy with the Peasants' Revolt of 1525, Grünewald left Albrecht's service in 1526. He spent the last two years of his life visiting in Frankfurt and Halle, cities sympathetic to the newly emerging Protestant cause. In Halle he was involved in supervising the town waterworks. Grünewald died in August 1528; among his effects were discovered several Lutheran pamphlets and documents.

Grünewald's painterly achievement remains one of the most striking in the history of northern European art. His 10 or so paintings (some of which are composed of several panels) and approximately 35 drawings that survive have been jealously guarded and carefully scrutinized in modern times. His dramatic and intensely expressive approach to subject matter can perhaps best be observed in his three other extant paintings of the Crucifixion, which echo the Isenheim Altarpiece in their depiction of the scarified and agonized body of Christ.

Despite his artistic genius, failure and confusion no doubt marked much of Grünewald's life. He seems not to have had a real pupil, and his avoidance of the graphic media also limited his influence and renown. Grünewald's works did continue to be highly prized, but the man himself was almost forgotten by the 17th century. The German painter Joachim von Sandrart, the artist's fervent admirer and first biographer (*Teutsche Akademie*, 1675), was responsible for preserving some of the scanty information that we have about the artist, as well as naming him, erroneously and from an obscure source, Grünewald. At the lowest ebb of his popularity, in the mid-19th century, Grünewald was labeled by German scholarship "a competent imitator of Dürer." However, the late 19th-century and early 20th-century artistic revolt against rationalism and naturalism, typified by the German Expressionists, led to a thorough and scholarly reevaluation of the artist's career. Grünewald's art is now recognized as an often painful and confused but always highly personal and inspired response to the turmoil of his times.

LORENZO LOTTO

(b. c. 1480, Venice [Italy]—d. 1556, Loreto, Papal States)

Lorenzo Lotto is best known for his perceptive portraits and mystical paintings of religious subjects. He represents one of the best examples of the fruitful relationship between the Venetian and Central Italian (Marche) schools.

In the earlier years of his life, he lived at Treviso, and, although he was influenced by the Venetians Giovanni Bellini and Antonello da Messina, he always remained somewhat apart from the main Venetian tradition. His earliest dated pictures, the *Madonna and St. Peter Martyr* (1503) and the *Portrait of Bishop Bernardo de' Rossi* (1505), both in Naples, have unmistakable Quattrocento traits in the treatment of the drapery and landscape and in the cool tonality.

Between 1508 and 1512, Lotto was in Rome, where he was influenced by Raphael, who was painting the Stanza della Segnatura in the Vatican palace. In the *Entombment* (1512) at Jesi and the *Transfiguration* (c. 1513) at Recanati,

Lotto abandoned the dryness and cool colour of his earlier style and adopted a fluid method and a rich, joyful colouring.

After 1513 Lotto lived primarily in Bergamo, where his style matured. His most successful works of this period are the altarpieces in San Bernardino and Santo Spirito, which show a new inventiveness, a greater competence in rendering light and shade, and a preference for opulent colours. The compositions of his Bergamo works are more self-assured, and the *Susanna and the Elders* (1517) exhibits his growing ability as a narrative painter.

In 1526 or 1527 Lotto returned to Venice, where he was briefly influenced by the glowing palette and grand compositional schemes of Titian. This is best seen in his *St. Nicholas of Bari in Glory* (1529). But Lotto's main interest was in the forceful depiction of emotions and psychological insights. This is evident in his many portraits and especially in the *Annunciation* (c. 1527), with its agitated figures, swirling drapery, dramatic lighting, and scant interest in perspective.

In this period his work became even more emotional, and many works, such as the *Madonna of the Rosary* (1539) and the *Crucifixion* (1531), exhibit a highly charged mysticism in their nervous, crowded compositions and pale colouring. His numerous portraits of this period are among his most incisively descriptive of the sitter's character; and the *Madonna Enthroned with Four Saints* (c. 1540) shows Lotto at the height of his narrative power.

Lotto was back in Venice in 1540, and his *St. Antonino Giving Alms* (1542) shows a renewed interest in Titian. But in 1549 he returned to the Marche, and his life became increasingly unsettled. He had a nervous, irritable temperament and seemed unable to stay long in one place or to sustain permanent relationships. In his old age he was destitute and was forced to paint numbers on hospital beds to earn a living. In 1554, partially blind, he entered the Santa Casa in Loreto as an oblate member with a permission to reside and work there. There he began one of his most sensitive masterpieces, the *Presentation in the Temple*, which remained unfinished at his death.

GIOVANNI GIROLAMO SAVOLDO

(b. *c.* 1480, Brescia, Republic of Venice [Italy] — d. *c.* 1548, Venice?)

G iovanni Girolamo Savoldo, also called Girolamo da Brescia, was a painter of the Brescian school whose style is marked by a quiet lyricism. Although his work was largely forgotten after his death, interest in Savoldo was revived in the 20th century and his work gained a place alongside that of other High Renaissance painters.

The first records of Savoldo's life show he was in Parma in 1506 and was recorded in the guild at Florence in 1508. Little else is known of his personal life except that he may have left Venice, where he spent most of his life, to live in Milan for a few years and that he had a Flemish wife through whom he may have made Northern contacts. Scholars have found it difficult to pinpoint Savoldo's training and artistic influences because his style changed very little during his career. His preoccupation with clearly defined shapes in light suggests he was influenced by Cima da Conegliano, who also used light with quiet exactitude and who may have also been based in Parma in 1506. Savoldo also may have been influenced by Flemish painters.

Savoldo's use of deep, rich colour gives his paintings dramatic tonal values. The influence of Giorgione can be felt in the dreamy, poeticized treatment in such works as *Portrait of a Knight* (*c.* 1525). Savoldo defined his luminous, meticulously detailed figures by setting them against darkened, twilit skies, a technique that culminated in *Saint*

Matthew and the Angel (1530–35) and *St. Mary Magdalene Approaching the Sepulchre* (*c.* 1535). The portrait long known as *Gaston de Foix* (*c.* 1532), but no longer identified with that duke of Nemours, attempted to give a sense of three-dimensionality by depicting a figure wearing a suit of armour reflected in a mirror.

Savoldo liked to depict unusual effects of light, and he paid particular attention to reflected or nocturnally lit scenes. His output was small (only about 40 paintings), and he had little influence on the course of Venetian painting, from which he had always stood somewhat aloof. For centuries after his death his work was typically either ignored or wrongly attributed to other artists, but in the early 20th century it was revived by art critics who grouped him, for the first time, with the High Renaissance artists. Exhibitions of his paintings followed, and a 1990 retrospective of his work, held in Brescia and Frankfurt am Main, continued to revitalize his reputation.

FRANCIABIGIO

(b. 1482/83, Florence [Italy]—d. 1525, Florence)

The Italian Renaissance painter Franciabigio is best known for his portraits and religious paintings. His style included early Renaissance, High Renaissance, and proto-Mannerist elements.

Franciabigio, also known as Francesco di Cristofano, Francesco Giudini, and Francesco Giudici, had completed an apprenticeship under his father, a weaver, by 1504. He probably then trained under the Italian painter Mariotto Albertinelli before forming a joint workshop with a leading Florentine painter, Andrea del Sarto, about 1506. Their relationship became tense after 1509, when Andrea began receiving more commissions and more praise for his work, and Franciabigio began to live in his shadow.

Franciabigio's early style is filled with movement and attention to descriptive detail strongly reminiscent of 15th-century Italian painting. He was attracted to the Florentine works of Raphael, as can be seen in his *Madonna del Pozzo* (c. 1508). In the atrium of the Annunziata in Florence he painted the *Marriage of the Virgin* (1513) as a portion of a series in which Andrea was chiefly concerned. When the friars uncovered this work before it was quite finished, Franciabigio was so incensed that, seizing a mason's hammer, he struck at the head of the Virgin and some other heads, and the fresco, which would otherwise be his masterpiece in that medium, was mutilated.

For a number of years, Franciabigio maintained the studio with Andrea. Together with Andrea's student, Jacopo da Pontormo, they decorated the Medici villa at Poggio a Caiano, where Franciabigio's *Triumph of Caesar* displays his talent for narrative painting. Andrea's influence on Franciabigio may be seen in the dark, smoky background and the soft, dramatic lighting of the St. Job Altar (1516). One of his best-known later paintings is his *Story of Bathsheba* (1523), which brings to mind the poses of some of Michelangelo's figures on the Sistine Chapel ceiling.

RAPHAEL

(b. April 6, 1483, Urbino, Duchy of Urbino [Italy] — d. April 6, 1520, Rome, Papal States [Italy])

A master painter and architect of the Italian High Renaissance, Raphael is best known for his Madonnas and for his large figure compositions in the Vatican in Rome. His work is admired for its clarity of form and ease of composition and for its visual achievement of the Neoplatonic ideal of human grandeur.

EARLY YEARS AT URBINO

Raffaello Sanzio, better known as Raphael, was the son of Giovanni Santi and Magia di Battista Ciarla; his mother died in 1491. His father was, according to the 16th-century artist and biographer Giorgio Vasari, a painter "of no great merit." He was, however, a man of culture who was in constant contact with the advanced artistic ideas current at the court of Urbino. He gave his son his first instruction in painting. Before his death in 1494, when Raphael was 11, he had introduced the boy to humanistic philosophy at the court.

Urbino had become a centre of culture during the rule of Duke Federico da Montefeltro, who encouraged the arts and attracted the visits of men of outstanding talent, including Donato Bramante, Piero della Francesca, and Leon Battista Alberti, to his court. Although Raphael would be influenced by major artists in Florence and Rome, Urbino constituted the basis for all his subsequent learning. Furthermore, the cultural vitality of the city probably stimulated the exceptional precociousness of the young artist, who, even at the beginning of the 16th century, when he was scarcely 17 years old, already displayed an extraordinary talent.

APPRENTICESHIP AT PERUGIA

The date of Raphael's arrival in Perugia is not known, but several scholars place it in 1495. The first record of Raphael's activity as a painter is found there in a document of Dec. 10, 1500, declaring that the young painter, by then called a "master," was commissioned to help paint an altarpiece to be completed by Sept. 13, 1502. It is clear from this that Raphael had already given proof of his mastery, so much so that between 1501 and 1503 he received a rather important commission—to paint the *Coronation of the Virgin* for the Oddi Chapel in the church of San Francesco, Perugia. The great Umbrian master Pietro Perugino was executing the frescoes in the Collegio del Cambio at Perugia between 1498 and 1500, enabling Raphael, as a member of his workshop, to acquire extensive professional knowledge.

In addition to this practical instruction, Perugino's calmly exquisite style also influenced Raphael. The *Giving of the Keys to St. Peter*, painted in 1481–82 by Perugino for the Sistine Chapel of the Vatican Palace in Rome, inspired Raphael's first major work, *The Marriage of the Virgin* (1504). Perugino's influence is seen in the emphasis on perspectives, in the graded relationships between the figures and the architecture, and in the lyrical sweetness of the figures. Nevertheless, even in this early painting, it is clear that Raphael's sensibility was different from his teacher's. The disposition of the figures is less rigidly related to the architecture, and the disposition of each figure in relation to the others is more informal and animated. The sweetness of the figures and the gentle relation between them surpasses anything in Perugino's work.

Three small paintings done by Raphael shortly after *The Marriage of the Virgin*—*Vision of a Knight*, *Three Graces*, and *St. Michael*—are masterful examples of narrative painting, showing, as well as youthful freshness, a maturing ability to control the elements of his own style. Although he had learned much from Perugino, Raphael by late 1504 needed other models to work from; it is clear that his desire for knowledge was driving him to look beyond Perugia.

MOVE TO FLORENCE

Vasari vaguely recounts that Raphael followed the Perugian painter Bernardino Pinturicchio to Siena and then went

Saint Michael Overwhelming the Demon (*also known as* The Small Saint Michael*), oil on wood by Raphael, c. 1505; in the Louvre, Paris.* ©
Photos.com/Jupiterimages

on to Florence, drawn there by accounts of the work that Leonardo da Vinci and Michelangelo were undertaking in that city. By the autumn of 1504 Raphael had certainly arrived in Florence. It is not known if this was his first visit to Florence, but, as his works attest, it was about 1504 that he first came into substantial contact with this artistic civilization, which reinforced all the ideas he had already acquired and also opened to him new and broader horizons. Vasari records that he studied not only the works of Leonardo, Michelangelo, and Fra Bartolomeo, who were the masters of the High Renaissance, but also "the old things of Masaccio," a pioneer of the naturalism that marked the departure of the early Renaissance from the Gothic.

Still, his principal teachers in Florence were Leonardo and Michelangelo. Many of the works that Raphael executed in the years between 1505 and 1507, most notably a great series of Madonnas including *The Madonna of the Goldfinch* (c. 1505), the *Madonna del Prato* (c. 1505), the *Esterházy Madonna* (c. 1505–07), and *La Belle Jardinière* (c. 1507), are marked by the influence of Leonardo, who since 1480 had been making great innovations in painting. Raphael was particularly influenced by Leonardo's *Madonna and Child with St. Anne* pictures, which are marked by an intimacy and simplicity of setting uncommon in 15th-century art. Raphael learned the Florentine method of building up his composition in depth with pyramidal figure masses; the figures are grouped as a single unit, but each retains its own individuality and shape. A new unity of composition and suppression of inessentials distinguishes the works he painted in Florence. Raphael also owed much to Leonardo's lighting techniques; he made moderate use of Leonardo's chiaroscuro (i.e., strong contrast between light and dark), and he was especially influenced by his sfumato (i.e., use of extremely fine, soft

Madonna del Prato, *oil on wood panel by Raphael, 1505; in the Kunsthistorisches Museum, Vienna.* Kunsthistorisches Museum, Vienna

shading instead of line to delineate forms and features). Raphael went beyond Leonardo, however, in creating new figure types whose round, gentle faces reveal uncomplicated and typically human sentiments but raised to a sublime perfection and serenity.

In 1507 Raphael was commissioned to paint the *Deposition of Christ* that is now in the Borghese Gallery in Rome. In this work, it is obvious that Raphael set himself deliberately to learn from Michelangelo the expressive possibilities of human anatomy. But Raphael differed from Leonardo and Michelangelo, who were both painters of dark intensity and excitement, in that he wished to develop a calmer and more extroverted style that would serve as a popular, universally accessible form of visual communication.

LAST YEARS IN ROME

Raphael was called to Rome toward the end of 1508 by Pope Julius II at the suggestion of the architect Donato Bramante. At this time Raphael was little known in Rome, but the young man soon made a deep impression on the volatile Julius and the papal court, and his authority as a master grew day by day. Raphael was endowed with a handsome appearance and great personal charm in addition to his prodigious artistic talents, and he eventually became so popular that he was called "the prince of painters."

Raphael spent the last 12 years of his short life in Rome. They were years of feverish activity and successive masterpieces. His first task in the city was to paint a cycle of frescoes in a suite of medium-sized rooms in the Vatican papal apartments in which Julius himself lived and worked; these rooms are known simply as the Stanze. The Stanza della Segnatura (1508–11) and Stanza d'Eliodoro (1512–14) were decorated practically entirely by Raphael himself;

the frescoes in the Stanza dell'Incendio (1514–17), though designed by Raphael, were largely executed by his numerous assistants and pupils.

The decoration of the Stanza della Segnatura was perhaps Raphael's greatest work. Julius II was a highly cultured man who surrounded himself with the most illustrious personalities of the Renaissance. He entrusted Bramante with the construction of a new basilica of St. Peter to replace the original 4th-century church; he called upon Michelangelo to execute his tomb and compelled him against his will to decorate the ceiling of the Sistine Chapel; and, sensing the genius of Raphael, he committed into his hands the interpretation of the philosophical scheme of the frescoes in the Stanza della Segnatura. This theme was the historical justification of the power of the Roman Catholic church through Neoplatonic philosophy.

The four main walls in the Stanza della Segnatura are occupied by the frescoes *Disputa* and the *School of Athens* on the larger walls and the *Parnassus* and *Cardinal Virtues* on the smaller walls. The two most important of these frescoes are the *Disputa* and the *School of Athens*. The *Disputa*, showing a celestial vision of God and his prophets and apostles above a gathering of representatives, past and present, of the Roman Catholic church, equates through its iconography the triumph of the church and the triumph of truth. The *School of Athens* is a complex allegory of secular knowledge, or philosophy, showing Plato and Aristotle surrounded by philosophers, past and present, in a splendid architectural setting, illustrating the historical continuity of Platonic thought.

The *School of Athens* is perhaps the most famous of all Raphael's frescoes, and one of the culminating artworks of the High Renaissance. Here Raphael fills an ordered and stable space with figures in a rich variety of poses and gestures, which he controls in order to make one group of

Plato and Aristotle surrounded by philosophers, detail from School of Athens, *fresco by Raphael, 1508–11; in the Stanza della Segnatura, the Vatican.* Erich Lessing/Art Resource, New York

figures lead to the next in an interweaving and interlocking pattern, bringing the eye to the central figures of Plato and Aristotle at the converging point of the perspectival space. The space in which the philosophers congregate is defined by the pilasters and barrel vaults of a great basilica that is based on Bramante's design for the new St. Peter's in Rome. The general effect of the fresco is one of majestic calm, clarity, and equilibrium.

About the same time, probably in 1511, Raphael painted a more secular subject, the *Triumph of Galatea* in the Villa Farnesina in Rome; this work was perhaps the High Renaissance's most successful evocation of the living spirit of Classical antiquity. Meanwhile, Raphael's decoration of the papal apartments continued after the death of Julius in 1513 and into the succeeding pontificate of Leo X until 1517. In contrast to the generalized allegories in the Stanza della Segnatura, the decorations in the second room, the Stanza d'Eliodoro, portray specific miraculous events in the history of the Christian church. The four principal subjects are *The Expulsion of Heliodorus from the Temple*, *The Mass at Bolsena*, *The Liberation of St. Peter*, and *Leo I Halting Attila*. These frescoes are deeper and richer in colour than are those in the earlier room, and they display a new boldness on Raphael's part in both their dramatic subjects and their unusual effects of light. *The Liberation of St. Peter*, for example, is a night scene and contains three separate lighting effects—moonlight, the torch carried by a soldier, and the supernatural light emanating from an angel. Raphael delegated his assistants to decorate the third room, the Stanze dell'Incendio, with the exception of one fresco, the *Fire in the Borgo*, in which his pursuit of more dramatic pictorial incidents and his continuing study of the male nude are plainly apparent.

The Madonnas that Raphael painted in Rome show him turning away from the serenity and gentleness of his earlier works in order to emphasize qualities of energetic movement and grandeur. His *Alba Madonna* (1508) epitomizes the serene sweetness of the Florentine Madonnas but shows a new maturity of emotional expression and supreme technical sophistication in the poses of the figures. It was followed by the *Madonna di Foligno* (1510) and the *Sistine Madonna* (1513), which show both the richness of colour and new boldness in compositional invention typical of Raphael's Roman period. Some of his other late Madonnas, such as the *Madonna of Francis I*, are remarkable for their polished elegance. Besides his other accomplishments, Raphael became the most important portraitist in Rome during the first two decades of the

Portrait of Dona Isabel de Requesens, Vice-Reine of Naples, *formerly* Portrait of Jeanne d'Aragon Raffaello, *oil on canvas (18th century) transferred from oil on wood by Raphael and Giulio Romano, 1518; in the Louvre, Paris.* © Photos.com/Jupiterimages

16th century. He introduced new types of presentation and new psychological situations for his sitters, as seen in the portrait of *Leo X with Two Cardinals* (1517–19). Raphael's finest work in the genre is perhaps the *Portrait of Baldassare Castiglione* (1516), a brilliant and arresting character study.

Leo X commissioned Raphael to design 10 large tapestries to hang on the walls of the Sistine Chapel. Seven of the 10 cartoons (full-size preparatory drawings) were completed by 1516, and the tapestries woven after them were hung in place in the chapel by 1519. Among these cartoons are *Christ's Charge to Peter*, *The Miraculous Draught of Fishes*, *The Death of Ananias*, *The Healing of the Lame Man*, *The Blinding of Elymas*, *The Sacrifice at Lystra*, and *St. Paul Preaching at Athens*. In these pictures Raphael created prototypes that would influence the European tradition of narrative history painting for centuries to come. The cartoons display Raphael's keen sense of drama, his use of gestures and facial expressions to portray emotion, and his incorporation of credible physical settings from both the natural world and that of ancient Roman architecture.

While he was at work in the Stanza della Segnatura, Raphael also did his first architectural work, designing the church of Sant' Eligio degli Orefici. In 1513 the banker Agostino Chigi, whose Villa Farnesina Raphael had already decorated, commissioned him to design and decorate his funerary chapel in the church of Santa Maria del Popolo. In 1514 Leo X chose him to work on the basilica of St. Peter's alongside Bramante; and when Bramante died later that year, Raphael assumed the direction of the work, transforming the plans of the church from a Greek, or radial, to a Latin, or longitudinal, design.

Raphael was also a keen student of archaeology and of ancient Greco-Roman sculpture, echoes of which are apparent in his paintings of the human figure during the Roman period. In 1515 Leo X put him in charge of the supervision of the preservation of marbles bearing valuable Latin inscriptions; two years later he was appointed commissioner of antiquities for the city, and he drew up an archaeological map of Rome. Raphael had by this time been put in charge of virtually all of the papacy's various artistic projects in Rome, involving architecture, paintings and decoration, and the preservation of antiquities.

Raphael's last masterpiece is the *Transfiguration* (commissioned by Cardinal Giulio de' Medici in 1517), an enormous altarpiece that was unfinished at his death and completed by his assistant Giulio Romano. It now hangs in the Vatican Museum. The *Transfiguration* is a complex work that combines extreme formal polish and elegance of execution with an atmosphere of tension and violence communicated by the agitated gestures of closely crowded groups of figures. It shows a new sensibility that is like the prevision of a new world, turbulent and dynamic; in its feeling and composition it inaugurated the Mannerist movement and tends toward an expression that may even be called Baroque.

Raphael died on his 37th birthday. His funeral mass was celebrated at the Vatican, his *Transfiguration* was placed at the head of the bier, and his body was buried in the Pantheon in Rome.

HANS BALDUNG

(b. c. 1484, Schwäbisch Gmünd, Württemberg [Germany]—d. 1545, Imperial Free City of Strasbourg [now Strasbourg, France])

The painter and graphic artist Hans Baldung was one of the most outstanding figures in northern Renaissance art. He served as an assistant to Albrecht Dürer, whose influence is apparent in his early works, although the demonic energy of his later style is closer to that of Matthias Grünewald.

Baldung was born into a successful family of doctors and lawyers that immigrated to Strasbourg from Swabia in the 1490s. He probably received his early artistic training in Strasbourg before entering Albrecht Dürer's workshop in Nürnberg about 1503. The "Grien" element that is sometimes seen in his name (it is sometimes given as "Baldung-Grien") was apparently an early nickname. After moving to Halle in 1507, he received commissions to produce the altarpieces *Epiphany*, or *Adoration of the Magi*, and *St. Sebastian* (1507), which were later displayed in the Collegiate Church there.

Baldung's paintings are equaled in importance by his extensive body of drawings, engravings, woodcuts, and designs for tapestries and stained glass. He is noted for his representations of the Virgin Mary, in which he combined landscapes, figures, light, and colour with an almost magical serenity. His portrayals of age, on the other hand, have a sinister character and a mannered virtuosity, as can be seen in his painting *Three Ages of Woman and Death* (c. 1510). His best-known painted work is the high altar (1516) of the cathedral at Freiburg im Breisgau, for which he also designed the stained-glass choir windows. The altarpiece consists of 11 large-scale paintings, including the *Coronation of the Virgin* in the centre. The dance-of-death (*Totentanz*) and the death-and-the-maiden themes occur frequently in his graphic works. An early supporter of the Reformation, he executed a woodcut in which Martin Luther is protected by the Holy Spirit in the form of a dove. In addition to his religious representations, Baldung's work also expressed his fascination with witchcraft, as can be seen in his woodcut *Witches' Sabbath* (1510) and in a series of drawings and prints he made on this theme between 1510 and 1544.

Baldung was a member of the Strasbourg town council and was official painter to the episcopate. His works also appear in the church at Elzach and the museums of Basel, Karlsruhe, Cologne, Freiburg, and Nürnberg.

JEAN CLOUET

(b. *c.* 1485—d. *c.* 1540, Paris, France)

The Renaissance painter of portraits Jean Clouet (whose byname was Janet, or Jehannet) is celebrated for the depth and delicacy of his characterization. Although he lived in France most of his life, records show that he was not French by origin and was never naturalized. He was one of the chief painters to Francis I as early as 1516 and was appointed groom of the chamber from 1523, thus enjoying the salary and social position granted to the most prominent poets and scholars of the time. In the early 1520s he lived in Tours and from 1529 in Paris. He painted chiefly portraits, but, at least in the earlier part of his career, he also produced religious subjects (a *St. Jerome* in 1522; designs for the *Four Evangelists*, 1523).

Until recently, the works attributed to Clouet consisted of a group of about 130 preparatory drawings representing members of the French court between 1514 and 1540 and a small group of miniatures and oil paintings, the drawings for which can be found among those of the first group. None of these, however, is signed or documented as the work of Jean Clouet. Consequently, their attribution to Clouet was merely tentative. But the discovery and cleaning of the well-documented *Portrait of Guillaume Budé* enabled the characteristics of Clouet's art to be established. Budé himself stated about 1536 that Jean Clouet had painted a portrait of him. Since the preparatory drawing for this picture exists in Chantilly and is obviously by the same hand as the other drawings, the attribution to Jean Clouet of all the aforementioned works ceased to be merely hypothetical.

In all these portraits the sitters' hands differ considerably and were probably executed by apprentices in Clouet's workshop. This body of works shows Clouet as one of the best 16th-century portrait painters, both incisive and delicate in the psychological characterization of sitters. His drawings are simple, broad, and subtle; his paintings are fresh in colour, subdued in modeling, and minute in execution. His technique seems fundamentally Flemish (he came probably either from Brussels or from the old Franco-Flemish region of Valenciennes), but the supple drawing, the calm plasticity, and the acute analysis of the individual in his portraits are typically French. In his youth he could have been influenced by the already ancient French tradition of portrait drawing. On the other hand, his monumental composition is influenced by the Italian Renaissance portraiture introduced into France by Andrea Solari. Some of Clouet's portraits also show similarities to those by Holbein, who in his turn borrowed the technique of portrait drawing in coloured chalks, or pastels, from Clouet.

SEBASTIANO DEL PIOMBO

(b. c. 1485, Venice [Italy] — d. July 21, 1547, Rome)

The Italian painter Sebastiano del Piombo is best known for his attempts to merge the rich colours of the Venetian school with the monumental form of the Roman school.

At first a professional lute player, Sebastiano, born Sebastiano Luciani, began his career as a painter later than most of his contemporaries. He was a pupil of Giovanni Bellini and of Giorgione, whose influence is apparent in his work. His works in fact were often confused with Giorgione's — e.g., *Salome* (1510). In 1511 Sebastiano went to Rome, where the Sienese banker Agostino Chigi had engaged him to decorate his newly built Villa Farnesina.

Shortly after completing this commission, Sebastiano settled permanently in Rome, where he became a member of Raphael's circle of artists and soon showed himself to be a notable portraitist.

About 1515 Sebastiano came under the influence of Michelangelo and began collaborating with that artist. From drawings and cartoons by Michelangelo he executed his best-known work, the *Pietà* (*c.* 1517), as well as the *Flagellation* (1516–24) and the *Raising of Lazarus* (1519). Michelangelo's opinion of him was so high that he thought by correcting his rather dull draftsmanship, he could make Sebastiano the best painter in Rome. In his Roman work Sebastiano combined the warm colouring of the Venetian school with the anatomical clarity and firm sculptural drawing probably resulting from his association with Michelangelo.

From 1519 to 1530 Sebastiano had an unparalleled reputation in Rome as a portraitist. Among the best of his later portraits are those of *Andrea Doria* (1526) and of *Clement VII* (1526). In 1531 Pope Clement VII bestowed upon Sebastiano the lucrative post of keeper of the papal seal (*piombino* is Italian for "lead seal," hence his nickname). During the last 17 years of his life this economic security seems to have been a significant contributing factor in Sebastiano's limited production of pictures.

ANDREA DEL SARTO

(b. July 16, 1486, Florence [Italy]—d. before Sept. 29, 1530, Florence)

The development of Florentine Mannerism was due in large part to the Italian painter and draftsman Andrea d'Agnolo, better known as Andrea del Sarto. His works exhibit exquisite composition and craftsmanship. Perhaps his most striking among other well-known works is the series of frescoes on the life of St. John the Baptist in the Chiostro dello Scalzo (*c.* 1515–26).

Sarto's family name was probably Lanfranchi, and his father was a tailor (hence "del Sarto"; Italian *sarto*, "tailor"). Little of real interest is known about his life, probably because it was for the most part uneventful. He was notably short in stature and known to his friends as Andreino. With two brief exceptions, his working life was spent in Florence. He was a pupil of Piero di Cosimo and was greatly influenced by Raphael, Leonardo da Vinci, and Fra Bartolommeo. His art, rooted in traditional Quattrocento (15th-century) painting, combined Leonardo's sfumato with Raphael's compositional harmony in a style that was typical of the Cinquecento (16th century). He began to produce independent work about 1506 — not precociously.

Almost immediately Sarto began a long association with the church and convent of Santissima Annunziata, for which he executed frescoes in 1509–14 (in the Chiostro dei Voti) and 1525 (in the Chiostro Grande), and he moved to a workshop near it in or about 1511. There, for five or six years, he shared the experiences and sometimes commissions of a major sculptor, Jacopo Sansovino, which led him to an increasingly and, in the end, exceptionally solidly structured style. These were the years in which Il Rosso and Pontormo were his pupils, and it may fairly be said that about 1513–14 the leadership in Florentine painting passed from the workshop of Fra Bartolommeo to that of Sarto.

In 1517 or 1518 Sarto married Lucrezia del Fede, a widow whom he had, according to her testimony, used as a model for several years. She brought him property and a useful dowry. In 1518 he was summoned by the king of France, Francis I, to Fontainebleau, where he was preceded by a reputation based upon pictures made for export. It is unlikely that he found the life of a court artist congenial, and he remained for a year or less without beginning any major commission. Soon after his return, his connections with the Medici family (powerful since their return to Florence from exile in 1512) led to the most significant contract of his career—for part of the decoration of the Villa Medici at Poggio a Caiano, near Florence. The patron was in fact the pope, Leo X, whom Sarto almost certainly visited in Rome in 1519–20; but the project, the only one that ever offered Florentine artists the scope that Raphael had in the Vatican Palace, collapsed when the pope died in December 1521. Sarto's fresco *Tribute to Caesar* is a fragment now incorporated into a much later decorational scheme.

In 1520 Sarto began to build himself a house in Florence, which was later inhabited and modified by several other painters; it was a substantial property without being a palace. By 1523 he had a manservant as well as apprentices. Throughout his life he was content to work, when it suited him, for nominal fees, for no remuneration at all, or for only part of a fee offered to him, probably because he was in comfortable circumstances. He would paint for a carpenter or a king. A plague in 1523–24 drove Sarto and his wife to seek security in the Mugello, a valley north of Florence, but the interruption was brief. After the expulsion of the Medici, once again, in 1527, he worked for the republican government of Florence. His *Sacrifice of Isaac*, intended as a political present to Francis I, was painted in this period. After the siege of Florence by imperial and papal forces, he succumbed to a new wave of plague and died in his house. Sources differ on the exact date of Sarto's death, but documents show that he was buried in Santissima Annunziata on Sept. 29, 1530.

Andrea del Sarto's most striking monument is the grisaille (gray monochrome) series of frescoes on the life of St. John the Baptist in the Chiostro dello Scalzo in Florence. Begun about 1511, the work was not completed until 1526, and almost all of it was painted by his own hand, so that it reads like an artistic autobiography covering the greater part of his career. His portraits of his wife, Lucrezia (*c.* 1513–14 and *c.* 1522), can be supplemented by many others disguised as Madonnas (e.g., the celebrated *Madonna of the Harpies*), just as his self-portraits in the Uffizi and in the National Gallery of Scotland at Edinburgh (both *c.* 1528) can possibly be extended by several others, more or less hidden in his paintings from 1511 onward. A badly damaged pair of circular portraits of Andrea and Lucrezia at the Art Institute of Chicago appear to be signed (completed about 1530).

Sarto's style is marked throughout his career by an interest in effects of colour and atmosphere and by sophisticated informality and natural expression of emotion. In his early works such as the *Marriage of St. Catherine*, the search for the expression of animation and emotion led to an ecstatic and nonidealistic style that proved immensely attractive to a younger generation of painters. Restraint increasing with maturity did not inhibit the achievement of such passionate later works as the *Pietà* (*c.* 1520), but the mood is always intimate and never rhetorical. In the 1520s his style, as a result of the influence of Michelangelo or of artistic events in Rome, became perceptibly more ideal and more polished and approximates what may properly be called a grand manner in the last of the Scalzo frescoes, the *Birth of the Baptist* (1526).

From first to last, Sarto's integrity as a craftsman, his sheer professionalism, is impressively consistent. It is characteristic of him that he refused to have his works engraved. His real quality is also vividly revealed in his drawings. Among his pupils and followers were most of the significant Florentine painters of the first half of the 16th century—Rosso Fiorentino, Pontormo, Francesco Salviati, and Giorgio Vasari, for example—and it is largely through his example that the tradition of Florentine art

Madonna of the Harpies, *tempera on wood by Andrea del Sarto, 1517; in the Uffizi Gallery, Florence.* SCALA/Art Resource, New York

was transmitted through to the end of the Renaissance and was able to embrace the stylistic innovations made about 1500 by Leonardo da Vinci and Michelangelo.

DOSSO DOSSI

(b. c. 1486, Tramuschio, Mirandola [Italy]—d. 1542, Ferrara, Duchy of Ferrara [Italy])

The late Italian Renaissance painter Dosso Dossi, born Giovanni Francesco di Niccolò di Luteri, was the leader of the Ferrarese school in the 16th century. Very little is known about his early life, and his artistic influences and training have long been open to speculation. His byname comes from the name of the family estate near his place of birth.

Dosso is first recorded in 1512, in Mantua, where he was commissioned to do a large painting for the palazzo of San Sebastiano. By that time he must have been in Venice and absorbed the art of Giorgione, whose style dominates Dosso's *Nymph and Satyr*. He may also have seen some of the early works of Titian. His style was founded on the romantic approach to landscape, which reached its highest expression in Giorgione's *Tempest*, but Dosso also added something of Titian's richness and a personal quality of fantasy, which reflects his knowledge of the works of the Ferrarese painters Cosmè Tura, Francesco del Cossa, and Ercole de' Roberti. He worked in Florence in 1517 and must have come once more under the influence of Titian, whose early mythologies were painted for Dosso's own patron Alfonso I of Ferrara. In service to Alfonso, Dosso visited Venice and Mantua (1516–19). In addition to work for his patron, he was commissioned to paint *Virgin and Child in Glory* for the Modena Cathedral (1518–21).

Although the event is not supported by documentary evidence, it is probable that Dosso traveled to Rome about

1520 with his brother Battista, who was also a painter. In Rome Dosso became acquainted with the works of Michelangelo, Giulio Romano, and Raphael, whose late style greatly influenced him. In Dosso's later works there is an unearthly light falling on melancholy figures arranged in a romantic dreamland, as can be seen in *Mythological Allegory* (*c.* 1529–32). Dosso was the friend of the great Ferrarese poet Ludovico Ariosto, who celebrated him in *Orlando Furioso* as one of the nine great living painters. Dosso's most famous work, *The Sorceress Circe* (*c.* 1530), has been seen as almost an illustration to Ariosto. After about 1530, Dosso frequently collaborated with his brother Battista, so it is difficult to know which painter is responsible for which elements of their joint work. Together they worked in Pesaro, Trento, and Ferrara.

ALONSO BERRUGUETE

(b. *c.* 1488, Paredes de Nava, Castile [now in Palencia, Spain]—d. 1561, Toledo, Castile)

The most important Spanish sculptor of the Renaissance was Alonso Berruguete, known for his intensely emotional Mannerist sculptures of figures portrayed in spiritual torment or in transports of religious ecstasy. After studying under his father, the painter Pedro Berruguete, Alonso went to Italy (*c.* 1504/08). Most of his sojourn was spent in Florence and Rome, where he was influenced by the works of Michelangelo and such examples of Hellenistic sculpture in the Vatican collections as the *Laocoön*. Berruguete's painting of Salome suggests that his Italian paintings were in the early Mannerist style of Jacopo da Pontormo and Rosso Fiorentino.

Berruguete returned to Spain in about 1517, and in 1518 he was made court painter to Charles V and settled at Valladolid. Because he did not follow the emperor to

Germany in 1520, however, he received no royal commissions for paintings. Berruguete turned, therefore, to sculpture and architecture, and in the period 1518–21 executed sculpture for the tomb of Juan Selvagio in the church of Santa Engracia at Zaragossa, carved the relief of the *Resurrection* in the cathedral of Valencia (*c.* 1517), and submitted plans in 1521 for the Capilla Real (Royal Chapel) in Granada, which, not meeting with official approval, were never realized. Among his major sculpture commissions of the Valladolid period were the retables, or altarpieces, for the monastery of La Mejorada at Olmedo (1526), for San Benito at Valladolid (1527–32), for the Colegio de los Irlandeses at Salamanca (1529–32), and for the Church of Santiago at Valladolid (1537).

In 1539 the great Spanish humanist and art patron Juan Pardo Cardinal Tavera asked Berruguete to Toledo to execute the choir stalls of the Toledo Cathedral (1539–43), as well as the alabaster *Transfiguration* at the west end of the choir (1543–48). These carvings are somewhat more moderate and Classical in feeling than his earlier works. At the time of his death Berruguete was working on the tomb for Cardinal Tavera (1552–61) in the Hospital de San Juan Bautista at Toledo. Berruguete's use of a rather rich and extravagant but delicate ornamentation in his church decorations is typical of Spain's Plateresque style.

TITIAN

(b. 1488/90, Pieve di Cadore, Republic of Venice [Italy] — d. Aug. 27, 1576, Venice)

Titian was the greatest Italian Renaissance painter of the Venetian school. He was recognized early in his own lifetime as a supremely great painter, and his reputation has in the intervening centuries never suffered a decline. In 1590 the art theorist Giovanni Lomazzo

Self Portrait, *oil on canvas by Titian, 1565–67; in the Prado, Madrid.* Alinari/Art Resource, New York

declared him "the sun amidst small stars not only among the Italians but all the painters of the world."

The universality of Titian's genius is not questioned today, for he was surpassingly great in all aspects of the painter's art. In his portraits he searched and penetrated human character and recorded it in canvases of pictorial brilliance. His religious compositions cover the full range of emotion from the charm of his youthful Madonnas to the tragic depths of the late *Crucifixion* and the *Entombment*. In his mythological pictures he captured the gaiety and abandon of the pagan world of antiquity, and in his paintings of the nude Venus (*Venus and Adonis*) and the Danae (*Danae with Nursemaid*) he set a standard for physical beauty and often sumptuous eroticism that has never been surpassed. Other great masters—Rubens and Nicolas Poussin, for example—paid him the compliment of imitation.

EARLY LIFE AND WORKS

The traditional date of Titian's birth was long given as 1477, but today most critics favour the later date of 1488/90. Titian was born Tiziano Vicelli, the son of a modest official, Gregorio di Conte dei Vecelli (or Vicellio), and his wife, Lucia, in the small Alpine village of Pieve di Cadore, straight north of Venice. At the age of nine he set out for Venice with his brother, Francesco, to live there with an uncle and to become an apprentice to Sebastiano Zuccato, a master of mosaics. The boy soon passed to the workshop of the Bellini, where his true teacher became Giovanni Bellini, the greatest Venetian painter of the day.

Titian's early works are richly evident of his schooling and also of his association as a young man with another follower of the elderly Giovanni Bellini, namely, Giorgione

Venus and Adonis, *oil on canvas by Titian, c. 1560; in the National Gallery of Art, Washington, D.C.* Courtesy of the National Gallery of Art, Washington, D.C., Widener Collection

of Castelfranco (1477–1510). Their collaboration in 1508 on the frescoes of the *Fondaco dei Tedeschi* (the German Exchange) is the point of departure for Titian's career, and it explains why it is difficult to distinguish between the two artists in the early years of the 16th century. Only ruined outlines of the frescoes survive, the *Allegory of Justice* being the chief scene assigned to Titian. The etchings (1760) of the frescoes by Antonio Maria Zanetti, already in a much faded condition, give a better notion of the idealism and the sense of physical beauty that characterize both artists' work.

It is certain that Titian's first independent commission was for the frescoes of three miracles of St. Anthony of

Padua. The finest in composition is the *Miracle of the Speaking Infant*; another, the *Miracle of the Irascible Son*, has a very beautiful landscape background that demonstrates how similar in topography and mood were Titian's and Giorgione's works at this time. In fact, after Giorgione's death in 1510, Titian assumed the task of adding the landscape background to Giorgione's unfinished *Sleeping Venus*, a fact recorded by a contemporary writer, Marcantonio Michiel. Still Giorgionesque is the somewhat more lush setting of Titian's *Baptism of Christ* (*c.* 1515), in which the donor, Giovanni Ram, appears at the lower right.

The authorship of individual portraits is the most difficult of all to establish, but the *Gentleman in Blue* (so-called *Ariosto*) is certainly Titian's because it is signed with the initials T.V. (Tiziano Vecelli). The volume and the interest in texture in the quilted sleeve seem to identify Titian's own style. On the other hand, *The Concert* has been one of the most debated portraits, because since the 17th century it was thought to be most typical of Giorgione. The pronounced psychological content as well as the notable clarity of modelling in the central figure led 20th-century critics to favour Titian. Technique and the clear intelligence of the young Venetian aristocrat in the *Young Man with Cap and Gloves* has led modern critics to attribute this and similar portraits to Titian.

The earliest compositions on mythological or allegorical themes show the young artist still under the spell of Giorgione in his creation of a poetic Arcadian world where nothing commonplace or sordid exists. The inspiration lies in the idyllic world of the love lyrics of the 16th-century Italian poets Jacopo Sannazzaro and Pietro Bembo. *The Three Ages of Man*, where the erotic relationship of the young couple is discreetly muted and a mood of tenderness and sadness prevails, is one of the most exquisite of these. The contemporary *Sacred and Profane Love* is likewise set in a landscape of extraordinary beauty, but here the allegory is less easily understood. The most generally accepted interpretation holds that the two women are the twin Venuses, according to Neoplatonic theory and symbolism. The terrestrial Venus, on the left, stands for the generative forces of nature, both physical and intellectual, while the nude Venus, on the right, represents eternal and divine love. Essentially an ideally beautiful young woman rather than a cruel biblical antiheroine is the lovely *Salome*.

MATURE LIFE AND WORKS

Sometime in the early 1520s Titian brought to his house in Venice a young woman from Cadore whose name was Cecilia. Two sons were born in 1524 and 1525, first Pomponio, who became a priest, and second Orazio, later a painter and Titian's chief assistant. During Cecilia's grave illness in 1525, Titian married her. She recovered and later gave birth to two daughters, Lavinia (born 1529/30) and another who died in infancy. Cecilia died in 1530, and the artist never remarried.

Titian's fame had spread abroad, and Alfonso I d'Este sought him as one of the chief masters in a cycle of mythological compositions for his newly rebuilt rooms called the Alabaster Chambers in the castle at Ferrara. Three of the canvases Titian produced for this purpose are the *Worship of Venus*, *The Bacchanal of the Andrians*, and, one of the most spectacular, the *Bacchus and Ariadne*. The gaiety of mood, the spirit of pagan abandon, and the exquisite sense of humour in this interpretation of an idyllic world of antiquity make it one of the miracles of Renaissance art. Warmth and richness of colour help to balance the intentionally asymmetrical grouping of the figures, placed in richly verdant landscape that is also an integral part of the design. At this time Titian partially repainted

The Bacchanal of the Andrians, *oil on canvas by Titian, c. 1523–26; in the Prado, Madrid.* Courtesy of Archivo Mas, Barcelona

the background of Giovanni Bellini's *Feast of the Gods*, so that the picture would better fit the series in the same room at Ferrara.

The standard for the reclining nude female obliquely placed in the picture space had been established by Giorgione in the *Sleeping Venus*. In Titian's *Venus of Urbino* the ideal rendering of the body and the position remain virtually unchanged, except that the goddess is awake and reclines upon a couch within the spacious room of a palace. For sheer beauty of form these two works were never surpassed. Despite the inherent eroticism of the subject, Titian managed it with restraint and good taste. Variations on the theme recur throughout his career.

Among the religious paintings Titian produced between 1516 and 1538 is one of his most revolutionary masterpieces, the *Assumption* (1516–18). This large and at the same time monumental composition occupies the high altar of St. Maria dei Frari in Venice, a position that fully justifies the spectacular nature of the Virgin's triumph as she ascends heavenward, accompanied by a large semi-circular array of angels, while the startled Apostles gesticulate in astonishment at the miracle. When the painting was unveiled it was quickly recognized as the work of a great genius.

The posture of the Madonna in the *Assumption* and the composition of Titian's *Madonna and Child with SS. Francis and Alvise and Alvise Gozzi as Donor* reveal the influence of Titian's contemporary Raphael; and the pose of St. Sebastian in the Resurrection Altarpiece, the influence of Michelangelo. These influences, however, are of secondary importance since the landscapes, the physical types, and the colour are totally Titian's own.

In the *Pesaro Madonna* (1519–26) Titian created a new type of composition, in which the Madonna and Saints with the male members of the Pesaro family are placed within a monumental columnar portico of a church. The picture is flooded with sunlight and shadows. This work established a formula that was widely followed by later Venetian Renaissance painters and served as an inspiration for some Baroque masters, including Rubens and Van Dyck.

Such a quantity of masterpieces by Titian followed that only a few can be mentioned. The poetic charm of the artist's pictures with landscape continues in the *Madonna and Child with St. Catherine and a Rabbit* and the *Madonna and Child with SS. John the Baptist and Catherine of Alexandria* (c. 1530). The *Entombment* is his first tragic masterpiece, where in a twilight setting the irrevocable finality of death and the despair of Christ's followers are memorably evoked. The stately *Presentation of the Virgin in the Temple*, a very large canvas, reflects the splendour of Venetian Renaissance society in the great architectural setting, partly in the latest style of the contemporary architects Serlio and Jacopo Sansovino. The pageantry of the scene also belongs to well-established tradition in Venetian art, but the organization, with its emphasis on verticals and horizontals, constitutes Titian's interpretation of the High Renaissance style.

One of Titian's great triumphs came when he answered the call to Bologna in 1530 at the time of Charles V's coronation as Holy Roman emperor. In 1531, in keeping with his social state, he moved to a Venetian palace known as the Casa Grande. Titian returned to Bologna to portray Charles V again on the occasion of the second meeting of Charles V and Pope Clement VII in the winter of 1532–33. The portrait of *Charles V in Armour* (1530) and another painted in January 1533 are lost, while only a less important work, *Charles V with Hound* (1532–33), a copy of a portrait by Jakob Seisenegger, survives. Charles was so pleased with Titian's work that in May 1533 he bestowed upon the artist the most extraordinary honour of knighthood. Thereafter, the Austrian-Spanish Habsburgs remained Titian's most important patrons. Charles attempted to induce Titian to go to Spain in 1534 to prepare a portrait of the empress, but the artist wisely refrained from undertaking the arduous journey.

Titian's other portraits in the 1520s and 1530s provide a gallery of the leading aristocrats of Italy. A splendid example is *Alfonso d'Avalos, Marques del Vasto* (1533), brilliantly rendered in gleaming armour ornamented with gold. He is accompanied by a small page whose head reaches his waist. Another refulgent portrait in armour is that of *Francesco Maria della Rovere, Duke of Urbino* (1536–38). Emphasis here is given to the duke's military career, not only by the armour but also by the baton in hand and the three others in the background. These works are essentially idealized state portraits, although the heads are very convincingly rendered. Doge Andrea Gritti is to a greater extent a symbol of the office—that is, that of ruler of Venice. The gigantic body in a canvas of large size is sweeping in design and commanding in presence. In later works, too, Titian very effectively managed the scaling of a figure to appear massive by filling the space of the canvas—in his portraits of Pietro Aretino, for example, where he gives his subject a leonine bulkiness. Allowing more space around the figure in *The Young Englishman*, he projected a personality of cultivated elegance and human warmth.

LATE LIFE AND WORKS

The large number of masterpieces in portraiture that Titian continued to create throughout the rest of his life is astounding. Pope Paul III and his grandson, Cardinal Alessandro Farnese, began to compete with Emperor Charles V for Titian's services. At the request of the pope, the painter traveled to Bologna in May 1543 and there prepared the celebrated official portrait of *Pope Paul III Without Cap*. Although a state symbol of the pontiff, the characterization of the crafty statesman, bent with age, comes through.

Titian's next major association with the Farnese came in 1545–46, when he made his only visit to Rome, lodged in the Belvedere Palace of the Vatican. For the first time Titian was able to see the archaeological remains of ancient Rome and also the Renaissance masterpieces of Michelangelo, Raphael, Sebastiano del Piombo, and others. The effect upon the master's own style was relatively slight, understandably enough, since he was already a mature and famous artist.

Of portraits of the Farnese family carried out at this time, few remain. The most celebrated of all is *Paul III and His Grandsons Ottavio and Cardinal Alessandro Farnese* (1546). A painting of a family group, it is most searching in psychological revelation. The feeble pope, then aged 78, appears to turn suddenly in his chair toward Ottavio Farnese, his 22-year-old grandson. Ottavio's overly obsequious bow and his shrewd Machiavellian profile demonstrate Titian's sheer genius in understanding and recording character. As a foil, the great churchman Cardinal Alessandro Farnese stands quietly by. It is no wonder that the portrait is not completely finished, for Paul III must have found it too revealing of the feud within the Farnese family.

Titian's two greatest portraits may well be the Farnese group and *The Vendramin Family*. Here the situation is quite different, for the two heads of the clan kneel in adoration of a reliquary of the Holy Cross, accompanied by seven sons ranging in age from about eight to 20. This portrait group is a tour de force in technical brilliance, richly beautiful in colour, running the emotional gamut from gravity to the innocence of childhood.

On his departure from Rome, in June 1546, Titian's association with the Farnese ended. He received no payment for his pictures, and his hopes for recompense in the form of a benefice for his son Pomponio were never realized. Titian decided to throw in his lot with the Habsburgs. Consenting to undertake the arduous journey to Augsburg, he set out in the depths of winter in January 1548 to cross the Alps to reach the emperor's court. There he carried out one of his most memorable works, the equestrian *Emperor Charles V at Mühlberg*, designed to commemorate the emperor's victory over the Protestants the year before. It is the great state portrait par excellence, intended to show the emperor as a Christian knight, as he wished posterity to remember him. Titian minimized the disfiguring lantern jaw and gave great dignity of bearing to his subject. In sheer mastery of the painter's art, the picture is unsurpassed. The handsome armour, with its gleaming highlights and reflected colour, the rose sash across the chest (a symbol of the Catholic party and the Holy Roman Empire), and the superb sunset landscape all contribute to make it one of the masterpieces of all time.

In December 1548 Charles instructed Titian to proceed to Milan to prepare likenesses of Prince Philip on his first trip outside of Spain. Once again, in the fall of 1550, Charles obliged Titian to travel to Augsburg to remain until May 1551, when he executed one of his greatest state portraits, the *Philip II* in full length. In this portrait of Philip, when still a prince aged 23, Titian achieved another tour de force in sheer beauty of painting, and he treated gently the surly face of the arrogant young man.

Like some of Titian's earlier religious paintings, *Christ Before Pilate* is a work in which Titian managed a large crowd in a processional manner leading to the focal point, the figure of Christ at the left. Here the people are in a state of turmoil as they demand Christ's crucifixion. The composition, however, marks a new phase in Titian's development, far removed from the Renaissance serenity of the *Presentation*, which is not explainable by the subject alone. The compact massing of figures, the oblique position of the steps and the wall at the left, and the general effect of excitement are indicative of the mid-16th-century style known as Mannerism. Titian assimilated and recreated, however, to produce a masterpiece far surpassing anything of which the Mannerist artists were capable.

Titian's religious compositions after his visit to Rome in 1545–46 reveal to some degree his contact with ancient art and the works of Michelangelo. In *Christ Crowned with*

Adam and Eve, *oil on panel by Titian, 1550; in the Prado, Madrid.* SCALA/
Art Resource, New York

Thorns the burly muscular figures are thus explained, as perhaps is the violence of the whole interpretation.

LAST YEARS IN VENICE

On his return to Venice in 1551, Titian remained there for the rest of his life except for summer visits to his native city of Pieve di Cadore. In his last 25 years his productivity was undiminished in quantity and in creative ideas.

Among his portraits is the full-length, dashingly rendered figure of the duke of Atri, who is dressed in red velvet. One of the latest and most dramatic was *Jacopo Strada*, in which this brilliant antiquarian, writer, and art collector is shown presenting a small statue, a Roman copy of an Aphrodite of Praxiteles. Here again, the scope and variety of Titian's invention is astonishing in this new composition, so notable for lively action, psychological perception, and pictorial beauty. Titian's *Self Portrait* presents himself with great dignity, wearing the golden chain of knighthood. The intelligent, tired face is fully rendered, while the costume is sketched in lightly with a free brush. One of the most remarkable late works is the *Triple Portrait Mask* or *Allegory of Prudence*, in which Titian, gray-bearded and wearing a rose-coloured cap, represents old age, his son Orazio, maturity, and presumably Marco Vecelli stands for youth.

The *Trinity* (or *La Gloria*), painted for Charles V's personal devotion, reflects central Italian art to a lesser degree than the earlier *Christ Crowned with Thorns*. The glowing richness of colour predominates in this adoration of the Trinity in which Charles V and his family appear among the elect. The *Martyrdom of St. Lawrence* marks a further step in new compositional directions that culminate in Baroque form in the following century. Although dramatic power invests the main action in the foreground, the night scene with the tall flares and mysterious light suggests the supernatural. In his late religious pictures Titian veils the human forms in shadowy light and so increases the dominant mood of spirituality. One sees this effect in the late *Entombment*, in which muted colour prevails, and in the awesome tragedy of the *Crucifixion*. The *Christ Crowned with Thorns*, employing essentially the same composition as in the earlier version, is now seen through a veil of darkness, and the colour is broken into tiny spots and areas.

All is miraculous in the *Annunciation*, in which Gabriel rushes in and an assembly of angels in glory hovers about the Virgin. Titian's final word and last testament is the *Pietà*, intended for his own burial chapel but left unfinished and completed by Palma il Giovane. The master and his son, Orazio, appear as tiny donors on the small plaque to the right. The monumentality of the composition is established by the great architectural niche flanked by Moses and the Hellespontic sibyl, while the figures are grouped in a long diagonal. The subdued colour befits the all-prevailing sorrow and the immutability of death in this, one of the artist's most profound achievements.

The *Venus and Cupid with an Organist* and the *Venus and the Lute Player* are variations on the theme of the earlier *Venus of Urbino*. The *Venus with a Mirror* is a natural theme for the goddess of love and beauty. Yet Titian is the first artist to show her with a mirror held by Cupid.

A group of several important pictures of mythological themes was created by the master in 1554–62 for Charles's successor, Philip II of Spain, who never bothered to pay Titian for any of them. From the letters of the artist to the king, it is clear that he planned the paintings in pairs, but otherwise they do not constitute a comprehensive iconographic program. The first pair consists of the *Danae with Nursemaid* and the *Venus and Adonis*. The magnificent nude Danae lies upon her couch, knees raised, as Jupiter descends to her in the form of golden rain, and her nursemaid rather amusingly attempts to catch the coins in her apron. This work (of which there exist numerous replicas and copies) is undoubtedly the most voluptuous in Titian's entire repertory. In colour and technique, as well, the *Danae* is one of Titian's greatest achievements. In the *Venus and Adonis*, the goddess, depicted from the back, attempts to restrain her muscular young lover as he is about to depart for the hunt, his dogs straining at the leash. The rose of his costume and the red velvet cushion beneath Venus are foils in the colour composition to the flesh tones and the sunlit landscape.

The *Perseus and Andromeda* was intended to be a companion to *Medea and Jason*, according to Titian's letter, but for some reason the second picture was never carried out. Andromeda, bound to the rock at the left, awaits deliverance as Perseus descends from the sky to slay the monster. Her powerful physique reflects Titian's familiarity with the work of Michelangelo, yet Andromeda's body is more feminine and graceful than any of the Florentine's masculine-looking women.

The Rape of Europa is surely one of the liveliest of Titian's "poesies," as he called them. Taken by surprise, Europa is carried off, arms and legs flying, on the back of Jupiter in the form of a garlanded white bull. A putto (a chubby, naked child, often with wings) on the back of a dolphin appears to be mimicking her, and cupids in the sky follow the merry scene. The sheer wizardry of Titian's technique is nowhere more fully demonstrated than in the misty distances shot through with blues and sunset rose and in the expanse of sea with its iridescent lights.

In *The Rape of Europa* Titian reached the climax of his powers, and by good fortune the picture has survived in almost perfect condition. On the contrary, two other great "poesies" done for Philip II are sadly abused by time and restorers, particularly the *Diana and Callisto*, and less so the *Diana and Actaeon*. The assembly of female nudes in a variety of poses, befitting the action, illustrates two episodes of the Diana legend as told by Ovid in his *Metamorphoses*, books II and III.

The latest of these compositions carried out for Philip II was the *Tarquin and Lucretia*, a dramatic work of great vigour that proves that the aged master had lost none of his creative powers. Rather than Lucretia's suicide because of her rape by Tarquin, which is the more common subject, Titian chose to represent Tarquin's violent attack upon her. Again the rich colour is equally as important as the action. Against the green curtain and white sheets the rose velvet breeches of Tarquin and his green and gold doublet stand out in rich brilliancy.

The great master died of old age in 1576, while a plague was raging in Venice. He was interred in the church of St. Maria dei Frari, where two of his most famous works may still be seen.

LUCAS VAN LEYDEN

(b. 1489/94, Leiden [the Netherlands]—d. before Aug. 8, 1533, Leiden)

The northern Renaissance painter Lucas van Leyden, also called Lucas Huyghenszoon (or Huyghensz), was also one of the greatest engravers of his time. Lucas is more highly regarded today as a printmaker than as a painter.

Lucas was first trained by his father, Huygh Jacobszoon. Later, he entered the workshop of Cornelis Engelbrechtsz, a painter of Leiden. Lucas's paintings, like his prints, reveal his unique approach to subject matter and style. He was extraordinarily precocious. Even such early prints as *Muhammed and the Monk Sergius* (1508) are compositionally clear and direct and show great technical skill. Such engravings as *Susanna and the Elders* (1508), *St. George Liberating the Princess* (c. 1508–09), and his famous series *The Circular Passion* (1510) are notable for their accurate rendering of space and subtly composed landscapes.

In 1510, under the influence of Albrecht Dürer, Lucas produced two masterpieces of engraving, *The Milkmaid* and *Ecce Homo*, the latter much admired by Rembrandt. Their sureness of line and modeling complement their strong, simple compositions and place them among the most forceful engravings of their time. But engravings such as the *Adoration of the Magi* (c. 1512), cluttered with awkward figures and architectural backgrounds, indicate a decline in conceptual power that lasted until about 1519, when he engraved the *Dance of the Magdalene*. This work also has a large number of figures, but they are tranquil and are lucidly composed in small groupings.

In 1521 Lucas met Dürer in Antwerp and again fell under his influence, as can be seen in the *Passion* series of the same year. Lucas may have learned the technique of etching from Dürer, for he produced a few etchings after their meeting. But Lucas himself is thought to have developed the technique of etching on copper, instead of iron, plates. The softness of the copper made it possible to combine etching and line engraving in the same print. His well-known portrait of the emperor Maximilian (1521) is one of the earliest examples of the use of that technique.

Lucas was also among the first to employ aerial perspective in prints. Impressed with the Italianate style of Jan Gossart, he produced engravings, such as *The Poet Virgil*

Suspended in a Basket (1521), characterized by a contrived monumentality. Such late prints, which often show the influence of the Italian engraver Marcantonio Raimondi, are generally considered to be his least successful.

The number of paintings attributed to Lucas has diminished considerably since the late 19th century. Once numbered in the hundreds, it is now believed to be under 25. Such early works as *The Chess Players* (*c.* 1508) reveal a predilection for narrative painting and characterization, which he used often at the expense of compositional unity. That was largely overcome in his *Moses Striking the Rock* (1527), the *Worship of the Golden Calf*, and above all in his masterpiece, the *Last Judgment* (commissioned 1526), in which the composition is unified by the clear, dominant rhythm of the figures and the logically rendered space.

JEAN COUSIN THE ELDER AND JEAN COUSIN THE YOUNGER

Respectively, (b. 1490, Sens, France—d. 1560/61, Paris) and (b. 1522, Sens, France—d. 1594, Paris)

The versatile French painter and engraver Jean Cousin the Elder was a man of many accomplishments. In the arts, he was noteworthy also for his tapestry, stained-glass design, sculpture, and book illustration. His son, Jean Cousin the Younger, was an artist and craftsman, like his father. He, too, achieved fame for his versatility and independent style.

RENAISSANCE ARTIST COUSIN THE ELDER

Early in his career, Cousin worked as an expert geometer in his native village of Sens in 1526 and designed a walled enclosure for the city of Courgenay in 1530. The same year, he repaired a clock and restored a tableau representing the Virgin for the cathedral of Sens. Cousin created several stained-glass windows in the chapels of Saint-Eutrope and Notre-Dame de Lorette, both in the Sens Cathedral.

About 1540 he ventured to Paris, where he soon qualified as a master painter and a citizen. In 1540 he helped design the decorations in honour of the Holy Roman emperor Charles V's entry into Paris. In 1541 he was commissioned to design three models of tapestries commemorating the life of St. Geneviève, and in 1543 he painted eight cartoons of tapestries depicting scenes from the life of St. Mammès. In 1549 Cousin designed a portal in front of the Chatelet to honour the entry of Henry II into Paris. He also painted the life of St. Germain and in 1557 was commissioned to design stained-glass windows for the hospital constructed by the Parisian goldsmiths. His engravings *Annunciation* and *Deposition* probably also date to this period. Despite his lengthy and productive career in Paris, he still managed to contribute work to his native city of Sens.

Few extant works can be definitely attributed to Cousin. The painting *Eva Prima Pandora* (1540s), now in the Louvre, is generally agreed to be his. It shows that he was not influenced by the dominant Fontainebleau school; rather, it reflects the influence of, among others, Leonardo da Vinci and Albrecht Dürer in composition, physiognomy, and lighting. Its style fits neatly into the French Renaissance and also shows the influence of Benvenuto Cellini, whose *Nymph of Fontainebleau* uses similar techniques. The painting *Charity* is also widely considered to be his creation. Cousin's *Traité de perspective* (1560; "Treatise of Perspective") summarizes his knowledge of art, science, and geometry.

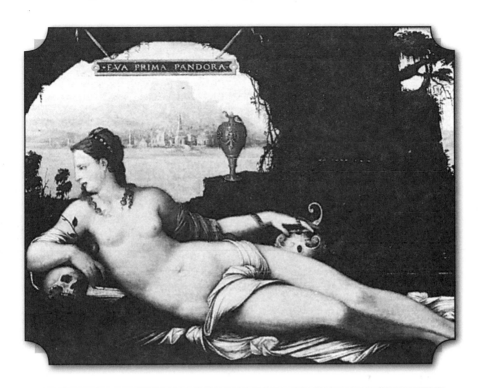

Eva Prima Pandora, *painting on panel by Jean Cousin the Elder, c. 1550; in the Louvre, Paris.* Giraudon/Art Resource, New York

YOUNGER JOINS ELDER IN PARIS

The younger Cousin followed his father to Paris and became a student in his studio, which he took over when his father died in 1560/61. Early in his career in Paris he achieved the title of master painter. Occasionally he left Paris to work in other locations: he journeyed to Sens in 1563 to consult on the preparations for the entrance of Charles IX, and he painted a series of portraits of his family there. Also in 1563 Cousin decorated the window and sculptures of the chapel of the Château de Fleurigny. From 1565 to 1572 he worked on a funeral monument for Admiral

Chabot; there is some controversy surrounding Cousin's exact contribution to the piece, though it is now believed he made the ornamental border.

Cousin's style generally remained faithful to his father's, so it is difficult to distinguish many of their works, which are undated. Jean Cousin's most important surviving work is the *Last Judgment*, the theme of which is the insignificance of human life; the composition suggests both Florentine Mannerism and Flemish influences. The younger Cousin also is noted for his drawing style, best represented in the emblematic style of his *Livre de Fortune* (1568). His other noted works include his engraving *Moses Showing the Serpent to the People*, his stained glass *Judgment of Solomon* (1586), and his illustrations for Ovid's *Metamorphoses*.

GIULIO ROMANO

(b. 1492/99, Rome [Italy]—d. Nov. 1, 1546, Mantua, Duchy of Mantua)

The late Renaissance painter and architect Giulio Romano, born Giulio Pippi, was the principal heir of Raphael and one of the initiators of the Mannerist style.

Giulio was apprenticed to Raphael as a child and had become so important in the workshop that by Raphael's death, in 1520, he was named with G. Penni as one of the master's chief heirs; he also became his principal artistic executor. After Raphael's death, Giulio completed a number of his master's unfinished works, including the *Transfiguration*. In his original work from these years, such as the *Madonna and Saints* (c. 1523) and the *Stoning of St. Stephen* (1523), Giulio developed a highly personal, anti-Classical style of painting.

In 1524 Giulio left Rome for Mantua, where he remained until his death, completely dominating the artistic affairs of that duchy. The most important of all his works is the Palazzo del Te, on the outskirts of Mantua, begun in 1525 or 1526 and built and decorated entirely by him and his pupils. This palace is almost a parody of the serene Classicism of Donato Bramante while retaining the forms of Roman antiquity. The building consists of a square block around a central court with a garden opening off at right angles to the main axis — in itself characteristic of the way in which all the elements are slightly different from what would be expected. The design is particularly famous for its capricious misuse of ancient Greek and Roman ornamental motifs.

The principal rooms of the Palazzo del Te are the Sala di Psiche, with erotic frescoes of the loves of the gods; the Sala dei Cavalli, with life-size portraits of some of the Gonzaga horses; and the fantastic Sala dei Giganti. This showpiece of trompe l'oeil (illusionistic) decoration is painted from floor to ceiling with a continuous scene of the giants attempting to storm Olympus and being repulsed by the gods. On the ceiling, Jupiter hurls his thunderbolts, and the spectator is made to feel that he, like the giants, is crushed by the mountains that topple onto him, writhing in the burning wreckage. Even the fireplace was incorporated into the decoration, and the flames had a part to play. This room was completed by 1534, with much help from Rinaldo Mantovano, Giulio's principal assistant. The colour is very crude; the subject is suited to facile virtuosity and tends to bring out the streak of cruelty and obscenity that runs just below the surface in much of Giulio's painting.

In Mantua itself he did a great deal of work in the huge Reggia dei Gonzaga. The decorations of the Sala di Troia are particularly noteworthy in that they look forward to the illusionistic ceiling decorations of the Baroque; this style was probably inspired by the presence in Mantua of the Camera degli Sposi by Andrea Mantegna. Giulio also built for himself a Mannerist version of the House of Raphael (1544–46) and began the rebuilding of the cathedral (1545 onward).

JACOPO DA PONTORMO

(b. May 24, 1494, Pontormo, near Empoli, Republic of Florence [Italy]—d. before Jan. 2, 1557, Florence)

The Florentine painter Jacopo Carrucci, better known as Jacopo da Pontormo, broke away from High Renaissance Classicism to create a more personal, expressive style that is sometimes classified as early Mannerism.

Pontormo was the son of Bartolommeo Carrucci, a painter. According to the biographer Giorgio Vasari, he was apprenticed to Leonardo da Vinci and afterward to Mariotto Albertinelli and Piero di Cosimo. At age 18 he entered the workshop of Andrea del Sarto, and it is this influence that is most apparent in his early works. In 1518 he completed an altarpiece in the Church of San Michele Visdomini, Florence, that reflects in its agitated—almost neurotic—emotionalism a departure from the balance and tranquillity of the High Renaissance. His painting of *Joseph in Egypt* (c. 1515), one of a series for Pier Francesco Borgherini, suggests that the revolutionary new style appeared even earlier.

Pontormo was primarily a religious painter, but he painted a number of sensitive portraits and in 1521 was employed by the Medici family to decorate their villa at Poggio a Caiano with mythological subjects. In the Passion cycle (1522–25) for the Certosa near Florence (now in poor condition), he borrowed ideas from Albrecht Dürer, whose engravings and woodcuts were circulating in Italy. His mature style is best exemplified in the *Deposition* painted soon after this for Santa Felicità, Florence.

Pontormo became more and more of a recluse in later life. A diary survives from 1554 to 1557, but the important frescoes in San Lorenzo on which he worked during the last decade of his life are now known only from drawings; in these the influence of Michelangelo is apparent. Numerous drawings survive, and paintings are to be found in various galleries in Europe and America, as well as in Florence.

CORREGGIO

(b. August 1494, Correggio, Modena [Italy]—d. March 5, 1534, Correggio)

Correggio was the most important Renaissance painter of the school of Parma, and his late works influenced the style of many Baroque and Rococo artists. His first important works are the convent ceiling of St. Paolo (1519), Parma, depicting allegories on humanist themes, and the frescoes in St. Giovanni Evangelista, Parma (1520–23), and the cathedral of Parma (1526–30). The *Mystic Marriage of St. Catherine* (*c.* 1526) is among the finest of his poetic late oil paintings.

EARLY LIFE AND CAREER

Correggio was born Antonio Allegri. His father was a tradesman living at Correggio, the small city in which Antonio was born and died, and whose name he took as his own. He was not, as it is often alleged, a self-taught artist. His early work refutes the theory, for it shows an educated knowledge of optics, perspective, architecture, sculpture, and anatomy. His initial instruction probably came from his uncle, Lorenzo Allegri, a painter of moderate ability, at Correggio. About 1503 he probably studied in Modena and then went to Mantua, arriving before the death in 1506 of the famed early Renaissance painter Andrea Mantegna. It has traditionally been said that he completed the decoration of Mantegna's family chapel in the church of St. Andrea at Mantua after the artist's death. It seems certain the two round paintings, or tondi, of the *Entombment of Christ* and *Madonna and Saints* are by the young Correggio.

Although his early works are pervaded with his knowledge of Mantegna's art, his artistic temperament was more akin to that of Leonardo da Vinci (1452–1519), who had a commanding influence upon almost all of the Renaissance painters of northern Italy. Where Mantegna uses tightly controlled line to define form, Correggio, like Leonardo, prefers chiaroscuro, or a subtle manipulation of light and shade creating softness of contour and an atmospheric effect. It is also fairly certain that early in his career he visited Rome and came under the influence of the Vatican frescoes of Michelangelo and Raphael.

Leaving Mantua, Correggio's time was divided between Parma and his hometown. His first documented painting, an altarpiece of the *Madonna of St. Francis*, was commissioned for St. Francesco at Correggio in 1514. The best known works of his youth are a group of devotional pictures that became increasingly luscious in colour. They include the *Nativity*, *Adoration of the Kings*, and *Christ Taking Leave of His Mother*.

MATURE WORKS

Correggio's mature style emerged with his first commission for Parma, the ceiling of the abbess' parlour in the convent of St. Paolo, which was probably executed about 1518–19. Although there are echoes in this work of

Mantegna's murals in the Castello at Mantua (1494), it was wholly original in conception. The abbess Giovanna de Piacenza secured for Correggio another important appointment, to decorate the dome of the church of St. Giovanni Evangelista at Parma. The dome fresco of the *Ascension of Christ* (1520–23) was followed by the decoration of the apse of the same church, of which only the segment entitled *Coronation of the Virgin* survives, the remainder having been destroyed in 1587. This work was still in the High Renaissance tradition and owed much to Michelangelo.

The fresco of the *Assumption of the Virgin* in the dome of the cathedral of Parma marks the culmination of Correggio's career as a mural painter. This fresco (a painting in plaster with water-soluble pigments) anticipates the Baroque style of dramatically illusionistic ceiling painting. The entire architectural surface is treated as a single pictorial unit of vast proportions, equating the dome of the church with the vault of heaven. The realistic way the figures in the clouds seem to protrude into the spectators' space is an audacious and astounding use for the time of foreshortening.

The remainder of Correggio's most famous works, the dates of few known with certainty, fall into three groups: the great altarpieces (and a few other large religious compositions); exquisite small works of private devotion; and a handful of mythological subjects of a lyrically sensuous character. Many of the altarpieces became so well known that they acquired nicknames. The *Adoration of the Shepherds* (c. 1530) is called *Night* (*La Notte*), and the *Madonna of St. Jerome* is popularly known as *Day* (*Il Giorno*). The late altarpieces are generally characterized by an intimate and domestic mood sustained between idealized figures. This intimate and homely poetry also distinguishes the small devotional works, such as the *Madonna of the Basket* or *The*

Virgin Adoring the Child Jesus, while the *Mystic Marriage of St. Catherine* is a visual essay in the mid-16th-century aesthetic of ideal feminine beauty.

In these late works Correggio fully exploited the medium of oil painting. He was intrigued with the sensual beauty of paint texture and achieved his most remarkable effects in a series of mythological works, including the *Danae*, *The Rape of Ganymede*, and *Jupiter and Io*. The sensuous character of the subject matter is enhanced by the quality of the paint, which seems to have been lightly breathed onto the canvas. These pictures carry the erotic to the limits it can go without becoming offensive or pornographic.

Although his influence can be detected in later Parmese painting, especially in the Mannerist style of Parmigianino (1503–40), Correggio had many imitators but no direct pupils who deserve mention. His decorative ideas were taken up by the Baroque painters of the 17th century, particularly in the ceiling painting of Giovanni Lanfranco (1582–1647), himself a native of Parma. Correggio became almost a tutelary deity of the French Rococo style, and his great altarpieces were among the works most abundantly copied by the travelling artists of the 18th century during their years of study in Italy.

ROSSO FIORENTINO

(b. March 8, 1494, Florence [Italy]—d. Nov. 14, 1540,
Fontainebleau, France)

The Italian painter and decorator Rosso Fiorentino was an exponent of the expressive style that is often called early, or Florentine, Mannerism. He also is one of the founders of the Fontainebleau school.

Rosso Fiorentino was the byname of Giovanni Battista di Jacopo. He received his early training in the studio of

Andrea del Sarto, alongside his contemporary Jacopo da Pontormo. Scholars have argued that he was influenced as much by Pontormo as by Sarto. The earliest works of these two young painters combined influences from Michelangelo and from northern Gothic engravings in a novel style, which departed from the tenets of High Renaissance art and was characterized by its highly charged emotionalism and departure from Classicism.

From 1513 to 1514, Rosso painted the fresco *Assumption* in the Annunziata, Florence. In 1518 he was commissioned to paint an altarpiece, *Virgin and Child Enthroned with Four Saints*, for a Florentine church. When his patrons saw what they perceived as harsh, devilish depictions of the saints in the picture, they rejected it. After this incident, Rosso left Florence for Volterra, and there he painted *Deposition* (1521). In 1521 or 1522 he returned to Florence, where he probably painted the dramatic *Moses Defending the Daughters of Jethro* (c. 1523).

At the end of 1523 Rosso moved to Rome, where his exposure to Michelangelo's Sistine ceiling, the late art of Raphael, and the work of Parmigianino resulted in a radical realignment of his style. His *Dead Christ with Angels* (c. 1526) exemplifies this new style with its feeling for rarefied beauty and subdued emotion. Fleeing from the sack of the city in 1527, he worked briefly in several central Italian towns. By 1530 Rosso was in Venice but desired to enter the artistic community centred on the court at Fontainebleau; he was fortunate to receive such an invitation from Francis I later that year. In exchange for a home in Paris, a handsome salary, and French citizenship, he went to France and remained in the royal service there until his death.

At court Rosso was responsible for all manner of artistic design, from costumes and scenery to architectural drawings and tableware. His principal surviving work is the decoration of the Galerie François I at the palace of Fontainebleau (c. 1534–37), where, in collaboration with Francesco Primaticcio, he developed an ornamental style whose influence was felt throughout northern Europe. His numerous designs for engravings also exercised a wide influence on the decorative arts both in Italy and in northern Europe.

JAN VAN SCOREL

(b. August 1495, Schoorel, near Alkmaar, Habsburg Netherlands — d. Dec. 6, 1562, Utrecht)

Dutch humanist, architect, engineer, and painter Jan van Scorel established the painting style of the Italian Renaissance in Holland, just as his teacher Jan Gossart did in Brussels.

Scorel (whose name is variously spelled Scoreel, Schorel, Schoreel, Schoorel, Schooreel, Schoorl, Scorelius, and Scorellius) studied with several local artists, but by 1517 he was in Utrecht working with Gossart, who encouraged Scorel to travel. He went to Germany in 1519 and while in Nürnberg visited Albrecht Dürer. He visited in Switzerland and then made his way to Venice. In Venice he was impressed by the work of Giorgione and Jacopo Palma but soon left on a pilgrimage to Jerusalem that took him to Cyprus, Rhodes, and Crete.

Scorel then journeyed to Rome during the brief pontificate of the Utrecht-born pope Adrian VI and was made keeper of the papal collection and inspector of the Belvedere. The pope gave Scorel a studio in the Vatican and sat for a portrait (1523). Scorel was deeply influenced by the work of both Michelangelo and Raphael while in Italy. In 1524, however, he returned to the Netherlands to become the canon of Utrecht, a position that guaranteed him an income for life.

In the large figurative compositions Scorel completed upon his return to Holland, he introduced such Italian elements as nudes, Classical draperies and architecture, and spacious imaginary landscapes. However, the genre he truly excelled at was portraiture; the surviving works are painted in a more conventionally northern style, and show his gift for characterization. His finest portraits were those of *Agatha Schoonhoven* (1529), a *Young Scholar*, and a *Venetian Nobleman*. Group portraits of pilgrims to Jerusalem are in Utrecht and Haarlem, although much of his work based on religious themes, especially the many altarpieces, was destroyed in the 16th century by Protestant iconoclasts. Scorel successfully combined the idealism of Renaissance Italy with the naturalism of northern European art in his painting, and bequeathed his style to succeeding generations of Dutch painters.

HANS HOLBEIN THE YOUNGER

(b. 1497/98, Augsburg, Bishopric of Augsburg [Germany]—d. 1543, London, England)

The German painter, draftsman, and designer Hans Holbein the Younger is renowned for the precise rendering of his drawings and the compelling realism of his portraits, particularly those recording the court of King Henry VIII of England.

Holbein was a member of a family of important artists. His father, Hans Holbein the Elder, and his uncle Sigmund were renowned for their somewhat conservative examples of late Gothic painting in Germany. One of Holbein's brothers, Ambrosius, became a painter as well, but he apparently died about 1519 before reaching maturity as an artist. The Holbein brothers no doubt first studied with their father in Augsburg; they both also began independent work about 1515 in Basel, Switzerland. It should be noted that this chronology places Holbein firmly in the second generation of 16th-century German artists. Albrecht Dürer, Matthias Grünewald, and Lucas Cranach the Elder all were born between 1470 and 1480 and were producing their mature masterpieces by the time Holbein was just beginning his career. Holbein is, in fact, the only truly outstanding German artist of his generation.

Holbein's work in Basel during the decade of 1515–25 was extremely varied, if also sometimes derivative. Trips to northern Italy (c. 1517) and France (1524) certainly affected the development of his religious subjects and portraiture, respectively. Holbein entered the painters' corporation in 1519, married a tanner's widow, and became a burgher of Basel in 1520. By 1521 he was executing important mural decorations in the Great Council Chamber of Basel's town hall.

Holbein was associated early on with the Basel publishers and their humanist circle of acquaintances. There he found portrait commissions such as that of the humanist scholar Bonifacius Amerbach (1519). In this and other early portraits, Holbein showed himself to be a master of the current German portrait idiom, using robust characterization and accessories, strong gaze, and dramatic silhouette.

In Basel, Holbein was also active in designing woodcuts for title pages and book illustrations. The artist's most famous work in this area, a series of 41 scenes illustrating the medieval allegorical concept of the *Dance of Death*, was designed by him and cut by another artist as early as about 1523 to 1526 but was not published until 1538. Its scenes display an immaculate sense of order, packing much information about the lifestyles and habits of Death's victims into a very small format. In portraiture, too, Holbein's minute sense of observation was soon evident. His first major portrait of Desiderius Erasmus (1523) portrays the

Dutch humanist scholar as physically withdrawn from the world, sitting at his desk engaged in his voluminous European correspondence; his hands are as sensitively rendered as his carefully controlled profile.

Protestantism, which had been introduced into Basel as early as 1522, grew considerably in strength and importance there during the ensuing four years. By 1526 severe iconoclastic riots and strict censorship of the press swept over the city. In the face of what, for the moment at least, amounted to a freezing of the arts, Holbein left Basel late in 1526, with a letter of introduction from Erasmus, to travel by way of the Netherlands to England.

Though only about 28 years old, he would achieve remarkable success in England. His most impressive works of this time were executed for the statesman and author Sir Thomas More and included a magnificent single portrait of the humanist (1527). In this image, the painter's close observation extends to the tiny stubble of More's beard, the iridescent glow of his velvet sleeves, and the abstract decorative effects of the gold chain that he wears. Holbein also completed a life-size group portrait of More's family; this work is now lost, though its appearance is preserved in copies and in preparatory drawing. This painting was the first example in northern European art of a large group portrait in which the figures are not shown kneeling—the effect of which is to suggest the individuality of the sitters rather than impiety.

Before Holbein journeyed to England in 1526, he had apparently designed works that were both pro- and anti-Lutheran in character. On returning to Basel in 1528, he was admitted, after some hesitation, to the new—and now official—faith. It would be difficult to interpret this as a very decisive change, for Holbein's most impressive religious works, like his portraits, are brilliant observations of physical reality but seem never to have been inspired by

Christian spirituality. This is evident in both the claustro-phobic, rotting body of the *Dead Christ in the Tomb* (1521) and in the beautifully composed *Family of Burgomaster Meyer Adoring the Virgin* (1526). In this latter painting, Holbein skillfully combined a late medieval German com-positional format with precise Flemish realism and a monumental Italian treatment of form. Holbein appar-ently quite voluntarily gave up almost all religious painting after about 1530.

In Basel from 1528 to 1532, Holbein continued his important work for the town council. He also painted what is perhaps his only psychologically penetrating por-trait, that of his wife and two sons (*c.* 1528). This picture no doubt conveys some of the unhappiness of that abandoned family. In spite of generous offers from Basel, Holbein left his wife and children in that city for a second time, to spend the last 11 years of his life primarily in England.

By 1533 Holbein was already painting court personali-ties, and four years later he officially entered the service of King Henry VIII of England. It is estimated that dur-ing the last 10 years of his life Holbein executed approximately 150 portraits, life-size and miniature, of royalty and nobility alike. These portraits ranged from a magnificent series depicting German merchants who were working in London to a double portrait of the French ambassadors to Henry VIII's court (1533) to por-traits of the king himself (1536) and his wives Jane Seymour (1536) and Anne of Cleves (1539). In these and other examples, the artist revealed his fascination with plant, animal, and decorative accessories. Holbein's prelimi-nary drawings of his sitters contain detailed notations concerning jewelry and other costume decorations as well. Sometimes such objects point to specific events or concerns in the sitter's life, or they act as attributes refer-ring to a sitter's occupation or character. The relation

Anne of Cleves, *portrait by Hans Holbein the Younger, 1539; in the Louvre, Paris.* © Giraudon/Art Resource, New York

between accessories and face is a charged and stimulating one that avoids simple correspondence.

In an analogous fashion, Holbein's mature portraits present an intriguing play between surface and depth. The sitter's outlines and position within the frame are carefully calculated, while inscriptions applied on the surface in gold leaf lock the sitter's head into place. Juxtaposed with this finely tuned two-dimensional design are illusionistic miracles of velvet, fur, feathers, needlework, and leather. Holbein acted not only as a portraitist but also as a fashion designer for the court. The artist made designs for all the state robes of the king; he left, in addition, more than 250 delicate drawings for everything from buttons and buckles to pageant weapons, horse outfittings, and bookbindings for the royal household. This choice of work indicates Holbein's Mannerist concentration on surface texture and detail of design, a concern that in some ways precluded the incorporation of great psychological depth in his portraits.

The fact that Holbein's portraits do not reveal the character or spiritual inclinations of his sitters is perfectly paralleled by knowledge of the artist's life. His biography is basically a recounting of disparate facts; about his personality practically nothing is known. Not one note or letter from his own hand survives. Other men's opinions of him are often equally inscrutable. Erasmus, one of Holbein's most renowned sitters, praised and recommended him on one occasion but scorned the artist as opportunistic at another time. Indeed, Henry VIII, who sent Holbein to the Continent to help select a bride by providing a dependable portrait for his scrutiny, was perhaps the only person who had absolute confidence in Holbein.

The artist's detachment and his refusal to submit to an authority that might inhibit his own creative (but very worldly) powers enabled him to produce paintings whose beauty and brilliance have never been questioned. Had he been a more devout Christian or more subject to the turmoil of his times, his artistic achievement might have been quite different. In recent times the lack of spiritual involvement in his work has been consistently noted, especially inasmuch as the 16th century was a time when few artists managed to remain above the religious conflict sweeping Europe. Thus, the effect of Holbein's art has often been felt to be more artistic and external than expressionistic or emotional. Only in that sense, however, is his achievement finally limited.

Holbein died in a London plague epidemic in 1543.

PARIS BORDONE

(b. *c.* 1500, Treviso, Republic of Venice [Italy] — d. Jan. 19, 1571, Venice)

Paris Paschalinus Bordone (Bordon) was a Venetian painter of religious, mythological, and anecdotal subjects, best known for his striking sexualized paintings of women. Bordone probably became a pupil of Titian about 1516 but remained in his workshop for under two years. There is evidence of tension between the two because Bordone was able to imitate his master's style so well. In 1523, when Bordone was offered his first commission to paint an altarpiece for a Venetian church, Titian took the work for himself.

Despite this rift, Bordone spent most of his working life in Venice, though he visited France to work temporarily at the court of Francis I in Fontainebleau in 1538. It was at court that he created many of his paintings of women. He is also said to have visited Augsburg and worked for the Fugger family sometime in the 1540s. Many of his pictures cannot be dated with any certainty. It is also difficult to ascertain whether he was influenced by working with other contemporary artists or merely by viewing prints of their work.

Bordone painted many scenes of the Madonna and saints seated in a landscape (a genre known as *sacra conversazione*), along with other religious subjects such as *Christ Among the Doctors*. His finest historical painting is *Fisherman Consigning a Ring to the Doge* (1534–35), and he first gained public attention after he won the competition to create it. The painting is characterized by typically bright colours, heavy Titianesque figures, and complex architectural motifs derived from the work of Sebastiano Serlio. Bordone's style gradually became more Mannerist, with warmer colours, tightly curled draperies, and figures in oddly tilted poses occupying the extreme foreground against a distant landscape. Though he continued to paint images of the Holy Family in outdoor settings, late in his career he also painted a series of groups of statuesque blonde female figures. Among these erotic paintings are *Diana with Two Nymphs* and *Venus with Flora*. Bordone worked from his studio in Venice after 1560, although many of his important commissions came from Treviso. He also painted portraits throughout his career.

BENVENUTO CELLINI

(b. Nov. 1, 1500, Florence [Italy]—d. Feb. 13, 1571, Florence)

The Florentine sculptor, goldsmith, and writer Benvenuto Cellini was one of the most important Mannerist artists. Because of the lively account of his life and artistic period revealed in his autobiography, Cellini is also one of the most picturesque figures of the Renaissance.

EARLY CAREER

Cellini, resisting the efforts of his father to train him as a musician, was apprenticed as a metalworker in the studio of the Florentine goldsmith Andrea di Sandro Marcone.

Saltcellar of Francis I, encrusted enamel and gold, by Benvenuto Cellini, 1540; in the Kunsthistorisches Museum, Vienna. Courtesy of the Kunsthistorisches Museum, Vienna

Banished to Siena as a result of a brawl in 1516, he returned to Florence during 1517–19 and then moved to Rome. Prosecuted for fighting in Florence in 1523 and condemned to death, he fled again to Rome, where he worked for the bishop of Salamanca, Sigismondo Chigi, and Pope Clement VII. Cellini participated in the defense of Rome in 1527, during which, by his own account, he shot the constable of Bourbon as well as the Prince of Orange.

After the sack of Rome he returned to Florence and in 1528 worked in Mantua, making a seal for Cardinal Gonzaga (Episcopal Archives of the City of Mantua). Moving back to Rome in 1529, he was appointed *maestro delle stampe* ("stamp master") at the papal mint and in 1530–31 executed a celebrated morse (clasp) for Clement VII. Like so many of Cellini's works in precious metals, this was melted down, but its design is recorded in three 18th-century drawings in the British Museum, London. The only survivors of the many works he prepared for the Pope are two medals made in 1534.

Guilty of killing a rival goldsmith, Cellini was absolved by Pope Paul III; but in the following year, having wounded a notary, he fled from Rome and settled in Florence, where he executed a number of coins for Alessandro de' Medici. After a further year in Rome, he paid a brief visit to France, where he was received by Francis I, a portrait medal of whom (1538) is the sole relic of the journey. On his return to Rome in 1537, he was accused of embezzlement and imprisoned. He escaped, was once more imprisoned, and was finally released in 1539 at the insistence of Cardinal d'Este of Ferrara, for whom he executed a seal (c. 1540).

Again invited to France by Francis I, he arrived at Fontainebleau in 1540, carrying with him an unfinished saltcellar, which he completed in gold for the king in 1540. This, Cellini's only fully authenticated work in precious metal, is the supreme example of the Renaissance goldsmith's work. In 1542 Cellini was granted letters of naturalization by the king and in 1544 received a royal commission for 12 silver candlesticks decorated with figures from mythology. Also in 1543–44 he modeled and cast his first large-scale work, a large bronze lunette of the Nymph of Fontainebleau for the entrance to the palace. For a projected fountain at Fontainebleau he prepared a model in 1543 for a colossal figure of Mars (lost).

LATER YEARS

In 1545 Cellini left Paris precipitately and returned to Florence, where he was welcomed by Cosimo de' Medici and entrusted with the commissions for his best known sculpture, the bronze *Perseus* in Florence's Loggia dei Lanzi, where it still stands, and for a colossal bust of the Grand Duke of Tuscany (Bargello, Florence). Fleeing to Venice in 1546 to escape charges of immorality, Cellini completed the bust by 1548. In the same period he restored an antique torso from Palestrina as *Ganymede* (1546–47) and carved his marble figures of *Apollo* and *Hyacinth* (1546) and of *Narcissus* (1546–47); all three works are now in the Bargello in Florence, as is a small relief of a greyhound made as a trial cast for the *Perseus* (1545). A bronze bust of a banker and patron of the arts, Bindo Altoviti (*c.* 1550), was also executed by Cellini in Florence.

After the unveiling of the *Perseus* (1554), he began work on a marble crucifix originally destined for his own tomb in the Florentine church of Santissima Annunziata; this is now in the church of the royal monastery of the Escorial (Spain). The *Escorial Crucifix* (1556) exemplifies the superiority of Cellini's art to the works of his rivals Bartolommeo Ammannati and Baccio Bandinelli. Two designs for the seal of the Academy of Florence date from 1563. His autobiography was begun in 1558 and completed in 1562; and in 1565 he began work on his important treatises dealing with goldsmiths' work and sculpture, the *Trattato dell'oreficeria* and the *Trattato della scultura*.

Cellini's lasting fame is due more to his record of his own life than it is to his work as an artist. First printed in Italy in 1728, Cellini's autobiography was translated into English (1771), German (1796), and French (1822) and, launched on the tide of the Romantic movement, gained immediate popularity. Dictated to a workshop assistant, it is composed in colloquial language with no literary artifice and gives a firsthand account of the writer's experience in the Rome of Clement VII, the France of Francis I, and the Florence of Cosimo de' Medici. Despite its manifest exaggerations and its often boastful tone, it is a human document of surprising frankness and incomparable authenticity, and thanks to it Cellini's character is more intimately known than that of any other figure of his time.

PARMIGIANINO

(b. Jan. 11, 1503, Parma, Duchy of Milan [Italy]—d. Aug. 24, 1540, Casalmaggiore, Cremona)

One of the first artists to develop the elegant and sophisticated version of Mannerist style that became a formative influence on the post-High Renaissance generation was Girolamo Francesco Maria Mazzola (Mazzuoli), better known as Parmigianino.

There is no doubt that Correggio was the strongest single influence on Parmigianino's early development, but Parmigianino probably was never his pupil. The influence is apparent in Parmigianino's first important work, the *Mystic Marriage of St. Catherine* (c. 1521). About 1522–23 he executed two series of frescoes: one series, in two side chapels of St. Giovanni Evangelista, in Parma, was executed contemporaneously with Correggio's great murals on the dome and pendentives of that church, and the other, representing the *Legend of Diana and Actaeon*, was executed on the ceiling of a room in the Rocca Sanvitale at Fontanellato just outside Parma. The scheme of the latter decoration recalls Correggio's work in the Camera di San Paolo in Parma.

After the summer of 1524, Parmigianino moved to Rome, taking with him three specimens of his work to impress the pope, including the famous self-portrait that he had painted on a convex panel from his reflection in a convex mirror. His chief painting done in Rome is the large *Vision of St. Jerome* (1527). Although this work shows the influence of Michelangelo, it was Raphael's ideal

Parmigianino, self-portrait from a convex mirror, oil on convex panel, 1524; in the Kunsthistorisches Museum, Vienna. Courtesy of the Kunsthistorisches Museum, Vienna

beauty of form and feature that influenced his entire oeuvre. While at work on the *Vision of St. Jerome* in 1527, he was interrupted by soldiers of the imperial army taking part in the sack of Rome, and he left for Bologna. There he painted one of his masterpieces, the *Madonna with St. Margaret and Other Saints.*

In 1531 he returned to Parma, where he remained for the rest of his life, the principal works of this last period being the *Madonna of the Long Neck* (1534) and the frescoes on the vault preceding the apse of St. Maria della Steccata. The latter were to have been only part of a much larger scheme of decoration in the church, but Parmigianino was extremely dilatory over their execution, and he was

Madonna of the Long Neck, *oil on wood by Parmigianino, c. 1535; in the Uffizi Gallery, Florence.* SCALA/Art Resource, New York

eventually imprisoned for breaking his contract, while the frescoes were contracted to Giulio Romano and Michelangelo Anselmi.

Parmigianino was one of the most remarkable portrait painters of the century outside Venice. Some of his best portraits are in Naples, in the National Museum and Gallery of Capodimonte, including the *Gian Galeazzo Sanvitale* (1524) and the portrait of a young woman called *Antea* (*c.* 1535–37). The style that he developed was, in its suave attenuations and technical virtuosity, one of the most brilliant and influential manifestations of Mannerism. It was an extreme development of Raphael's late manner and opposed the naturalistic basis inherent in High Renaissance art.

Parmigianino's works are distinguished by ambiguity of spatial composition, by distortion and elongation of the human figure, and by the pursuit of what the art historian Giorgio Vasari called "grace"; that is to say, a rhythmical, sensuous beauty beyond the beauty of nature. This last quality of attenuated elegance is evident not only in Parmigianino's paintings but also in his numerous and sensitive drawings. One of the first Italian artists to practice etching, Parmigianino used the etching needle with the freedom of a pen, usually to reproduce his own drawings, which were in great demand.

IL BRONZINO

(b. Nov. 17, 1503, Florence [Italy] — d. Nov. 23, 1572, Florence)

The Florentine painter known as Il Bronzino created polished and elegant portraits that are outstanding examples of the Mannerist style. Classic embodiments of the courtly ideal under the Medici dukes of the mid-16th century, they influenced European court portraiture for the next century.

Bronzino was born Agnolo (Agniolo) di Cosimo di Mariano Tori. He studied separately under the Florentine painters Raffaellino del Garbo and Jacopo da Pontormo before beginning his career as an artist. His early work was greatly influenced by Pontormo. He adapted his master's eccentric, expressive style (early Mannerism) to create a brilliant, precisely linear style of his own that was also partly influenced by Michelangelo and the late works of Raphael. Between 1523 and 1528, Bronzino and Pontormo collaborated on interior decorations for two Florentine churches. In 1530 Bronzino moved to Pesaro, where he briefly painted frescoes in the Villa Imperiale before returning to Florence in 1532.

From 1539 until his death in 1572, Bronzino served as the court painter to Cosimo I, duke of Florence. He was engaged in a variety of commissions, including decorations for the wedding of the duke to Eleanora of Toledo (1539) as well as a Florentine chapel in her honour (1540–45). Frescoes he painted there include *Moses Striking the Rock*, *The Gathering of Manna*, and *St. John the Evangelist*. He also created mythological paintings such as *The Allegory of Luxury* (also called *Venus, Cupid, Folly, and Time*; c. 1544–45), which reveals his love of complex symbolism, contrived poses, and clear, brilliant colours. By the 1540s he was regarded as one of the premier portrait painters in Florence. His *Eleanor of Toledo with Her Son Giovanni* and *Portrait of a Young Girl with a Prayer Book* (1545) are preeminent examples of Mannerist portraiture: emotionally inexpressive, reserved, and noncommittal yet arrestingly elegant and decorative. Bronzino's great technical proficiency and his stylized rounding of sinuous anatomical forms are also notable. His many other portraits of the royal family include *Cosimo in Armour* (1543), *Giovanni with a Goldfinch* (1545), and *Cosimo at Age Thirty-Six* (1555–56).

Bronzino's last Mannerist painting was *Noli me tangere* (1561). As Italian artists abandoned Mannerism in the 1560s, Bronzino attempted to adjust his characteristic style by adding clarity to his work. This can be seen in his final paintings, including a *Pietà* (*c.* 1569) and *Raising of the Daughter of Jairus* (*c.* 1571–72), an altarpiece.

FRANCESCO PRIMATICCIO

(b. April 30, 1504, Bologna, Emilia [Italy]—d. 1570, Paris, France)

The Italian Mannerist painter, architect, and sculptor Francesco Primaticcio was the leader of the first school of Fontainebleau.

Primaticcio, also called Primadizzi, or Bologna, was first trained as an artist in Bologna, under Innocenzo da Imola and later Bagnacavallo. He also studied with Giulio Romano and assisted him in his work on the decorations of the Palazzo del Te in Mantua. When the French king Francis I invited Romano to assist in the redecoration of the Fontainebleau Palace in 1532, Romano sent Primaticcio in his place, and, once there, Primaticcio became one of the principal artists in France. He would remain an artist at Fontainebleau, where he was known as Le Primatice, for the rest of his life.

In his initial work at Fontainebleau, Primaticcio employed a decorative style that combined stucco work and mural painting. He returned to Rome for a couple of years to purchase artworks for Francis I, and on his return he decorated the Cabinet du Roi with a series of paintings, now lost, that flouted rational perspective in painting and stressed the primacy of the human figure. Primaticcio's stylistic use of exaggerated musculature and active, elongated figures in these works was to exert great influence on French painting for the remainder of the 16th century.

In 1543 Primaticcio completed a number of decorations, most depicting scenes from the life of Alexander the Great, for the bedchamber of the duchesse d'Étampes; all of these works survive. During this period he also completed work on the Galerie d'Ulysse (1541–70) and the Salle de Bal (or Galerie Henri II). The former was completely destroyed under Louis XV, and the latter has been heavily restored. Primaticcio increased his use of foreshortening and illusionistic treatment of subjects in his later work. His design for the ceiling of the chapel of the Hotel de Guise in Paris (1557) was to be the artist's last major work. For the last decade of his life, Primaticcio collaborated with the sculptor Germain Pilon on the tomb of Henry II in the abbey church of St. Denis near Paris. In his decorations Primaticcio was one of the first artists in France to replace religious themes with those of Classical mythology. He subdued the violence of Italian Mannerism, investing it with a quiet and characteristic French elegance.

NICCOLÒ DELL'ABATE

(b. c. 1509, Modena, duchy of Modena [Italy]—d. 1571, Fontainebleau, France)

Niccolò dell'Abate (Nicolò dell'Abbate) was painter of the Bolognese school who, along with others, introduced the post-Renaissance Italian style of painting to France. He helped to inspire the French Classical school of landscape painting.

Abate probably received early training from his father, the stuccoist Giovanni dell'Abate. He began his career in Modena as a student of the sculptor Antonio Begarelli. He was greatly influenced by the Ferrarese school of painting and particularly by Dosso Dossi. Sometime after 1537 he began working in Modena with Alberto Fontana, often painting building facades, including that of the Pratonieri Palace. He also decorated a castle near Modena (*c.* 1540) with large-scale scenes from Virgil's *Aeneid*. In 1546 he worked with Fontana to decorate a building of the Town Hall (Palazzo Pubblico) in Modena. Abate's *Martyrdom of St. Peter and St. Paul* in the church of San Pietro, Modena (1547), probably established his reputation. During his stay in Bologna (1548–52), his style, influenced by his contemporaries Correggio and Parmigianino, matured. His stucco-surface landscapes (*c.* 1550) in the Poggi Palace (now Palazzo dell'Università), which depict scenes from *Life of*

The Story of Aristaeus, *oil painting by Niccolò dell'Abate; in the National Gallery, London.* Courtesy of the trustees of the National Gallery, London; photograph, A.C. Cooper Ltd.

Camilla and again from the *Aeneid*, survive to show his understanding of nature.

In 1552 Abate was called to the court of the king of France, Henry II, at Fontainebleau, and he remained in France for the rest of his life. With Francesco Primaticcio he composed immense murals, most of them later lost. He decorated both the Galerie d'Ulysse (destroyed 1738) and the Galerie Henri II (1552–56). He also painted portraits of the royal family, including *Henry II and Catherine de' Medici* (1553). His easel works, which included an enormous number of lyrical landscapes based upon pagan themes, were burned in 1643 by the Austrian regent, Anna. Among his later paintings executed for Charles IX were a series of landscapes with mythologies that influenced the 17th-century French painters Claude Lorrain and Nicolas Poussin. He also designed a series of tapestries, *Les Mois arabesques*, and some of his designs were adopted by the painted enamel industry of Limoges. His last works are believed to be 16 murals (1571) in which he was assisted by his son, Giulio Camillo. His work in France is recognized as a principal contribution to the first significant, wholly secular movement in French painting, the Fontainebleau style.

DANIELE DA VOLTERRA

(b. 1509, Volterra [Italy]—d. April 4, 1566, Rome)

The Italian Mannerist painter and sculptor Daniele da Volterra is noted for his finely drawn, highly idealized figures done in the style of Michelangelo.

It is believed that Daniele first studied in Siena under the painter Il Sodoma. His fresco *Justice*, completed for the Palazzo dei Priori after 1530, reflects Sodoma's influence. Sometime after 1535 he moved to Rome, where he worked outside the city to decorate a villa for Agostino Cardinal Trivulzio. He might have become a student of Baldassare Peruzzi, the architect who designed the villa; his work mimics Peruzzi's style.

While in Rome he became a pupil and close friend of Michelangelo. The latter's influence is apparent in the exaggerated musculature and strong linear rhythms of the figures in Volterra's fresco frieze (1541) in the Massimi Palace depicting the story of Fabius Maximus. That same year he painted his most famous work, the *Descent from the Cross*, in the Orsini Chapel of the church of Trinità dei Monti in Rome. The dynamically posed, monumental figures in this powerful and agitated composition make it one of the most important works done by the younger generation of Mannerist painters in Rome. Daniele's other major paintings include *Massacre of the Innocents* and *David Killing Goliath*. In the 1540s he also assisted the Italian artist Perino del Vaga on various projects in Rome, including decorating the Sala Regia in the Vatican.

About 1555 Daniele began work on the Ricci Chapel in Rome. With the help of assistants, he created paintings for altarpieces and frescoes and also designed two statues, *St. Peter* and *St. Paul*. The chapel was not completed until 1568, two years after his death. In 1559 Pope Paul IV assigned him the task of painting in draperies to cover the nudity of many of the figures in Michelangelo's *Last Judgment* in the Sistine Chapel. For his performance of this task Daniele earned the nickname Il Braghettone (or Brachettone; "The Breeches Maker"), as well as an undeserved posthumous reputation as a prude. Using Michelangelo's death mask for his model, Daniele made a bronze portrait bust of Michelangelo; it was his last work. The bust is considered to be the finest surviving representation of that great artist.

GIORGIO VASARI

(b. July 30, 1511, Arezzo [Italy] — d. June 27, 1574, Florence)

Giorgio Vasari, himself a Renaissance painter, architect, and writer, is best known for his important biographies of a number of Italian Renaissance artists. When still a child, Vasari was the pupil of Guglielmo de Marcillat, but his decisive training was in Florence, where he enjoyed the friendship and patronage of the Medici family, trained within the circle of Andrea del Sarto, and became a lifelong admirer of Michelangelo.

As an artist Vasari was both studious and prolific. His painting is best represented by the fresco cycles in the Palazzo Vecchio in Florence and by the so-called 100-days fresco, which depicts scenes from the life of Pope Paul III, in the Cancelleria in Rome. Vasari's paintings, often produced with the help of a team of assistants, are in the style of the Tuscan Mannerists and have often been criticized as being facile, superficial, and lacking a sense of colour. Contemporary scholars regard Vasari more highly as an architect than as a painter. His best-known buildings are the Uffizi in Florence, begun in 1560 for Cosimo I de' Medici, and the church, monastery, and palace created for the Cavalieri di San Stefano in Pisa. These designs show the influence of Michelangelo and are outstanding examples of the Tuscan Mannerist style of architecture.

Vasari's fame rests on his massive book *Le Vite de' più eccellenti architetti, pittori, et scultori italiani* ... (1550, 2nd ed., 1568; *Lives of the Most Eminent Painters, Sculptors, and Architects*, 1850–52, trans. of the 2nd ed.), which was dedicated to Cosimo de' Medici. In it Vasari offers his own critical history of Western art through several prefaces and a lengthy series of artist biographies. These discussions present three periods of artistic development: according to Vasari, the excellence of the art of Classical

Self-portrait by Giorgio Vasari, oil on canvas; in the Uffizi Gallery, Florence.
SCALA/Art Resource, New York

antiquity was followed by a decline of quality during the so-called Dark Ages, which was in turn reversed by a renaissance of the arts in Tuscany in the 14th century, initiated by Cimabue and Giotto and culminating in the works of Michelangelo. A second and much-enlarged edition of *Lives*, which added the biographies of a number of artists then living, as well as Vasari's own autobiography, is now much better known than the first edition and has been widely translated.

Vasari's writing style in the *Lives* is anecdotal and eminently readable. When facts were scarce, however, he did not hesitate to fill in the gaps with information of questionable veracity. His bias toward Italian (and more specifically Tuscan) art is also undeniable. Despite these flaws, Vasari's work in *Lives* represents the first grandiose example of modern historiography and has proven to be hugely influential. The canon of Italian Renaissance artists he established in the book endures as the standard to this day. Moreover, the trajectory of art history he presented has formed the conceptual basis for Renaissance scholarship and continues to influence popular perceptions of the history of Western painting.

FRANÇOIS CLOUET

(b. *c.* 1515/20, Tours, France—d. 1572, Paris)

François Clouet was a French painter who immortalized in his portraits the society of the court of the royal house of Valois. The son of Jean Clouet, François was known also under his father's byname, Janet, a circumstance that created a persistent confusion between the works of these two painters. François worked with Jean possibly as early as 1536 and replaced him in 1540 as official painter to Francis I. He continued in this office, serving under Henry II, Francis II, and Charles IX. He directed a

Portrait of Marguerite de Valois, *chalk drawing by François Clouet, c. 1559; in the Musée Condé, Chantilly, France.* Giraudon/Art Resource, New York

large workshop in which miniaturists, enamel designers, and decorators carried out his projects. In addition to making portraits, he painted genre subjects, including nude figures (e.g., *Diane de Poitiers*) and theatrical scenes— the latter attested by an engraving, as well as by a picture entitled *Scene of the Commedia dell'Arte*. He also supervised the decorations for funeral ceremonies and for the triumphal entries of the French kings.

It has been possible to identify his work on the basis of two signed pictures, *Diane de Poitiers* and the *Portrait of Pierre Quthe* (1562), and of another one bearing a 16th-century ascription to him, *Portrait of Charles IX, Full-Length* (probably 1569). The identification of the preparatory drawing for the last picture has enabled experts to attribute 50 portrait drawings and several painted portraits to François.

François Clouet was a typical Renaissance painter, closely related to the humanistic circles and praised by many poets of his day, including Pierre de Ronsard and Joachim du Bellay. As a portrait painter he was less profound than Jean Clouet, although he was able to render a more vivid, fleeting expression of the face. His drawings are characteristic of the French Renaissance with their almost dry precision, elegant stylization, and clear-cut plasticity.

JACOPO BASSANO

(b. *c.* 1517, Bassano del Grappa, Republic of Venice [Italy]—d. Feb. 13, 1592, Bassano del Grappa)

The late Renaissance painter Jacopo Bassano, also called Jacopo da Ponte, is known for his religious paintings, lush landscapes, and scenes of everyday life. The son of a provincial artist, Francesco the Elder, who adopted the name Bassano, he was the outstanding member of a thriving family workshop.

His early works, such as the *Susannah and the Elders* (1534–36) and the *Flight into Egypt* (*c.* 1536), reveal the influence of his master, Bonifacio Veronese (Bonifacio de' Pitati), a minor Venetian painter, as well as the art of Lorenzo Lotto and the atmospheric light of Titian. As Bassano's art matured, his brushstrokes became looser and the forms and masses of his compositions became larger and more lively—a development that resulted in such frescolike canvases as his *Calvary* (*c.* 1538–40). About 1540, he was greatly influenced by the elegance of the Florentine and Roman Mannerists. He especially admired the graceful attenuation of Parmigianino's figures, as can be seen in his *Adoration of the Shepherds*. But the robust modeling, vibrant colour, and thick impasto of his *Rest on the Flight into Egypt* (*c.* 1545) lend such works a vigour his Mannerist models lack.

After 1560 Jacopo painted a large number of works, such as the *Madonna with SS. Roch and Sebastian* and *The Adoration of the Magi*, characterized by an unearthly pale light, colours, and nervous, attenuated figures in affectedly sophisticated poses. Landscape and genre subjects became particularly important about 1565–70, when his first paintings of rural life were produced. One of the finest is his *Pastoral*. These works elaborated the genre and landscape elements that had been incidental in his religious works.

Jacopo's four sons were all painters, and Francesco the Younger (1549–92) and Leandro (1557–1622) were important in the continuity of the workshop; many Bassano paintings are the product of a family collaboration. Francesco the Younger had a predilection for the rural scenes begun by his father, and he developed this aspect of the workshop. He was entrusted with the Venetian branch of the workshop until his death by suicide in 1592. Leandro, who settled in Venice in 1582, was also successful there, receiving a number of commissions for canvases for the Doges' Palace. He is best known now for his portraits in a style based on that of Tintoretto.

TINTORETTO

(b. *c.* 1518, Venice [Italy] — d. May 31, 1594, Venice)

Tintoretto, byname of Jacopo Robusti, was an Italian Mannerist painter of the Venetian school and one of the most important artists of the late Renaissance. His paintings include *Vulcan Surprising Venus and Mars*, the Mannerist *Christ and the Adulteress*, and his masterpiece of 1594, *The Last Supper* of St. Giorgio Maggiore. Increasingly concerned with the drama of light and space, he achieved in his mature work (e.g., *The Law and the Golden Calf, c.* 1562) a luminous, visionary quality.

BACKGROUND AND EARLY YEARS

Little is known of Tintoretto's life. In a will of 1539 he called himself an independent professional man — not a surprising description in view of his imposing and forceful personality. No documents have survived regarding his artistic education. His biographers, among them Carlo Ridolfi, whose book was published in 1648, speak of an apprenticeship with Titian that was broken off because of the master's resentment of the pupil's proud nature and exceptional accomplishment. On the other hand, a contemporary pointed out that Tintoretto's style was formed by studying formal elements of the Tuscan school, especially those of Michelangelo, and pictorial elements derived from Titian.

Most probably, Tintoretto's precocious talent prompted his father to place him in the workshop of some undistinguished painter, but one with a solid artisan tradition so that his son might learn the foundations of his craft. Traces of an absolute style in his youthful works tend to corroborate this hypothesis. But he soon became aware of the variety of approaches tried by painters working between 1530 and 1540 in Venice, already reacting against the style of Giorgione, who was the first to merge forms and to subordinate local colour to its pervading tone.

The early works of Tintoretto were affected by a number of influences. The emigration of Roman artists to Venice in 1527 after the sack of Rome by imperial troops, as well as subsequent contacts with painters from Tuscany and Bologna, induced the painters of the Venetian school to return to greater plasticism, without altering the fundamental chromatic nature of the Venetian tradition. The influence of Michelangelo, the visit of the art historian and biographer Giorgio Vasari to Venice in 1541, and the journeys of Venetian artists to central Italy renewed Venetian painting in depth, giving it means of expression adapted to different types of pictures. In the renewed idiom, form and colour were blended in a synthesis in which light dominated so as to express a richly fantastic and visionary spirit.

Critics have identified a group of youthful works by Tintoretto, above all *Sacre Conversazioni*. One of these, painted in 1540, represents the Virgin with the Child on her knees, facing away from her, and six saints. While the style echoes various elements of the Venetian art of Tintoretto's time, it also shows a definite Michelangelesque influence.

CAREER

Tintoretto's first phase includes a group of 14 octagonal ceiling paintings with mythological themes (originally painted for a Venetian palace), which exhibit singular refinement in perspective and narrative clarity. Among other influences, they recall the fashion of partitioned ceiling paintings imported to Venice by Vasari. This was also the period of Tintoretto's closest collaboration with Andrea Meldolla; together they decorated the Palazzo Zen with frescoes. The fresco technique had an important part in the formation of Tintoretto's idiom, for it suggested to him the quickness of execution that was to become fundamental to his manner of painting. Unfortunately only some 18th-century prints of his frescoes and a few fragments of the numerous frescoed facades that adorned Venice survive.

Tintoretto's drawing exercises were made from nature, from statues, and from small wax models posed in various ways and artificially illuminated, as in tiny stage sets. These methods were suited to the painter's concern with resolving problems of form and light. The indefatigable draftsman acquired a narrative fluency that allowed him to trace with a brisk brushstroke and fanciful inspiration the series of biblical stories, the mythological episodes for the poet Pietro Aretino's house in Venice (1545), and sacred compositions such as *Christ and the Adulteress*, in which figures set in vast spaces in fanciful perspectives are illuminated in a distinctly Mannerist style. Tintoretto returned to an earlier form of composition in his *Last Supper* of St. Marcuola (1547), in which the choice of rough and popular types succeeds in endorsing the scene with a portrayal of ordinary everyday reality struck with wonder by the revelation of the miracle.

A few months later Tintoretto became the centre of attention of artists and literary men with his *S. Marco Freeing the Slave*. A letter from Aretino, full of praise, yet also intended to temper Tintoretto's youthful exuberance, confirmed the fame of the 30-year-old painter. Relations between Tintoretto and Aretino did not come to an end at this point, even though one of Aretino's letters contains hints of dissension. Although Aretino was no longer to write laudatory letters to Tintoretto, he commissioned him to execute family portraits, and after his death, his likeness was to appear in Tintoretto's huge *Crucifixion* of the Scuola Grande di St. Rocco (1565). The painting *S. Marco Freeing the Slave* is so rich in structural elements of post-Michelangelesque Roman art that it is reasonable to assume that Tintoretto had visited Rome. He did not, however, interrupt his artistic experiments. Stories from Genesis, painted for the Scuola della Trinità (1550–53), show a new attention to Titian's manner of painting as well as a palpable awareness of nature. The masterpiece of this phase is undoubtedly *Susanna and the Elders* (1555–56); the light creates Susanna's form in crystalline clarity against a background evoked with a fresh poetic sense.

FAMILY AND FAME

In 1555 Tintoretto, now a famous and sought-after painter, married Faustina Episcopi, who, affectionate and devoted, bore him eight children. At least three of them—Marietta, Domenico, and Marco—learned their father's trade and became his associates. An artist of indefatigable activity and a veritable fury of creativity, Tintoretto spent most of his life in the bosom of his family and in his workshop. But the love of solitude to which his biographer alludes did not prevent the painter from forming friendships with several artistic personalities. This particular period in Tintoretto's career—marked by greater vivacity of colour, by a predilection for a variegated perspective, and by a highly decorative quality—coincided with his growing admiration for the art of Paolo Veronese, who had been working in the Doges' Palace. The assimilation and transformation of the Veronesian elements in Tintoretto's work are discernible in his beautiful ceiling paintings of Bible stories.

The use of a colour that absorbs light yielded new possibilities for suggesting spaces no longer structured by the
pure play of perspective. And in those spaces the painter
introduced crowds in harmonized order with the rest of
the picture, a feature that had until then been missing in
Venetian art. It was at that time that Tintoretto began to
participate in the decoration of the church of the Madonna
dell'Orto and the private chapel of the Contarini family
contained within it, which in 1563 became the final resting
place of the great cardinal Gasparo.

Tintoretto's works for the Madonna dell'Orto, which
occupied him for approximately a decade, also give an idea
of the evolution of the idiomatic elements of his art; the
Presentation of the Virgin in the Temple (1552) was, according
to Vasari, "a highly finished work, and the best executed
and most successful painting that there is in the place"; in
St. Peter's Vision of the Cross and in *The Decapitation of St.
Paul* (c. 1556), the figures stand out dramatically on a space
suffused with a vaporous, unreal light. In the two enormous canvases depicting the Jews worshipping the golden
calf while Moses on Mt. Sinai receives the tables of the law
and a Last Judgment, Tintoretto painted two works of the
highest rank with a great richness of narrative means, with
an awareness of the thematic link between the two scenes
that attests to a knowledge of scripture and of contemporary spiritual movements. The high figurative quality of
the two paintings implies that Tintoretto made a number
of experiments in this decade.

Proof of this is, above all, the dramatic style in which
the scenes are executed, a style that firmly impresses their
romantic pathos on the beholder. Tintoretto's spatial conception has a dynamic character. As a modern critic has
noted, Tintoretto conveys a feeling of an almost precipi-
tate falling forward or of an equally swift rise. The
contrasted movements give the figures a similar instability.

To achieve such effects Tintoretto used formulas that were invariably different: in *The Pool of Bethesda* in the church of St. Rocco (1559) the evangelical episode is realized in a compressed space through which the foreshortened ceiling seems to weigh upon the milling crowd; in *St. George and the Dragon* Tintoretto sets the fable in a landscape of considerable depth, intersected by the white walls of the city. A series of canvases that the philosopher and physician Tommaso Rangone, grand guardian of the Scuola di St. Marco, commissioned from Tintoretto in 1562 contains similar elements.

In May 1564 the councillors of the Scuola Grande di St. Rocco decided to have the Sala dell'Albergo decorated with paintings, in place of the movable decorations used during feast days. St. Rocco (St. Roch) is the protector against plagues; the numerous epidemics of that period had given new impetus to the cult of the saint and caused great riches to flow to the Scuola, which built a splendid centre to assist the poor and the infirm. When Tintoretto presented the Scuola with his oval painting the *Glorification of S. Rocco*, the directors decided to entrust him with the decoration of the Sala. Vasari relates that designs were invited from various prominent artists, including Paolo Veronese, but Tintoretto, who presented his work already installed in the Sala, won hands down over his competitors. Similar episodes are counted by contemporary sources as proof that when it came to his work the painter knew no scruples. He was indeed a man devoured by a passion for painting and not for pecuniary gain, for he committed himself to grandiose undertakings for exceedingly modest remuneration.

The question of who assisted Tintoretto in his dizzying activity is still open; at that time Marietta was only about nine and Domenico four, but it is known that in 1560 Tintoretto's studio began to be visited by young painters, especially from the Netherlands and Germany. In 1565 his immense *Crucifixion* was displayed in the Sala dell'Albergo. Around Christ, in the centre, many figures revolve in a livid light that, muting the picture's colours, invests it with dramatic power. The decoration of the chamber was completed in 1567; it included other scenes of Christ's Passion, remarkable for their thematic innovations.

LATER YEARS

Vasari, who visited Venice in 1566 to bring his *Lives of the Most Eminent Painters, Sculptors, and Architects* up to date, had an opportunity to follow Tintoretto's work in progress. Undoubtedly he had the painter's most recent works in mind when he wrote that Tintoretto was "the most extraordinary brain that the art of painting has produced." For all his fundamental reservations about Tintoretto's style, Vasari sensed his greatness.

In 1576, with renewed zeal, Tintoretto resumed the decoration of the Scuola Grande di St. Rocco. He had finished the huge central panel of the upper hall with *The Erection of the Brazen Serpent* in time for the feast of the saint on August 16 and promised to paint a certain number of canvases, "wishing to demonstrate the great love that I bear for the saint and our venerable school, because of my devotion to the glorious Messer San Rocho." In 1581 all the ceiling paintings (10 ovals and 8 rhomboid chiaroscuro panels; the latter restored in the 18th century) and 10 *teleri* (large narrative paintings on canvas) on the walls were completed. Certainly the fundamental idea goes back to the conception elaborated in the rough illustrations of the *Biblia Pauperum*—i.e., the concordance of the Old and New Testaments.

It seems almost impossible that in the same year the painter should have executed the four mythological allegories for the Doges' Palace, of which the most famous is that of *Ariadne, Bacchus, and Venus*. All are works of great elegance, with an almost academic finishing touch. But the real Tintoretto is certainly to be found in St. Rocco, where he bears witness to his great faith and, like the medieval mosaicists, offers an illustrated Bible to the crowds of the poor who frequented the beneficent institution. His deep but independent faith in the religious myths, unrestricted by any rules of the Counter-Reformation, is apparent as much in the striking sketch of *The Council of Trent*, executed for the Doge Da Ponte, as in the altarpiece of St. Trovaso, executed in 1577 for Milledonne, a participant and historian of the Council, with the seminude women who tempt St. Anthony.

By 1577 Marietta and Domenico, already officers of the painters' guild, could help their father, together with other future artists of the close of the 16th and the beginning of the 17th century. Certainly the presence of collaborators is obvious in two cycles: the eight scenes of the Gonzaga Cycle, with vivid scenes of battles, painted between 1579 and 1580, and the many paintings for the halls of the Scrutinio and of the Maggior Consiglio in the Doges' Palace, which the Republic wanted to adorn with new canvases after the fire of 1577. It was certainly more his wish to finish his immense work in the decoration of St. Rocco than it was his advanced age that induced the painter to leave the canvases of the Doges' Palace largely to his workshop.

In the canvases executed between 1583 and 1587 for the lower hall of the Scuola Grande di St. Rocco, depicting episodes of the life of Mary and Christ, Tintoretto follows a new direction: light in its most lyrical meaning dominates the paintings, dissolving the colour in a flash of diaphanous brushstrokes. Space is multiplied in unlimited successions of perspectives; the scenery at times prevails over the human figure, as in the two great works in the ground floor hall, with the *St. Mary of Egypt* and the *St. Mary Magdalene* immersed in an incandescent hazy atmosphere in which things are animated with a life of their own: an invitation to the contemplative life of the 70-year-old painter, more than ever leaning toward the view of humanity and its destiny offered by the Christian faith. A marvelous model (in the Louvre) of the *Paradise* for the Doges' Palace and *The Last Supper* of St. Giorgio Maggiore, with the incorporeal apparitions of angelic creatures, finished a few months before his death, are proof of Tintoretto's deep spiritual bent. He died in 1594 and was buried in the church of Madonna dell'Orto next to his favourite child, Marietta.

ASSESSMENT

Tintoretto was a painter with a wholly personal, constantly evolving technique and vision. Although it is almost certain that his family was originally from Lucca, Tintoretto (a nickname meaning "little dyer," after his father's profession of silk dyer, or *tintore*) is considered a Venetian painter, not only by birth but because he always lived in Venice and because with his innumerable works he contributed to creating the face of that city. He was not only an exponent of the witness to the life of the city, of the sacred and profane complex pictorial developments of Venetian art, but of the myths of a society that formed a part of the dramatic history of 16th-century Italy.

Tintoretto's art was much discussed and highly appreciated in Venice in the years after his death, above all in the acute evaluations of Marco Boschini, the great 17th-century critic of Venetian painting. Roger de Piles, following in the latter's footsteps, exalted Tintoretto's luministic idiom. But to 18th-century critics, the closer they drew to

19th-century Neoclassical rationality, Tintoretto's art appeared excessive and too remote from its own sensibility. John Ruskin's romantic enthusiasm inaugurated a new attitude toward the art of Tintoretto, and contemporary art historiography has come to recognize in him one of the greatest representatives of that wide-ranging European movement that was Mannerism, interpreted in accordance with the great Venetian tradition.

PIETER BRUEGEL THE ELDER

(b. *c.* 1525, probably Breda, Duchy of Brabant [now in the Netherlands]—d. Sept. 5/9, 1569, Brussels [now in Belgium])

Considered the greatest Flemish painter of the 16th century, Pieter Bruegel the Elder (whose name has been spelled Breugel, Brueghel, and Breughel) is noted for his landscapes and particularly for his vigorous, often witty scenes of peasant life. Since Bruegel signed and dated many of his works, his artistic evolution can be traced from the early landscapes, in which he shows affinity with the Flemish 16th-century landscape tradition, to his last works, which are Italianate. He exerted a strong influence on painting in the Low Countries, and through his sons Jan and Pieter he became the ancestor of a dynasty of painters that survived into the 18th century.

LIFE

There is but little information about his life. According to Carel van Mander's *Het Schilderboeck* (*Book of Painters*), published in Amsterdam in 1604 (35 years after Bruegel's death), Bruegel was apprenticed to Pieter Coecke van Aelst, a leading Antwerp artist who had located in Brussels. The head of a large workshop, Coecke was a sculptor, architect, and designer of tapestry and stained glass who had traveled in Italy and in Turkey. Although Bruegel's earliest surviving works show no stylistic dependence on Coecke's Italianate art, connections with Coecke's compositions can be detected in later years, particularly after 1563, when Bruegel married Coecke's daughter Mayken. In any case, the apprenticeship with Coecke represented an early contact with a humanistic milieu. Through Coecke, Bruegel became linked indirectly to another tradition as well. Coecke's wife, Maria Verhulst Bessemers, was a painter known for her work in watercolour or tempera, a suspension of pigments in egg yolk or a glutinous substance, on linen. The technique was widely practiced in her hometown of Mechelen (Malines) and was later employed by Bruegel.

It is also in the works of Mechelen's artists that allegorical and peasant thematic material first appear. These subjects, unusual in Antwerp, were later treated by Bruegel. In 1551 or 1552, Bruegel set off on the customary northern artist's journey to Italy, probably by way of France. From several extant paintings, drawings, and etchings, it can be deduced that he traveled beyond Naples to Sicily, possibly as far as Palermo, and that in 1553 he lived for some time in Rome, where he worked with a celebrated miniaturist, Giulio Clovio, an artist greatly influenced by Michelangelo and later a patron of the young El Greco. The inventory of Clovio's estate shows that he owned a number of paintings and drawings by Bruegel as well as a miniature done by the two artists in collaboration. It was in Rome, in 1553, that Bruegel produced his earliest signed and dated painting, *Landscape with Christ and the Apostles at the Sea of Tiberias*. The holy figures in this painting were probably done by Maarten de Vos, a painter from Antwerp then working in Italy.

The earliest surviving works, including two drawings with Italian scenery sketched on the southward journey and dated 1552, are landscapes. A number of drawings of Alpine regions, produced between 1553 and 1556, indicate the great impact of the mountain experience on this man from the Low Countries. With the possible exception of a drawing of a mountain valley by Leonardo da Vinci, the landscapes resulting from this journey are almost without parallel in European art for their rendering of the over-powering grandeur of the high mountains. Very few of the drawings were done on the spot, and several were done after Bruegel's return, at an unknown date, to Antwerp. The vast majority are free compositions, combinations of motifs sketched on the journey through the Alps. Some were intended as designs for engravings commissioned by Hiëronymus Cock, an engraver and Antwerp's foremost publisher of prints.

Bruegel was to work for Cock until his last years, but, from 1556 on, he concentrated, surprisingly enough, on satirical, didactic, and moralizing subjects, often in the fantastic or grotesque manner of Hiëronymus Bosch, imitations of whose works were very popular at the time. Other artists were content with a more or less close imitation of Bosch, but Bruegel's inventiveness lifted his designs above mere imitation, and he soon found ways to express his ideas in a much different manner. His early fame rested on prints published by Cock after such designs. But the new subject matter and the interest in the human figure did not lead to the abandonment of landscape. Bruegel, in fact, extended his explorations in this field. Side by side with his mountain compositions, he began to draw the woods of the countryside, turned then to Flemish villages, and, in 1562, to townscapes with the towers and gates of Amsterdam.

The double interest in landscape and in subjects requiring the representation of human figures also informed, often jointly, the paintings that Bruegel produced in increasing number after his return from Italy. All of his paintings, even those in which the landscape appears as the dominant feature, have some narrative content. Conversely, in those that are primarily narrative, the landscape setting often carries part of the meaning. Dated paintings have survived from each year of the period except for 1558 and 1561. Within this decade falls Bruegel's marriage to Mayken Coecke in the Church of Notre-Dame de la Chapelle in Brussels in 1563 and his move to that city, in which Mayken and her mother were living. His residence recently was restored and turned into a Bruegel museum. There is, however, some doubt as to the correctness of the identification.

In Brussels, Bruegel produced his greatest paintings, but only few designs for engravings, for the connection with Hiëronymus Cock may have become less close after Bruegel left Antwerp. Another reason for the concentration on painting may have been his growing success in this field. Among his patrons was Cardinal Antione Perrenot de Granvelle, president of the council of state in the Netherlands, in whose palace in Brussels the sculptor Jacques Jonghelinck had a studio. He and Bruegel had traveled in Italy at the same time, and his brother, a rich Antwerp collector, Niclaes, was Bruegel's greatest patron, having by 1566 acquired 16 of his paintings. Another patron was Abraham Ortelius, who in a memorable obituary called Bruegel the most perfect artist of the century. Most of his paintings were done for collectors.

Bruegel died in 1569 and was buried in Notre-Dame de la Chapelle in Brussels.

ARTISTIC EVOLUTION AND AFFINITIES

In addition to a great many drawings and engravings by Bruegel, 45 authenticated paintings from a much larger output now lost have been preserved. Of this number, about a third is concentrated in the Vienna Kunsthistorisches Museum, reflecting the keen interest of the Habsburg princes in the 16th and 17th centuries in Bruegel's art.

In his earliest surviving works, Bruegel appears as essentially a landscape artist, indebted to, but transcending, the Flemish 16th-century landscape tradition, as well as to Titian and to other Venetian landscape painters. After his return from Italy, he turned to multifigure compositions, representations of crowds of people loosely disposed throughout the picture and usually seen from above. Here, too, antecedents can be found in the art of Hiëronymus Bosch and of other painters closer in time to Bruegel.

In 1564 and 1565, under the spell of Italian art and especially of Raphael, Bruegel reduced the number of figures drastically, the few being larger and placed closely together in a very narrow space. In 1565, however, he turned again to landscape with the celebrated series known as *Labours of the Months*. In the five of these that have survived, he subordinated the figures to the great lines of the landscape. Later on, crowds appear again, disposed in densely concentrated groups.

Bruegel's last works often show a striking affinity with Italian art. The diagonal spatial arrangement of the figures in *Peasant Wedding* recalls Venetian compositions. Though transformed into peasants, the figures in such works as *Peasant and Bird Nester* (1568) have something of the grandeur of Michelangelo. In the very last works, two trends appear; on the one hand, a combined monumentalization and extreme simplification of figures and, on the other hand, an exploration of the expressive quality of the various moods conveyed by landscape. The former trend is evident in his *Hunters in the Snow* (1565), one of his winter paintings. The latter is seen in the radiant, sunny atmosphere of *The Magpie on the Gallows* and in the threatening and sombre character of *The Storm at Sea*, an unfinished work, probably Bruegel's last painting.

He was no less interested in observing the works of man. Noting every detail with almost scientific exactness, he rendered ships with great accuracy in several paintings and in a series of engravings. A most faithful picture of contemporary building operations is shown in the two paintings of *The Tower of Babel* (one 1563, the other undated). The Rotterdam *Tower of Babel* illustrates yet another characteristic of Bruegel's art, an obsessive interest in rendering movement.

It was a problem with which he constantly experimented. In the Rotterdam painting, movement is imparted

The Tower of Babel, *oil painting by Pieter Bruegel the Elder, 1563; in the Kunsthistorisches Museum, Vienna.* Courtesy of the Kunsthistorisches Museum, Vienna

to an inanimate object, the tower seeming to be shown in rotation. Even more strikingly, in *The Magpie on the Gallows*, the gallows apparently take part in the peasants' dance shown next to them. The several paintings of peasant dances are obvious examples, and others, less obvious, are the processional representations in *The Way to Calvary* and in *The Conversion of St. Paul*. The latter work also conveys the sensation of the movement of figures through the constantly changing terrain of mountainous regions. This sensation had appeared first in the early mountain drawings and later, in different form, in *The Flight into Egypt* (1563). Toward the end of his life, Bruegel seems to have become fascinated by the problem of the falling figure. His studies reached their apogee in a rendering of successive stages of falling in *The Parable of the Blind*. The perfect unity of form, content, and expression marks this painting as a high point in European art.

The subject matter of Bruegel's compositions covers an impressively wide range. In addition to the landscapes, his repertoire consists of conventional biblical scenes and parables of Christ, mythological subjects as in *Landscape with the Fall of Icarus* (two versions), and the illustrations of proverbial sayings in *The Netherlands Proverbs* and several other paintings. His allegorical compositions are often of a religious character, as the two engraved series of *The Vices* (1556–57) and *The Virtues* (1559–60), but they included profane social satires as well. The scenes from peasant life are well known, but a number of subjects that are not easy to classify include *The Fight Between Carnival and Lent* (1559), *Children's Games* (1560), and *Dulle Griet*, also known as *Mad Meg* (1562).

It has recently been shown how closely many of Bruegel's works mirror the moral and religious ideas of Dirck Coornhert, whose writings on ethics show a rationalistic, commonsense approach. He advocated a Christianity free from the outward ceremonies of the various denominations, Roman Catholic, Calvinist, and Lutheran, which he rejected as irrelevant. In an age of bitter conflicts arising out of religious intolerance, Coornhert pleaded for toleration. Bruegel, of course, castigated human weakness in a more general way, with avarice and greed as the main targets of his criticism that was ingeniously expressed in the engraving *The Battle Between the Money Bags and Strong Boxes*. This would have been in keeping with Coornhert's views as well, which permitted taking part outwardly in the old forms of worship and accepting the patronage of Cardinal Granvelle.

GIUSEPPE ARCIMBOLDO

(b. c. 1527, Milan [Italy] — d. 1593, Milan)

One of the most unusual painters of the Renaissance was the Italian Mannerist painter Giuseppe Arcimboldo (Arcimboldi), whose grotesque compositions of fruits, vegetables, animals, books, and other objects were arranged to resemble human portraits. In the 20th century these double images were greatly admired by Salvador Dali and other Surrealist painters.

Beginning his career as a cartoon designer of stained-glass windows for the Milan Cathedral, Arcimboldo moved to Prague, where he became one of the favourite court painters to the Habsburg rulers Maximilian II and Rudolph II. He also painted settings for the court theatre there and developed an expertise for illusionistic trickery. His paintings contained allegorical meanings, puns, and jokes that were appreciated by his contemporaries but lost upon audiences of a later date. His eccentric vision is epitomized in his portraits *Summer* and *Winter*.

PELLEGRINO TIBALDI

(b. 1527, Puria, Duchy of Milan [Italy] — d. April 27, 1596, Milan)

The Italian painter, sculptor, and architect Pellegrino Tibaldi, also called Il Pellegrini, spread the style of Italian Mannerist painting in Spain during the late 16th century.

Tibaldi grew up in Bologna in a family of Lombard stonemasons. He was trained as a painter under minor Emilian artists who imitated the style of Raphael. His early paintings seem to reflect the influence of a number of artists. The classical style of *Mystic Marriage of St. Catherine* (c. 1545) brings to mind Raphael, or even Parmigianino. *The Adoration of the Shepherds* (c. 1546), one of Tibaldi's earliest-known paintings, shows the influence of Michelangelo and possibly Giorgio Vasari. His later works reveal the influence of Niccolò dell'Abate.

About 1547 Tibaldi went to Rome to work with Perino del Vaga. Together they decorated the living quarters of Pope Paul III in the Castel Sant'Angelo (1545–49). Upon the pope's death in 1549, Tibaldi assisted in decorating his funeral. While in Rome he also decorated the villa of Giovanni Poggi (c. 1550) as well as a room in the Vatican (1551–52) for Julius III. Tibaldi was in Loreto in 1554 to decorate the chapel of St. John the Baptist (now chapel of the Assumption). When he returned to Bologna about 1555, he revealed his talent in decorative painting at the Palazzo Poggi (now the University of Bologna). The series of frescoes he painted depict themes as varied as *The Life of St. Paul* and scenes from *The Odyssey*. He also created a set of male nudes similar to those Michelangelo had painted on the Sistine Chapel ceiling. He then completed several architectural projects in Bologna, Pavia, Milan, and other Italian cities.

In 1587 Tibaldi answered the summons of Philip II of Spain to supervise the decorating of the Escorial Library near Madrid. While there, he painted 46 frescoes in the cloister alone, executed many sculptural projects, and superintended the architectural details. Rich and ennobled, Tibaldi returned to Milan in 1596 at the summons of the archbishop, Federico, who wanted help with his new plan for the city, but he died shortly after his arrival.

Tibaldi's use of figures in violent and artificial poses is similar to that of Giulio Romano. The decorative, audacious, and absurd poses of his earlier figures are repeated in his frescoes for the Escorial. Tibaldi's architectural work is regarded as competent but unoriginal.

PAOLO VERONESE

(b. 1528, Verona, Republic of Venice [Italy] — d. April 9, 1588, Venice)

Paolo Veronese was one of the major painters of the 16th-century Venetian school. His works usually are huge, vastly peopled canvases depicting allegorical, biblical, or historical subjects in splendid colour and set in a framework of classicizing Renaissance architecture. A master of the use of colour, he also excelled at illusionary compositions that extend the eye beyond the actual confines of the room.

THE EARLY YEARS

Paolo Caliari became known as Veronese after his birthplace. Though first apprenticed as a stonecutter, his father's trade, he showed such a marked interest in painting that in his 14th year he was apprenticed to a painter named Antonio Badile, whose daughter Elena he later married. From Badile Veronese derived a sound basic painting technique as well as a passion for paintings in which people and architecture were integrated. The style of his first known work, the Bevilacqua-Lazise Altarpiece, reflects Badile's influence. Veronese was also influenced by a group of painters that included Domenico Brusasorci, Giambattista Zelotti, and Paolo Farinati; attracted by Mannerist art, they studied the works of Giulio Romano, Raphael, Parmigianino, and Michelangelo. Fragments of a fresco decoration executed by Veronese in 1551 for the Villa Soranza in Treville, with their elegant decorative figures, suggest that he was already creating a new idiom. The influence of Michelangelo is evident in a splendid canvas, *Temptation of St. Anthony*, painted in 1552 for the cathedral of Mantua.

In 1553 Veronese was introduced to Venice and launched on a long collaboration with the Venetian authorities in connection with the decoration of different parts of the Palazzo Ducale. The first of these commissions, the partitioned ceiling of the Sala del Consiglio dei Dieci (Hall of the Council of Ten), reveals characteristics of Veronese's mature style: skillful foreshortenings that make figures appear to be actually floating in space above the viewer, chromatic splendour, and luminous passages that endow even the shadows with colour.

In 1555, probably at the summons of the prior of St. Sebastiano in Venice, Veronese began the decoration of the church that was later to become his burial place. Whereas in the Palazzo Ducale he had often worked in collaboration with Zelotti, Veronese worked alone in St. Sebastiano. In the *Story of Esther*, depicted on the ceiling, appear the first of his rigorous compositions of foreshortened groups in luminous architectural frameworks and his decorative fancies that juxtapose animated, almost stereometric foregrounds and background figures wrought with a few strokes of light. The skilled fresco painter, who had worked in the villas and palaces of Venetian noblemen, including the beautiful boudoir of the Trevisan family in Murano, recounted the stories of St. Sebastian in elegantly fluent frescoes painted for the church (1558). In his decoration of the two shutters of the organ (1559), he again revealed his mastery of rhythmic composition and illusionistic perspective through extreme foreshortening. Contemporaneously with the decoration of St. Sebastiano, Veronese received numerous commissions for altarpieces, devotional paintings, and some Last Suppers. The theme of the latter—depicted in such paintings as *The Pilgrims of Emmaus* and *Feast in the House of Levi*—allowed him to compose large groups of figures in increasingly complex Renaissance architectural settings that attest to his knowledge of the works of the 16th-century Venetian architects Michele Sanmicheli, Andrea Palladio, and Jacopo Sansovino.

THE LATER YEARS

The decoration of the villa at Maser (1561), built by Palladio for Daniele and Marcantonio Barbaro, the former a scholar and translator of the works of the Roman architect Vitruvius, marked a fundamental stage in the evolution of the art of Veronese and in the development of Venetian painting. Assisted by his brother Benedetto in the execution of the architectural framework, Paolo brilliantly interpreted the villa's Palladian rhythms, breaking through the walls with illusionistic landscapes and opening the ceilings to blue skies with figures from Classical mythology. Mannerism had given way to harmonious rhythms and a superb handling of colour that imbued his frescoes with glowing vitality: the mythological scenes exalting human pleasures, the depiction of Barbaro's wife with the children and the wet nurse, and the landscapes, rendered in illusionistic perspective and detailed with Classic ruins.

The Classic compositions at Maser were succeeded by paintings with a tendency to monumentality and with a love for decorative pomp, as in *The Marriage at Cana*, executed in 1562 and 1563 for the refectory of St. Giorgio Maggiore. In this work the planes are multiplied, space is dilated, and an assembly of people is accumulated in complex but ordered movements. In their solemn monumentality, *The Family of Darius Before Alexander* and the canvases executed for the Cuccina family (c. 1572), which contain splendid portraits, are more organic in structure.

The wealth of whimsical and novel narrative details characteristically incorporated into Veronese's paintings and particularly in the *Last Supper* commissioned in 1573 by the convent of Saints Giovanni e Paolo aroused the suspicion of the Inquisition's tribunal of the Holy Office, which summoned Veronese to defend the painting. The tribunal objected to the painting on grounds that it included irreverent elements, inappropriate to the holiness of the event; for example, a dog, a jester holding a parrot, and a servant with a bleeding nose. Replying that "we painters take the same liberties as poets and madmen take," Veronese adroitly and staunchly defended the artist's right to freedom of imagination. The tribunal, perhaps influenced by the civil authority, elegantly resolved the question by suggesting that the theme be changed to a *Feast in the House of Levi*.

The nocturnal tone in the *Adoration of the Kings* in the church of St. Corona (Vicenza) endows the painting with a new intimacy, without renunciation of the characteristic Veronesian richness of colour, laid on with the minute, precious brushstrokes also used in small canvases, both sacred and profane, executed during this period. These paintings represent the most authentic expressions of the last 15 years of Veronese's life; for discernible in the large decorations for the Palazzo Ducale begun during this period—including the *Rape of Europa* and the *Apotheosis of Venice*—is a greater participation of his workshop, where his brother Benedetto, his sons Carlo and Gabriele, his nephew Alvise dal Friso, and others were employed. In 1588 Veronese contracted a fever and died after a few days of illness. His brother and sons had him buried in St. Sebastiano, where a bust was placed above his grave.

The sons continued their father's work, signing it *haeredes Pauli* ("Paul's heirs"). They were able to make use of a quantity of splendid sketches and drawings. Among Veronese's last works were superb allegorical fables, such as a series for Rudolph II that included *The Choice of Hercules* and *Allegory of Wisdom and Strength*; and *Mars and Venus United by Love*, in which the figures are bound to each other by harmonious rhythms. His final work also included biblical scenes with agitated, gloomy landscapes. A pathos-filled small altarpiece of *St. Pantaleon Healing a Sick Boy* and versions of the *Pietà* exhibit a dramatic quality and a meditative mood unusual in Veronese's works. It is the other, the serene Veronese, characterized by splendid colour and a luminosity that animates groups of figures and pure architectural structures, who above all was loved in his time and in the following centuries. Various leading artists of the 17th century found him a source of inspiration—as did Sebastiano Ricci and Giovanni Battista Tiepolo, who renewed the vital chromatic idiom of Venetian decorative painting. Nineteenth-century French painters from Eugène Delacroix to Paul Cézanne looked to Veronese, inspired by his use of colour to express exuberance as well as to model form.

GIAMBOLOGNA

(b. 1529, Douai, Spanish Netherlands [now in France]—d. Aug. 13, 1608, Florence [Italy])

The preeminent Mannerist sculptor in Italy during the last quarter of the 16th century was Giambologna, also called Giovanni da Bologna, or Jean Boulogne. First trained under Jacques Dubroeucq, a Flemish sculptor who worked in an Italianate style, Giambologna went to Rome about 1550, where his style was influenced by Hellenistic sculpture and the works of Michelangelo. Settling in Florence (1552), where he spent the rest of his life, he attracted the notice of Francesco de' Medici, for whom many of his most important works were made. Among his earliest Florentine works were a bronze Bacchus, later placed on a fountain in the Borgo San Jacopo, and a bronze Venus, made for the Villa di Castello and now at the Villa Medicea della Petraia, near Florence.

The Fountain of Neptune at Bologna (1563–66), which emulated Michelangelo's *Victory*, established his reputation. The full-scale plaster model of this work, initially set up with the *Victory* in the Palazzo Vecchio, was replaced in 1570 by the marble version, now in the Museo Nazionale. His *Samson and a Philistine* (1567) displays violence and anguish in a masterfully contrived composition that recalls such complex Hellenistic pieces as the *Laocoön*. *Rape of a Sabine* (1579–83), while uncluttered and monumental, is even more complex. The composition is subtly designed so that it can be viewed from any side with equal effect. In his fountain *Mercury* (c. 1580) Giambologna uses the shimmering play of light on the figure's smooth surface to enhance the effect of fleetness. His bronze equestrian portrait of Cosimo I de' Medici (1587–94) is also notable.

Rape of a Sabine *(two views), marble sculpture by Giambologna, 1579–83; in the Loggia dei Lanzi, Florence.* Alinari/Art Resource, New York

Giambologna enjoyed great popularity as a maker of garden sculpture for the Boboli Gardens, Florence (*Fountain of Oceanus*, 1571–76; *Venus of the Grotticella*, 1573), and for the Medici villas at Pratolino (the colossal *Apennine*, 1581), Petraia, and Castello. He was also a prolific manufacturer of bronze statuettes. In addition to his secular commissions, Giambologna was responsible for a large number of religious sculptures, which include (in marble) the fine Altar of Liberty in Lucca Cathedral (1577–79) and several bronze reliefs.

An Italian sculptor in all but birth, Giambologna transformed the Florentine Mannerism of the mid-16th century into a style of European significance. His ability to capture fleeting expression and the vivacity and sensual delight of his mature style anticipate the Baroque sculpture of Gian Lorenzo Bernini. For three centuries his work was more generally admired than that of any sculptor except Michelangelo.

SOFONISBA ANGUISSOLA

(b. *c.* 1532, Cremona [Italy]—d. November 1625, Palermo)

Sofonisba Anguissola was a late Renaissance painter best known for her portraiture. She was one of the first known female artists and one of the first women artists to establish an international reputation. Among other female painters, she was unusual in that her father was a nobleman rather than a painter.

The oldest of seven—six girls and one boy—Anguissola was born into a wealthy family. Like a true Renaissance man, her father, Amilcare Anguissola, was guided by the words of Baldassare Castiglione in *Il cortegiano* (*The Courtier*) not least in his consideration regarding the proper education of a young woman. In 1546 both Sofonisba and Elena, his second daughter, were sent to board in the household of

Bernardino Campi, a prominent local painter. They remained under instruction with Campi for three years until he moved from Cremona to Milan. Sofonisba continued her training with Bernardino Gatti, through whom she gained an appreciation of the work of Correggio. During this period of her life, through the influence of her father, she also received encouragement from Michelangelo, copying a drawing he sent her and sending it to him for his appraisal. While beginning to earn a living, Sofonisba also taught her sisters Lucia, Europa, and Anna Maria to paint. About 30 of her paintings from this period, including many self-portraits and the well-known *Lucia, Minerva, and Europa Anguissola Playing Chess* (1555), survived into the 21st century.

Anguissola's reputation spread, and in 1559 she was invited to Madrid, to the court of Philip II, where in addition to painting portraits she was an attendant to the Infanta Isabella Clara Eugenia (later the archduchess of Austria) and a lady-in-waiting to Philip's third wife, Elizabeth of Valois. Most of Anguissola's paintings of this period are no longer extant, having burned in a fire in the Prado during the 17th century. About 1571, while still in Madrid and with a dowry provided by the king, she married a Sicilian, Fabrizio de Moncada. Although she was once thought to have settled with him in Sicily, recent scholarship suggests that she may have remained in Spain after her marriage. She was widowed about 1579.

Aboard a ship bound for Cremona late in 1579, Anguissola met the captain, a Genoese nobleman by the name of Orazio Lomellino, and in January 1580 she married him. From 1584 until about 1616–20 the couple is known to have lived in Genoa. During this later period, she was influenced by the work of the Genoese painter Luca Cambiaso. Her work, like that of many early female painters, was often attributed to male painters of the period, in Anguissola's case painters as various as Titian, Leonardo da Vinci, Giovanni Battista Moroni, Alonso Sánchez Coello, and Francisco de Zurbarán. Near the end of her life, on July 12, 1624, she was visited by the young Flemish painter Anthony Van Dyck, who recorded her advice to him and sketched the elderly painter in his notebook.

Doubtless Anguissola was among the most accomplished painters of the late Renaissance. No less a commentator than Giorgio Vasari, who saw her work in her father's house in 1566, noted in his *Lives of the Most Eminent Painters, Sculptors, and Architects* that she had "worked with deeper study and greater grace than any woman of our times at problems of design, for not only has she learned to draw, paint, and copy from nature, and reproduce most skillfully works by other artists, but she has on her own painted some most rare and beautiful paintings."

GERMAIN PILON

(b. 1535, Paris, France—d. Feb. 3, 1590, Paris)

The French sculptor Germain Pilon, known principally for his monumental tombs, forms a transitional link between the Gothic tradition and the sculpture of the Baroque period. A sculptor's son, Pilon was employed at age 20 on the decoration of the tomb of King Francis I at Saint-Denis. His earlier work clearly shows an Italian influence, but eventually he developed a more distinctively French expression by fusing elements from Classical art, Gothic sculpture, and Michelangelo with the Fontainebleau adaptation of Mannerism, a style characterized by subjective conceptions, studied elegance, and virtuoso artifice.

Pilon's best-known works are funerary sculptures for Henry II. It was a custom of the period for men of high estate to assign their remains to more than one burial site—often one for the body, one for the heart, and one for the entrails. Pilon's monument for the heart of Henry II (*c.* 1561) consists of three marble Graces of great elegance supporting an urn. It was perhaps based on a design by Primaticcio. For the principal tomb of Henry II and Catherine de Médicis at Saint-Denis (1563–70), also designed by Primaticcio, Pilon created four bronze corner figures and, above, the kneeling figures of the king and queen in bronze. Most important, however, are the seminude, marble gisants, or figures of the royal pair recumbent in death. Considered by some to be his most sublime achievement, the gisants are a Renaissance idealization of a Gothic convention and possess a depth of emotion that Pilon perhaps never again attained.

Sculptor royal from 1568, Pilon had a successful career as a portraitist, his finest work in the genre being the kneeling figure of René de Birague (1583–85). Pilon also created an effigy, *Valentine Balbiani*, of Birague's wife. It is also believed that his bronze relief *Deposition* was created for Birague's private chapel. Appointed controller of the mint in 1572, he contributed to French medal casting a distinguished series of bronze medallions in 1575. Pilon was commissioned to decorate the Valois Chapel (1559, destroyed 1719) in Saint-Denis Abbey, and he worked on several marble statues, among them *Risen Christ* (begun 1572), that were probably intended for the chapel but were unfinished at the time of his death in 1590.

FEDERICO ZUCCARO

(b. *c.* 1540, Sant'Angelo in Vado, Urbino [Italy]—d. July 20, 1609, Ancona)

The central figure of the Roman Mannerist school and, after the death of Titian, possibly the best known painter in Europe was Federico Zuccaro (Zuccari). Between 1555 and 1563 Zuccaro was the helper and pupil of his older brother, the painter Taddeo Zuccaro. Because of Taddeo's close supervision of his brother's work, the two had an intense rivalry for a time. Federico was offended, for example, when his brother retouched some of his work on the facade of Tizio da Spoleto's home (1558). By the time he was 18, Zuccaro was already working in the Vatican, painting various rooms for Pius IV. In 1564 he traveled to Venice to decorate the Grimani Chapel in San Francesco della Vigna with various paintings, including *Adoration of the Magi* and *Conversion of Mary Magdalene*.

By 1565 Zuccaro had moved to Florence, where he worked under the painter, architect, and biographer Giorgio Vasari and codified the theory of Mannerism in *L'idea de' scultori, pittori e architetti* (1607; "The Idea of Sculptors, Painters, and Architects") and in a series of frescoes in his own house in Rome (Palazzo Zuccaro). After Taddeo's death in 1566, Federico completed some of his brother's unfinished commissions, including in the Villa Farnese at Caprarola; in the Sala Regia, where he painted *Henry IV Before Gregory VII* (1566); and at San Lorenzo (1568–70). He traveled through Spain, England, and the Netherlands in 1574.

In England in 1575 Zuccaro painted portraits of Queen Elizabeth I and the earl of Leicester (and probably no one else—the hundreds of portraits in England that bear his name are ascribed without foundation). His later commissions included the painting of the dome of Florence Cathedral, left unfinished by Vasari's death (1575–79), the Pauline Chapel in the Vatican (1580), and a large work in the Palazzo Ducale at Venice in 1582. In 1585 he was commissioned by Philip II to decorate El Escorial (1585–88) in

Madrid. Zuccaro's Mannerist style was considered too formal, though, and much of his work was later replaced. In 1593 Zuccaro became the first president of the Academy of St. Luke in Rome, which is to some extent the parent body of modern art academies. His late paintings are much quieter and less mannered in style, and he lived to see Mannerism fade from the scene.

EL GRECO

(b. 1541, Candia [Iráklion], Crete—d. April 7, 1614, Toledo, Spain)

The master of Spanish painting, whose highly individual dramatic and expressionistic style met with the puzzlement of his contemporaries but gained newfound appreciation in the 20th century was El Greco. He also worked as a sculptor and as an architect.

EARLY LIFE AND WORKS

El Greco never forgot that he was of Greek descent and usually signed his paintings in Greek letters with his full name, Doménikos Theotokópoulos. He is, nevertheless, generally known as El Greco ("the Greek"), a name he acquired when he lived in Italy, where the custom of identifying a man by designating country or city of origin was a common practice. The curious form of the article (*El*), however, may be the Venetian dialect or more likely from the Spanish.

Because Crete, his homeland, was then a Venetian possession and he was a Venetian citizen, he decided to go to Venice to study. The exact year in which this took place is not known, but speculation has placed the date anywhere from 1560, when he was 19, to 1566. In Venice he entered the studio of Titian, who was the greatest painter of the day. Knowledge of El Greco's years in Italy is limited. A letter of Nov. 16, 1570, written by Giulio Clovio, an illuminator in the service of Cardinal Alessandro Farnese, requested lodging in the Palazzo Farnese for "a young man from Candia, a pupil of Titian." On July 8, 1572, "the Greek painter" is mentioned in a letter sent from Rome by a Farnese official to the same cardinal. Shortly thereafter, on Sept. 18, 1572, "Dominico Greco" paid his dues to the guild of St. Luke in Rome. How long the young artist remained in Rome is unknown, because he may have returned to Venice, c. 1575–76, before he left for Spain.

The certain works painted by El Greco in Italy are completely in the Venetian Renaissance style of the 16th century. They show no effect of his Byzantine heritage except possibly in the faces of old men—for example, in the *Christ Healing the Blind.* The placing of figures in deep space and the emphasis on an architectural setting in High Renaissance style are particularly significant in his early pictures, such as *Christ Cleansing the Temple.* The first evidence of El Greco's extraordinary gifts as a portraitist appears in Italy in a portrait of Giulio Clovio and Vincentio Anastagi.

MIDDLE YEARS

El Greco first appeared in Spain in the spring of 1577, initially at Madrid, later in Toledo. One of his main reasons for seeking a new career in Spain must have been knowledge of Philip II's great project, the building of the monastery of San Lorenzo at El Escorial, some 26 miles (42 km) northwest of Madrid. Moreover, the Greek must have met important Spanish churchmen in Rome through Fulvio Orsini, a humanist and librarian of the Palazzo Farnese. It is known that at least one Spanish ecclesiastic who spent some time in Rome at this period—Luis de

Castilla—became El Greco's intimate friend and was eventually named one of the two executors of his last testament. Luis' brother, Diego de Castilla, gave El Greco his first commission in Spain, which possibly had been promised before the artist left Italy.

In 1578 Jorge Manuel, the painter's only son, was born at Toledo, the offspring of Doña Jerónima de Las Cuevas. She appears to have outlived El Greco, and, although he acknowledged both her and his son, he never married her. That fact has puzzled all writers, because he mentioned her in various documents, including his last testament. It may be that El Greco had married unhappily in his youth in Crete or Italy and therefore could not legalize another attachment.

For the rest of his life El Greco continued to live in Toledo, busily engaged on commissions for the churches and monasteries there and in the province. He became a close friend of the leading humanists, scholars, and churchmen. Antonio de Covarrubias, a Classical scholar and son of the architect Alonso de Covarrubias, was a friend whose portrait he painted. Fray Hortensio Paravicino, the head of the Trinitarian order in Spain and a favourite preacher of Philip II of Spain, dedicated four sonnets to El Greco, one of them recording his own portrait by the artist. Luis de Góngora y Argote, one of the major literary figures of the late 16th century, composed a sonnet to the tomb of the painter. Another writer, Don Pedro de Salazar de Mendoza, figured among the most intimate circle of El Greco's entourage.

The inventories compiled after his death confirm the fact that he was a man of extraordinary culture—a true Renaissance humanist. His library, which gives some idea of the breadth and range of his interests, included works of the major Greek authors in Greek, numerous books in

Latin, and others in Italian and in Spanish: Plutarch's *Lives*, Petrarch's poetry, Ludovico Ariosto's *Orlando Furioso*, the Bible in Greek, the proceedings of the Council of Trent, and architectural treatises by Marcus Vitruvius Pollio, Giacomo da Vignola, Leon Battista Alberti, Andrea Palladio, and Sebastiano Serlio. El Greco himself prepared an edition of Vitruvius, accompanied by drawings, but the manuscript is lost.

In 1585 and thereafter El Greco lived in the large, late-medieval palace of the Marqués de Villena. Although it is near the site of the now-destroyed Villena Palace, the museum in Toledo called the Casa y Museo del Greco ("Home and Museum of El Greco") was never his residence. It can be assumed that he needed space for his atelier more than for luxurious living. In 1605 the palace was listed by the historian Francisco de Pisa as one of the handsomest in the city; it was not a miserable ruined structure, as some romantic writers have presumed. El Greco surely lived in considerable comfort, even though he did not leave a large estate at his death.

El Greco's first commission in Spain was for the high altar and the two lateral altars in the conventual church of Santo Domingo el Antiguo at Toledo (1577–79). Never before had the artist had a commission of such importance and scope. Even the architectural design of the altar frames, reminiscent of the style of the Venetian architect Palladio, was prepared by El Greco. The painting for the high altar, *Assumption of the Virgin*, also marked a new period in the artist's life, revealing the full extent of his genius. The figures are brought close into the foreground, and in the Apostles a new brilliance of colour is achieved. The technique remains Venetian in the laying on of the paint and in the liberal use of white highlights; yet the intensity of the colours and the manipulation of contrasts, verging on dissonance, is distinctly El Greco. For the first time the importance of his assimilation of the art of Michelangelo comes to the fore, particularly in the painting of the *Trinity*, in the upper part of the high altar, where the powerful sculpturesque body of the nude Christ leaves no doubt of the ultimate source of inspiration. In the lateral altar painting of the *Resurrection*, the poses of the standing soldiers and the contrapposto (a position in which the upper and lower parts of the body are contrasted in direction) of those asleep are also clearly Michelangelesque in inspiration.

At the same time, El Greco created another masterpiece of extraordinary originality—the *Espolio* (*Disrobing of Christ*). In designing the composition vertically and compactly in the foreground he seems to have been motivated by the desire to show the oppression of Christ by his cruel tormentors. He chose a method of space elimination that is common to middle and late 16th-century Italian painters known as Mannerists, and at the same time he probably recalled late Byzantine paintings in which the superposition of heads row upon row is employed to suggest a crowd. The original altar of gilded wood that El Greco designed for the painting has been destroyed, but his small sculptured group of the *Miracle of St. Ildefonso* still survives on the lower centre of the frame.

El Greco's tendency to elongate the human figure becomes more notable at this time—for example, in the handsome and unrestored *St. Sebastian*. The same extreme elongation of body is also present in Michelangelo's work, in the painting of the Venetians Tintoretto and Paolo Veronese, and in the art of the leading Mannerist painters. The increased slenderness of Christ's long body against the dramatic clouds in *Crucifixion with Donors* foreshadows the artist's late style.

El Greco's connection with the court of Philip II was brief and unsuccessful, consisting first of the *Allegory of the Holy League* (*Dream of Philip II*; 1578–79) and second of the *Martyrdom of St. Maurice* (1580–82). The latter painting did not meet with the approval of the king, who promptly ordered another work of the same subject to replace it. Thus ended the great artist's connection with the Spanish court. The king may have been troubled by the almost shocking brilliance of the yellows as contrasted to the ultramarine in the costumes of the main group of the painting, which includes St. Maurice in the centre. On the other hand, to the modern eye El Greco's daring use of colour is particularly appealing. The brushwork remains Venetian in the way that the colour suggests form and in the free illusionistic and atmospheric creation of space.

The *Burial of the Count de Orgaz* (1586–88) is universally regarded as El Greco's masterpiece. The supernatural vision of Gloria ("Heaven") above and the impressive array of portraits represent all aspects of this extraordinary genius's art. El Greco clearly distinguished between heaven and earth: above, heaven is evoked by swirling icy clouds, semiabstract in their shape, and the saints are tall and phantomlike; below, all is normal in the scale and proportions of the figures. According to the legend, Saints Augustine and Stephen appeared miraculously to lay the Count de Orgaz in his tomb as a reward for his generosity to their church. In golden and red vestments they bend reverently over the body of the count, who is clad in magnificent armour that reflects the yellow and reds of the other figures. The young boy at the left is El Greco's son, Jorge Manuel; on a handkerchief in his pocket is inscribed the artist's signature and the date 1578, the year of the boy's birth. The men in contemporary 16th-century dress who attend the funeral are unmistakably prominent members of Toledan society. El Greco's Mannerist method of composition is nowhere more clearly expressed than here, where all of the action takes place in the frontal plane.

LATER LIFE AND WORKS

From 1590 until his death El Greco's painterly output was prodigious. His pictures for the churches and convents of the Toledan region include the *Holy Family with the Magdalen* and the *Holy Family with St. Anne*. He repeated several times the *Agony in the Garden*, in which a supernatural world is evoked through strange shapes and brilliant, cold, clashing colours. The devotional theme of *Christ Carrying the Cross* is known in 11 originals by El Greco and many copies. El Greco depicted most of the major saints, often repeating the same composition: St. Dominic, Mary Magdalen, St. Jerome as cardinal, St. Jerome in penitence, and St. Peter in tears. St. Francis of Assisi, however, was by far the saint most favoured by the artist; about 25 originals representing St. Francis survive and, in addition, more than 100 pieces by followers. The most popular of several types was *St. Francis and Brother Leo Meditating on Death*.

Two major series (*Apostolados*) survive representing Christ and the Twelve Apostles in 13 canvases: one in the sacristy of Toledo Cathedral (1605–10) and another, unfinished set (1612–14) in the El Greco House and Museum at Toledo. The frontal pose of the Christ blessing in this series suggests a medieval Byzantine figure, although the colour and brushwork are El Greco's personal handling of Venetian technique. In these works the devotional intensity of mood reflects the religious spirit of Roman Catholic Spain in the period of the Counter-Reformation. Although Greek by descent and Italian by artistic preparation, the artist became so immersed in the religious environment of Spain that he became the most vital visual representative of Spanish mysticism. Yet, because of the combination of these three cultures, he developed into an artist so individual that he belongs to no conventional school but is a lonely genius of unprecedented emotional power and imagination.

Several major commissions came El Greco's way in the last 15 years of his life: three altars for the Chapel of San José, Toledo (1597–99); three paintings (1596–1600) for the Colegio de Doña María de Aragon, an Augustinian monastery in Madrid; and the high altar, four lateral altars, and the painting *St. Ildefonso* for the Hospital de la Caridad at Illescas (1603–05).

Extreme distortion of body characterizes El Greco's last works—for example, the *Adoration of the Shepherds*, painted in 1612–14 for his own burial chapel. The brilliant, dissonant colours and the strange shapes and poses create a sense of wonder and ecstasy, as the shepherd and angels celebrate the miracle of the newly born child. In the unfinished *Vision of St. John*, El Greco's imagination led him to disregard the laws of nature even more. The gigantic swaying figure of St. John the Evangelist, in abstractly painted icy-blue garments, reveals the souls of the martyrs who cry out for deliverance. In like manner, the figure of the Madonna in the *Immaculate Conception* (1607–14), originally in the Church of San Vicente, floats heavenward in a paroxysm of ecstasy supported by long, distorted angels. The fantastic view of Toledo below, abstractly rendered, is dazzling in its ghostly moonlit brilliance, and the clusters of roses and lilies, symbols of the Virgin's purity, are unalloyed in their sheer beauty.

In his three surviving landscapes, El Greco demonstrated his characteristic tendency to dramatize rather than to describe. The *View of Toledo* (*c.* 1595) renders a city stormy, sinister, and impassioned with the same dark, fore-boding clouds that appear in the background of his earlier *Crucifixion with Donors*. Painting in his studio, he rear-ranged the buildings depicted in the picture to suit his compositional purpose. *View and Plan of Toledo* (1610–14) is almost like a vision, all of the buildings painted glistening white. An inscription by the artist on the canvas explains quite fancifully that he had placed the Hospital of San Juan Bautista on a cloud in the foreground so that it could bet-ter be seen and that the map in the picture shows the streets of the city. At the left, a river god represents the Tagus, which flows around Toledo, a city built on rocky heights. Although El Greco had lived in Italy and in Rome itself, he rarely used such Classical Roman motives.

The one picture by El Greco that has a mythological subject, so dear to most Renaissance artists, is the *Laocoön* (1610–14). For ancient Troy he substituted a view of Toledo, similar to the one just discussed, and he displayed little regard for Classical tradition in painting the highly expres-sive but great, sprawling body of the priest.

Although El Greco was primarily a painter of religious subjects, his portraits, though less numerous, are equally high in quality. Two of his finest late works are the por-traits of *Fray Felix Hortensio Paravicino* (1609) and *Cardinal Don Fernando Niño de Guevara* (c. 1600). Both are seated, as was customary after the time of Raphael in portraits presenting important ecclesiastics. Paravicino, a Trinitarian monk and a famous orator and poet, is depicted as a sensitive, intelligent man. The pose is essentially frontal, and the white habit and black cloak provide highly effective pictorial contrasts. Cardinal Niño de Guevara, in crimson robes, is almost electrical in his inherent energy, a man accustomed to command. El Greco's portrait of *Jeronimo de Cevallos* (1605–10), on the other hand, is most sympathetic. The work is half-length, painted thinly and limited to black and white. The huge ruff collar, then in fashion, enframes the kindly face. By such simple means, the artist created a memorable characterization that places him in the highest rank as a portraitist, along with Titian and Rembrandt.

No followers of any consequence remained in Toledo after El Greco's death in 1614. Only his son and a few unknown painters produced weak copies of the master's work. His art was so personally and so highly individual that it could not survive his passing. Moreover, the new Baroque style of Caravaggio and of the Carracci soon supplanted the last surviving traits of 16th-century Mannerism.

NICHOLAS HILLIARD

(b. 1547, Exeter, Devon, England—d. Jan. 7, 1619, London)

The first great native-born English painter of the Renaissance was Nicholas Hilliard. His lyrical portraits raised the art of painting miniature portraiture (called limning in Elizabethan England) to its highest point of development and did much to formulate the concept of portraiture there during the late 16th and early 17th centuries.

Hilliard had a tumultuous childhood due to the Reformation, the spread of Protestantism that occurred during the 16th century. His father, a proponent of the Reformed religion, sent him to Geneva to escape persecution in England. In Geneva the young Hilliard lived with the family of John Bodley—who would later become a publisher of the Geneva Bible—and was first exposed to the French language, French art, and a humanist education. He probably returned to England about 1559. His earliest known attempts at miniature painting were made

A Young Man Among Roses, *watercolour miniature by Nicholas Hilliard, c. 1588; in the Victoria and Albert Museum, London.* Courtesy of Victoria and Albert Museum, London

in 1560, and his talent is obvious in *Self Portrait Aged 13* and *Edward Seymour, Duke of Somerset*. Hilliard became miniature painter to Queen Elizabeth I about 1570 and made many portraits of her and of the leading members of her court. He paid a short visit to France in the service of the duc d'Alençon but returned early in 1578 because his wife was expecting a child.

Throughout his life Hilliard practiced as goldsmith and jeweller as well as miniaturist, and in 1584 he designed Queen Elizabeth's second great seal. On the accession of James I, in 1603, his appointment as limner to the crown was continued, but he seems to have found the atmosphere of the new court less congenial to his art.

In his *Treatise on the Arte of Limning* (c. 1600) he gives an account of his method and many sidelights on his own mercurial and engaging temperament. Throughout his life he had financial difficulties, and he was imprisoned for debt for a short period in 1617. His *Treatise* also states that he derived his sensibility from that of the painter Hans Holbein the Younger, a German portraitist working in England, whose influence doubtless accounts for Hilliard's preference for even, nondramatic lighting and firm contours, as seen in the miniatures *A Young Man Among Roses* and *An Unknown Man Against a Background of Flames*.

Hilliard's son Laurence (c. 1582–1640) also practiced miniature painting, but a much more eminent pupil of Hilliard's was the French-born miniaturist Isaac Oliver.

LAVINIA FONTANA

(b. 1552, Bologna [Italy]—d. Aug. 11, 1614, Rome)

I talian Mannerist Lavinia Fontana was one of the most important portraitists in Bologna during the late 16th century. She was one of the first women to execute large, publicly commissioned figure paintings.

Fontana studied with her father, Prospero Fontana (*c.* 1512–97), a minor painter of the school of Bologna, who taught his daughter to paint in the Mannerist style. By the late 1570s she was known in Bologna for painting fine portraits, including *Self-portrait at the Harpischord* and the very formal *Gozzadini Family* (1584). The attention to detail in her portraits is reminiscent of the work of another northern Italian Renaissance painter, Sofonisba Anguissola. Fontana's works were admired for their vibrant colour and the detail of the clothes and jewelry that her subjects wore.

Fontana also produced many religious paintings; among her best was *Noli me tangere* (1581). Some of her most famous works are large altarpieces executed for the churches of her native city. In addition, in 1589 she painted the altarpiece *Holy Family with the Sleeping Christ Child* for El Escorial in Madrid. After about 1600 —when she executed *Vision of St. Hyacinth*, a work commissioned by the cardinal of Ascoli—Fontana's work was introduced to Rome; she moved to Rome three years later and continued painting portraits and altarpieces. In 1604 she painted her largest work, the *Martyrdom of St. Stephen*, an altarpiece for San Paolo Fuori le Mura in Rome, a basilica that was destroyed in the fire of 1823. Her *Visit of the Queen of Sheba to Solomon* is her most ambitious surviving narrative work. She was elected a member of the Roman Academy, a rare honour for a woman.

In 1577 Fontana married the minor painter Gian Paolo Zappi. He was willing to subordinate his career to her own; he also became her agent. After her marriage, Fontana sometimes signed her work with her married name. She enjoyed the patronage of the family of Pope Gregory XIII and painted the likenesses of many eminent people. In addition to her career as an artist, she was the mother of 11 children.

GLOSSARY

altarpiece A large painting or carving that is placed above and behind the altar of a church; traditionally depicting religious/ecumenical subject matter.

bas-relief A sculpture that is shallow cut from wood or stone, so that the subject is slightly raised over the background material.

byname A name by which a person is more familiarly known; usually a diminutive or a nickname based on a physical attribute or an occupation.

chiaroscuro A strong contrast between light and dark.

dilatory Tending to delay or postpone; tardy.

drapery The depiction of clothing folds in drawing, painting, and sculpture; drapery techniques distinguish not only artistic periods and styles but the work of individual artists.

fresco A painting done on fresh plaster with pigments diluted by water.

humanism A cultural and intellectual movement of the Renaissance that emphasized secular (human) concerns as a result of the rediscovery and study of the literature, art, and civilization of ancient Greece and Rome.

Mannerism A style of art characterized by excessive elongation of the human figure and spatial inconsistency.

perspective The artistic technique of representing three-dimensional objects and depth on a flat surface.

plasticism The use of three-dimensional effects in art.

polyptych Four or more painted/carved panels usually hinged together; used for any number of panels greater than three (triptych).

quatrefoil A symmetrical shape that forms the overall outline of four partially overlapping circles of the same diameter.

sarcophagus A stone coffin.

sfumato The fine shading that produces soft, imperceptible transitions between colours and tones.

tondo A round painting; the plural is tondi.

triptych Three panels, on each of which is a painting or carving; the three together form a complete scene or work of art.

wool carder One who cleans up and prepares raw wool fibres for use in textiles.

FOR FURTHER READING

Ames-Lewis, Francis, ed., and Paul Joannides, ed. *Reactions to the Master: Michelangelo's Effect on Art and Artists in the Sixteenth Century*. Farnham, England: Ashgate Publishing, 2003.

Aronberg Lavin, Marilyn. *Artists' Art in the Renaissance*. New York, NY: Pindar Press, 2009.

Bober, Phyllis, and Ruth Rubinstein. *Renaissance Artists and Antique Sculpture: A Handbook of Sources*. Rev. ed. New York, NY: Harvey Miller Publishers, 2009.

Campbell, Lorne, et. al. *Renaissance Faces: Van Eyck to Titian*. London, England: National Gallery London, 2009.

Hancock, Lee. *Lorenzo De' Medici: Florence's Great Leader and Patron of the Arts*. New York, NY: Rosen Publishing Group, 2004.

Hartt, Frederick. *History of Italian Renaissance Art*. Upper Saddle River, NJ: Prentice Hall, 2006.

Kemp, Martin. *Leonardo da Vinci: The Marvellous Works of Nature and Man*. Oxford, England: Oxford University Press, 2007.

Lubbock, Jules. *Storytelling in Christian Art from Giotto to Donatello*. New Haven, CT: Yale University Press, 2006.

Murphy, Caroline P. *Lavinia Fontana: A Painter and Her Patrons in Sixteenth-century Bologna*. New Haven, CT: Yale University Press, 2003.

O'Malley, Michelle. *The Business of Art: Contracts and the Commissioning Process in Renaissance Italy*. New Haven, CT: Yale University Press, 2005.

Schroth, Sarah, and Ronni Baer. *El Greco to Velazquez: Art During the Reign of Philip II*. Boston, MA: MFA Publications, 2008.

Toman, Rolf, ed. *The Art of the Italian Renaissance: Architecture, Sculpture, Painting, Drawing*. Duncan, SC: h.f. ullman, 2008.

Eichler, Anja. *Albrecht Dürer: 1471–1528*. Duncan, SC: h.f. ullman, 2008.

Vasari, Giorgio. *Vasari's Lives of the Artists: Giotto, Masaccio, Fra Filippo Lippi, Botticelli, Leonardo, Raphael, Michelangelo, Titian*. New York, NY: Dover Publications, 2005.

Zirpolo, Lilian H. *Historical Dictionary of Renaissance Art*. Lanham, MD: The Scarecrow Press, Inc., 2007.

Zollner, Frank. *Botticelli*. New York, NY: Prestel Publishing, 2009.

INDEX